Bob Marshall in the Adirondacks

Writings of a Pioneering Peak-Bagger,
Pond-Hopper and Wilderness Preservationist

Bob Marshall on Wright Peak.

Bob Marshall
in the Adirondacks

Writings of a Pioneering Peak-Bagger,
Pond-Hopper and Wilderness Preservationist

*With additional articles
by George Marshall*

Edited by Phil Brown

Lost Pond Press, Saranac Lake, N.Y.

Lost Pond Press
40 Margaret St.
Saranac Lake, New York 12983
www.lostpondpress.com

First edition

ISBN-13: 978-0-9789254-0-6
ISBN-10: 0-9789254-0-8

Cover photo: Bob Marshall as a teenage hiker,
used with the permission of the Adirondack Museum.

Book and jacket design by Susan Bibeau/Beehive Productions.

Library of Congress Control Number: 2006933037

*We feel the indomitable spirit of
Bob Marshall with us constantly, still
lighting on every front where wilderness
values are threatened.*

– Sigurd Olson

Editor's Preface

It was a cool, clear morning in September. On a day like this you can see forever from a mountaintop. Starting down the trail at Heart Lake, I felt a slight regret that I would not be going to a bald summit. My destination was Lost Pond, and I would spend a good part of the day thrashing about in a dense spruce forest. When I got to the register I met a man heading for Nye and Street mountains. Neither peak has great views. Like me, this fellow seemed to be going out of his way to avoid the inspiring panoramas that could be seen that day from a number of mountains in the vicinity. How to explain such behavior? After the trail forked and we parted, the answer struck me: Each of us was following in the footsteps of Bob Marshall.

Like many Adirondack hikers, I became interested in Bob Marshall when I started climbing the forty-six High Peaks. Marshall, along with his younger brother, George, and their guide, Herb Clark, were the first to ascend them all, starting with Whiteface Mountain in 1918 and finishing on Mount Emmons in 1925.[1] Bob's booklet on the High Peaks (reprinted here) was the first publication of the fledgling Adirondack Mountain Club. Over the next decade, only two people duplicated their feat. In time, bagging the forty-six evolved into an Adirondack tradition. More than five thousand hikers have now done it.

Bob Marshall loved all wilderness, regardless of its elevation. When he was a forestry student at Cranberry Lake, he spent his weekends trekking through the wilds of the northwestern Adirondacks, visiting nearly a hundred ponds and rating their scenic beauty. His account of these hikes, in the form of a typewritten manuscript, can be found at the New York State College of Environmental Science and Forestry in Syracuse. My initial idea for a book was to retrace these hikes and publish Marshall's manuscript, supplemented by my own observations. But soon after undertaking my research, I discovered that Marshall wrote a good deal more about the Adirondacks, and I decided that my book could perform a greater service by collecting these writings in one volume.

Those who know Marshall solely by his national reputation will discover in these pages the source of the passion that inspired him to become a leader of the wilderness movement. Although he grew up in New York City, he spent his boyhood summers at the family's camp, Knollwood, on Lower Saranac Lake. The camp became a base for explorations. At first, these were limited to walks in the adjacent woods, but as he grew older, Bob began venturing deeper into the wilderness and up mountains. By age seventeen, he had decided to go into forestry, because, as he wrote in a high-school essay, "I love the woods and solitude."

His decision must have been influenced by his father, Louis Marshall, a prominent attorney who helped found the New York State College of Forestry,[2] where Bob enrolled in 1920. Louis Marshall instilled in all his children an appreciation of the importance of preserving the natural world. (Both of Bob's brothers, George and James, devoted much of their lives to conservation in the Adirondacks and elsewhere.) At the New York State constitutional convention of 1894, Louis Marshall fought successfully for amending the constitution to declare that the Adirondack Forest Preserve "shall be forever kept as wild forest lands," thus making them among the most protected lands in the world. Writing to Bob in 1927, he recounts a discussion with a potential developer of his beloved Adirondacks:

> I said half jocularly in the course of my argument that I would continue the fight as long as I lived, and if I did not succeed in finishing it I would put a clause in my will in which I would ask my children to continue the fight. I am quite sure that they would do so whether I asked them or not.[3]

By then, of course, Bob had already joined the fight, and he would go on, in 1935, to organize the Wilderness Society, which became one of the nation's leading preservationist groups. His earliest writings about the Adirondacks evince a wilderness aesthetic that he stayed true to his entire life. In *The High Peaks of the Adirondacks*, written while a sophomore in college, he rails against the ravages to the forest caused by logging and fires and longs for vistas that lack any sign of man. "It's a great thing these days," he says, "to leave civilization for a while and return to nature." In "Recreational Limits to Silviculture in the Adirondacks," published just after he graduated, Marshall sets forth arguments for preservation that he would develop and refine in later essays, culminating in the celebrated "The Problem of the Wilderness."

Marshall's work with the U.S. Forest Service and the Bureau of Indian Affairs introduced him to the country's grandest scenery—in the Rockies, the Southwest and Alaska—but he never lost his affection for the Adirondacks.

Louis Marshall, right, and guide Ed Cagle with the day's catch.

He returned often, and he picked up his pen whenever he felt compelled to defend the Forest Preserve against those who would trammel it. In various articles, he opposes the construction of truck trails and cabins in the Preserve and argues for leaving large tracts entirely natural, with no trails or campsites. And when he cataloged the nation's major roadless areas in 1936, in order to call for their protection, he remembered to include his old haunts: the High Peaks and the territory south of Cranberry Lake.

Marshall's enthusiasm for nature turned him into a hiking machine. He thought nothing of trekking thirty or forty miles through wild country—a habit he developed as a youth in the Adirondacks. He and George once walked sixty miles in a day: They left Knollwood at 5:40 a.m. to circumambulate Whiteface Mountain and straggled back after midnight. Herb Clark led the young men on numerous big hikes in the High Peaks, including a traverse of the largely trailless Dix Range. In 1934, on a trip back to the Adirondacks, Marshall set a record by climbing fourteen peaks in a single day. In a remarkable coincidence, he met another ardent conservationist, Paul Schaefer, on top of Mount Marcy that afternoon. This book contains both Marshall's account of his marathon hike and, in an appendix, Schaefer's article about their summit meeting.

Those who share Marshall's love of the Adirondacks should get a kick out of reading about his adventures and comparing his experiences with their own. Anyone who has climbed Haystack or visited the Five Ponds, for example, will recognize much in his portrayals of these places. But it's striking how much has changed since the 1920s—and for the better. In his wanderings, Marshall often encountered slash left behind by lumbermen and gazed out over land that had been burned or clear cut. Time has healed most of the scars. Overall, the Adirondack Park is a wilder place today, thanks in part to conservationists like Bob Marshall.

Marshall's accounts of his Adirondack adventures and his polemics for preservation take up the bulk of this book, but we've rounded it out with several others of his pieces, including profiles of Herb Clark and Mills Blake, the 19th-century surveyor; notes from a dinner with Albert Einstein, who vacationed in Saranac Lake; excerpts from an unpublished novel partially set in the Adirondacks, and "Contribution to the Life History of the Northwestern Lumberjack," a humorous article that exhibits one of Marshall's salient personality traits, a finely honed sense of the absurd. Though not about the Adirondacks, it might just as well have been written about the Adirondack lumberjack.

Like his brother, George Marshall grew up to become a staunch conservationist and defender of the Adirondacks. He, too, was a writer. His heartfelt portrait, "Adirondacks to Alaska: A Biographical Sketch of Bob Marshall," is the ideal introduction to this book, for it provides an overview not only of Bob's life, but also of Bob's writings. At the end of the book, I've included two other articles by George Marshall in which he reminisces about hiking in the Adirondacks.

Which brings me back to Lost Pond. In one of those articles, George extols this remote jewel, located high on a trailless peak. He and Bob bushwhacked to it more than once. George remarks that Lost Pond, "surrounded as it is by a splendid forest and with high hills rising from its steep banks, seemed one of the most beautiful and wildest spots we had ever seen." That was enough to get me to go—even if it meant skipping a panoramic vista.

As for the other fellow on the trail that morning, he completed his High Peaks circuit that very day on Nye and Street. I imagine he'll be designated Forty-Sixer No. 5,601 or whatever. I hope he takes the time to get to know the first three.

Phil Brown

NOTES

1 George Marshall, letter to Grace Hudowalski, March 1, 1951. It was the Marshalls' intention to climb all the Adirondack mountains that are four thousand feet or higher. Later surveys indicated that four of the original forty-six peaks are below four thousand feet and that one not on the list, MacNaughton Mountain, is in fact four thousand feet. In the letter to Hudowalski, George Marshall notes that the three men climbed MacNaughton two days after ascending Emmons. Despite the new measurements, Forty-Sixers continue to follow the traditional list.

2 The forerunner of the New York State College of Environmental Science and Forestry.

3 Quoted in Glover 1986, p. 86.

George, James and Bob Marshall in 1939, the year that Bob died.

Note on Marshall texts and photos

I treated Bob Marshall's writings with the deference due historical documents. For the most part, my editing was limited to standardizing punctuation, correcting spelling and syntactical errors and adding footnotes and introductions. Unless noted, I left intact variant spellings of topographical names, such as *Racquette* instead of *Raquette*. In some cases, the toponyms themselves have changed: Marshall refers to Algonquin Peak as MacIntyre, for example.

The book contains numerous photographs taken by Bob and George Marshall. These include scenic shots from their hikes in and around the High Peaks, preserved in fragile glass slides in the possession of the Adirondack Room of the Saranac Lake Free Library. Because these photos have rarely, if ever, been seen by the public, we think it appropriate to distinguish them from other photos in the book that were taken of or by the Marshalls. Therefore, all of them (and no others) will carry the following credit line: "Marshall Collection, Saranac Lake Free Library." It is unknown which brother took which pictures.

CONTENTS

Adirondack Writings of Bob Marshall

I. Peak-Bagger

II. Pond-Hopper

III. Preservationist

IV. Portrait Artist

V. Novelist

SUPPLEMENTARY MATERIAL

Related Articles

Bibliographical Information

Bob Marshall Great Wilderness

The big idea for the western Adirondacks.

Acknowledgments

I'll begin by thanking three organizations that are helping to preserve Bob Marshall's beloved Adirondacks and that, each in its own way, contributed to this book: the Adirondack Council, for it financial support; the Adirondack Mountain Club, for originally publishing many of the writings contained herein, and the Association for the Protection of the Adirondacks, for making available its treasure trove of historical documents and photographs. I was fortunate in that I was able to conduct most of my research in the Adirondack Room of the Saranac Lake Free Library, located just a few blocks from my home. Thanks to Michelle Tucker and her staff for putting up with me day after day. Two other libraries invaluable in my research were the Bancroft Library at the University of California at Berkeley, the keeper of most of Marshall's papers, and the Moon Library at the New York State University College of Environmental Science and Forestry, which counts Marshall as an alumnus. Other organizations that aided me one way or another were the Wilderness Society, Adirondack Museum, U.S. Forest Service and American Jewish Archives. I'd also like to acknowledge all the publications that first printed articles found in this book. For a list of the original sources, see Page 299.

I am extremely grateful to Carl Heilman II for his expert photographs and to Susan Smeby for her antiquarian postcards. I made liberal use of both in the pages that follow. I'd like to single out several other individuals who contributed directly to this book: Ellen Scholle and Roger Marshall, the niece and nephew of Bob Marshall, for use of documents and photographs in the family's possession; Steve Scholle, Ellen's son, for the photograph of Bob Marshall with his two brothers (the last one taken of Bob); Philip G. Terrie, for his article on Mount Marshall and for providing his notes on Marshall; Bill McKibben, for his droll verse; Lynda McIntyre, for her photograph of Elk Lake; Mike Storey, for his panther track, and Nancy Bernstein, for her elegantly drawn maps.

I owe a big debt to three people who found a number of errors in the manuscript and who offered useful suggestions: Dick Beamish, publisher of the *Adirondack Explorer*; Betsy Dirnberger, associate publisher of the same, and Mike Virtanen, my lifelong friend. Dick also gave me much encouragement in this project. Three others I must thank are my daughters, Becky and Martha, for relieving me of some of the typing, and my son, Nathan, for backpacking to the Five Ponds with me.

A number of other people answered questions, offered advice or encouragement, or otherwise assisted in the making of this book. They are listed alphabetically: Ben Beach, Neal Burdick, Nick Burns, Chad Dawson, Angela Donnelly, Bill Frenette, Jared Gange, Dave Gibson, Tony Goodwin, Evelyn Greene, Brian Houseal, Mike Laddin, Brian Mann, Ed Niedhammer, Elise Nienaber, Flora Nyland, Jerry Pepper, Clarence Petty, Paul Grondahl, Wray Rominger, Douglas W. Scott, John Sheehan and Neil Woodworth. I also am indebted to James M. Glover for his having written *A Wilderness Original: The Life of Bob Marshall*, which I cite many times in footnotes.

Finally, I want to say thank you to Sue Bibeau of Beehive Productions, Saranac Lake, for her design of the book and the dust jacket. She lived with this project almost as long as I did and always remained professional and enthusiastic.

–Phil Brown

Bob Marshall on North Doonerak in Alaska, 1939.

Adirondacks to Alaska:
A Biographical Sketch
of Robert Marshall

By George Marshall

For years the reddish-brown reports of the *Topographical Survey of the Adirondack Wilderness* were obscured in shadow at the bottom of the bookcase until one day Bob discovered them. Immediately he became enthralled by these accounts of the explorations of Verplanck Colvin and Mills Blake. Their adventures were not in distant Himalayas or Rockies, but were among the mountains which surrounded us. The heroes of these explorations were not the contemporaries of Columbus or Daniel Boone, but of our father. This opened our eyes to new possibilities and, when soon thereafter Bob read Longstreth's *The Adirondacks*,[1] we determined to penetrate those mountains, which previously had been accepted as a scenic backdrop along the skyline across the lake, and see what lay beyond.

Robert Marshall first came to the Adirondacks in 1901 when he was six months old. He returned for at least part of each summer for the next quarter-century and at every opportunity thereafter. Going to Knollwood, our father's "camp" on Lower Saranac Lake, was the great event of the year. Life in New York City could never approach the joys of the Adirondacks. Here we entered a world of freedom and informality, of living plants and spaces, of fresh greens and exhilarating blues, of giant, slender pines and delicate pink twinflowers, of deer and mosquitoes, of fishing and guide boats and tramps through the woods.

First walks were down to the lake with a steep climb home. Then came the walk around "The Paths"—by "The Fish Pond" surrounded by high hills and floating bog with an amphitheater of spruce and tamarack

This article is reprinted from the May-June 1951 issue of *Ad-i-ron-dac*.

to the north, "The Temple" with dim light filtering through graceful hemlock colonnades, and "The Big Rock." We learned where to find shinleaf and rattlesnake plantain, dalibarda and lady's slipper, pipsissewa and broadleaf green orchis. Annually we recorded the date on which we first saw each variety of flower and identified each new species.

The discovery of pathless woods brought new freedom and joys. Before breakfast, in the early hours of the day when everything in the forest is freshest, Bob tramped the trailless woods of Knollwood. Every ridge and hollow and deer runway within the forest where we lived became familiar to him, and he gave them such names as Found Knife Pass, Squashed Berry Valley and Hidden Heaven Rock.

After breakfast was time for studies and then tennis or more walking and swimming; in the afternoons we took long walks or rows up the lake or a combination of the two, unless it was an afternoon for baseball. It was not unusual to row on the lake after supper or walk to the Fish Pond hoping to see a deer. Bob was not strong as a child, but these long, active days helped develop that great stamina which made him a legend in the West in later years.

In the years before we could take frequent trips into the mountains, many of our most enjoyable adventures were on road walks; each new road traversed meant discovery. We ranged over a fairly wide area on half-day and full-day hikes, the longest being our sixty-mile Wilmington Walk in 1920 on which we circled Whiteface Mountain.[2]

Our first mountain climbed was Ampersand on August 15, 1916; our first trailless peak, Boot Bay Mountain, the following year; our first High Peaks, Whiteface, Marcy, Algonquin and Iroquois, in August 1918. This was followed by six of our seven most enjoyable Adirondack summers and included climbs among the High Peaks, trips along the Raquette and Cold rivers and into the Moose River wilderness.

Herbert K. Clark, the great Saranac Lake guide and our close friend, trained us from early childhood in the arts of woodcraft and boatmanship and accompanied us on most of our longer trips. His understanding of people, his delightful sense of humor and his creative accounts of North Woods lore were a welcome counterpoint to the silent grandeur of the forests. With Herb we climbed the forty-six High Peaks and made eight first ascents.[3] It was about our climbs to the summits over four thousand feet that Bob wrote *The High Peaks of the Adirondacks*, which was published by the Adirondack Mountain Club in 1922.[4]

The Marshall family's camp on Lower Saranac Lake.

Bob seldom lost an opportunity for a trip into the woods. He spent his free time on weekends to make an intensive survey of the ponds in the Cranberry Lake area while attending the Sophomore Summer Camp of the New York State College of Forestry[5] and to see new ponds and mountains in the southern and western Adirondacks while making a sample plot study in 1923 for the New York Conservation Commission.

Later in the West, he spent most of his spare time climbing mountains and exploring wilderness areas, and I fear he walked the legs off more than one of his colleagues while tramping through the woods on official duties. On one trip, however, the entire party rode, except Bob, who went on foot. He not only kept up with the horses but climbed an extra mountain for good measure.

By the beginning of October 1937, Bob had taken two hundred thirty-mile walks, fifty-one forty-mile walks and a number of longer walks, including at least one of seventy miles. He always kept elaborate statistics of his adventures and added to his record during the last two years of his life. He made numerous first ascents in Alaska and the West as well as in the Adirondacks.

Bob made his first explorations of the hitherto unmapped Koyukuk drainage in north-central Alaska in the summer of 1929. He became so enthusiastic about the dramatic country which he discovered near the Arctic Divide and about the extraordinary happy people he met in the Wiseman area that he returned the following summer and remained thirteen months. His book, *Arctic Village*, a brilliant and entertaining study of the Koyukuk community in which he lived, was a bestseller and was acclaimed alike by explorers and sociologists. Bob made his final trips to the Arctic in the summers of 1938 and 1939 and privately published an account of his exciting wilderness explorations in his two "Doonerak" booklets. These Alaskan adventures were a culmination of Bob's years of searching for certain fundamental aesthetic and spiritual values.

At fifteen, Bob decided to become a forester so that he might spend the greater part of his life in the woods he loved.[6] He attended the New York State College of Forestry, was graduated in 1924, received his master's degree from the Harvard Forest in 1925 and his Ph.D. from the Johns Hopkins University Laboratory of Plant Physiology in 1930. He joined the U.S. Forest Service in the summer of 1924 and was on the staff of the Northern Rocky Mountain Forest Experiment Station from 1925-1928.

As director of the Forestry Division of the U.S. Office of Indian Affairs, 1933-1937, Bob helped integrate the preservation and utilization of Indian forestlands into the rebuilding of tribal life on the principle of self-government and the raising of levels of living of the Indians. The U.S. Forest Service established the position of chief of the Division of Recreation and Lands for Bob, in May 1937, and he occupied this post until his death in November 1939. He created a system of wilderness areas in Indian reservations and the National Forests and developed projects to make certain other parts of the National Forests much more available to low-income groups.

During these years, Bob spent about half his time in the field and half in Washington, D.C. He felt that this was necessary for good administration. It was also a good way of life for him because he enjoyed people just as much as the wilderness and needed both. He had a splendid sense of humor, great gusto and infectious enthusiasms, thoroughly enjoyed living and made everyone about him feel the same way. Dancing and bringing his friends together for good conversation gave him equal pleasure. He delighted in introducing controversial issues and encouraging the expression of conflicting points of view.

Perhaps Bob Marshall's greatest contribution was his creative leadership in developing a greater understanding of the multiple use of forests—particularly the importance of wilderness areas for water and soil conservation and for essential ecological, recreational, aesthetic and psychological needs—and his initiative in building a movement for wilderness preservation. He made this contribution through helping found the Wilderness Society, through his work as a public official, and as a speaker and writer. His most important articles established a philosophical basis for wilderness preservation, particularly "The Problem of the Wilderness" in the February 1930 *Scientific Monthly*.[7] Soon after his death, these accomplishments were recognized in the naming of the largest wilderness in the country the "Bob Marshall Wilderness Area."[8]

He wrote on a variety of other subjects, including land and forest policy, technical forestry, sociology, Alaskan policy and the Adirondacks. They ranged from his important book, *The People's Forests* (1933), to his delightful "Contribution to the Life History of the Northwestern Lumberjack."[9] He was also deeply interested in the preservation of civil liberties and in social reform.

Only eleven of his voluminous Adirondack articles and journals have been published. One was an obituary on Mills Blake in *High Spots* of March 1930. The longer article on Blake in this issue of the *Adirondac* was written by Robert Marshall about 1928 but was found only recently among his unpublished manuscripts.[10] It will be a further tribute to Bob if those who read his article will share some of his early enthusiasm for Colvin and Blake and thereby be encouraged to discover more of the beauty of the Adirondacks for themselves.

NOTES

1 *The Adirondacks* by T. Morris Longstreth was published in 1919.

2 See the hitherto unpublished "Wilmington Walk," p. 79.

3 Russell Carson credits them with the first ascents of Marshall, Street, Nye, South Dix, East Dix, Hough, Allen and Couchsachraga (Carson 1927, 263).

4 For the text of this booklet, see p. 3.

5 Marshall's descriptions of his hikes in the Cranberry Lake region begin on p. 99.

6 For Marshall's schoolboy essay on his career choice, see p. 169.

7 See p. 205.

8 The Bob Marshall Wilderness Area now encompasses more than a million acres in Montana. It remains the nation's largest Wilderness Area outside Alaska.

9 This whimsical article appears on p. 257.

10 Both the profile of Blake (p. 229) and his obituary (p. 237) are reprinted in this volume.

Bob Marshall Chronology

1901 Born Jan. 2 in New York City, to Louis and Florence Marshall.

1915 Herb Clark, the family's guide, takes Bob and his younger brother, George, up their first peak, 3,352-foot Ampersand Mountain.

1916 Florence Marshall dies of cancer.

1918 On Aug. 1, climbs first peak over four thousand feet, Whiteface Mountain, with George, Herb and a friend, Carl Poser. Later that month, the Marshall brothers and Clark climb three other High Peaks: Algonquin Peak, Iroquois Peak and Mount Marcy.

1920 Enrolls in the New York College of Forestry in Syracuse, a school his father helped found.

1921 Bob, George and Herb finish climbing all forty-two Adirondack peaks believed to be over four thousand feet.

1922 Spends summer at forestry camp on Cranberry Lake. On weekends, he explores the surrounding wilderness, rating the beauty of ninety-four ponds. Adirondack Mountain Club publishes his booklet *The High Peaks of the Adirondacks*.

1924 Graduates from college, finishing fourth in a class of fifty-nine. The senior yearbook describes him as "the Champion Pond Hound of all time, a lad with a mania for statistics and shinnying mountain peaks." Climbs four four-thousand-footers previously overlooked, bringing the number of High Peaks to forty-six.

1925 Receives master's degree in forestry from Harvard. Climbs Mount Emmons, last High Peak. Leaves in June for a job with the U.S. Forest Service in Montana.

1927 Flees grizzly bear in Selway Wilderness in Montana by climbing a tree. When branch breaks, he falls to ground and feigns death. Grizzly lumbers away.

1928 Sends announcement to friends informing them that he just completed his hundreth hike of at least thirty miles. Enrolls at Johns Hopkins University to pursue doctorate in plant physiology.

1929 First trip to Wiseman, Alaska, tiny community north of Arctic Circle. Explores nearby Brooks Range. Louis Marshall dies in Switzerland.

1930 Publishes "The Problem of the Wilderness," a celebrated defense of preservation, in *The Scientific Monthly*. Receives Ph.D. In July, Bob and George climb nine High Peaks in a day, setting an Adirondack record. In August, Bob returns to Wiseman for a year.

1932 Returns to Adirondacks and climbs thirteen High Peaks and one lesser peak in a single day, ascending 13,600 feet. Takes job with U.S. Forest Service and compiles list of the nation's largest roadless areas. Three are in the Adirondacks.

1933 Publishes *Arctic Village*, about Wiseman. The book is a Literary Guild selection. Takes job with U.S. Indian Bureau, overseeing forestry and grassland management on reservations.

1934 Publishes his second book, *The People's Forests*, in which he argues that the federal government should acquire and manage most of the nation's forestland.

1935 Organizes the Wilderness Society.

1936 Sister Ruth (nicknamed Putey) dies of cancer at thirty-eight.

1937 Transfers from Indian Bureau back to Forest Service.

1938 Returns to Wiseman. Tries to climb 7,547-foot Mount Doonerak but is turned back by incessant rains. He and three companions nearly drown when raft capsizes on a swollen river.

1939 Returns to Wiseman. Tries and fails again to climb Doonerak. On Nov. 10, boards train in Washington, D.C., for New York City. He is found dead in his berth the next day, at age thirty-eight.

1940 U.S. Agriculture Secretary Henry Wallace designates a 950,000-acre tract in Montana the Bob Marshall Wilderness Area.

Bob Marshall and Herb Clark.

Part One

PEAK
BAGGER

*"It's a great thing these days
to leave civilization for a while
and return to nature."*

– Bob Marshall THE HIGH PEAKS OF THE ADIRONDACKS

An aerial view of the High Peaks. Some of the names in the photograph differ from those used by Marshall.

The High Peaks
of the Adirondacks

Bob Marshall was seventeen when he climbed his first High Peak, 4,867-foot Whiteface Mountain, on August 1, 1918, accompanied by his younger brother, George, and their family's guide, Herbert Clark. By the month's end, they had scrambled up four other major Adirondack peaks, including Mount Marcy and Algonquin Peak, the only two surpassing five thousand feet. Eventually, they decided to climb all the peaks over four thousand feet. Not only had this never been done, but most of the mountains were trailless and had rarely or never been climbed. They counted as a separate peak any that rose at least three hundred feet on all sides or that was at least three-quarters of a mile from the nearest higher peak. At the time they believed there were forty-two such peaks over four thousand feet. They finished the round in 1922,[1] and that year Bob Marshall wrote his booklet The High Peaks of the Adirondacks, *the first publication of the newly formed Adirondack Mountain Club.*

The scars of lumbering and forest fires were still much in evidence in those days. In rating the views from the summits, Marshall and his companions gave more weight to primitiveness than to expansiveness. Thus, they ranked the limited view from wooded Mount Redfield seventh and that from wide-open Rocky Peak Ridge thirtieth. They later discovered that four other peaks attained at least four thousand feet: Couchsachraga, Gray, Cliff and Blake. The Marshalls and Clark knocked those off in 1924. In the decades since, the forty-six High Peaks have become the holy grail of Adirondack hikers. More than five thousand have bagged them all, according to the Adirondack Forty-Sixers, which keeps track of such things. Although later surveys found that four of the traditional High Peaks fall short of four thousand feet,[2] hikers who want to join the organization must climb the original forty-six. All the photographs in this chapter were taken by the Marshall brothers during their hikes.

In every mountain section in the country there is a certain elevation, arbitrarily selected, which divides the monarchs of the region from the ordinary mountains. Thus in the Colorado Rockies fourteen thousand feet is generally chosen as the height which enables a mountain to get on the roll of honor. In the East no peaks rise nearly to that height, and so, of course, the elevation necessary to make a mountain a monarch is lowered. In the Appalachians of North Carolina it is about five thousand feet; in the White Mountains of New Hampshire it is four thousand; in our own Adirondacks it is also four thousand. Here there are forty-two peaks which fall in this category. But, unlike the other sections, these peaks are comparatively little known and, with a few exceptions, almost never climbed.

Many believe that mountaineering in the Adirondacks is more or less of a joke. They explain that there are any number of Western peaks over twice four thousand feet high; that the city of Denver is at the same elevation as the summit of Marcy; and that six hundred square miles of wilderness are insignificant in the Rockies or the Sierras. It is true, nevertheless, that the Adirondacks are capable of furnishing worthwhile mountaineering experiences.

Of course one cannot find any mountain which rises eight thousand feet above the starting point, as do some of our Western summits. The greatest rise is in climbing Marcy from Keene Valley, and this is but 4,300 feet. However, one who really wants to climb need not be contented with one mountain a day. Close at hand are many other summits. We started one morning from the foot of Haystack below Panther Gorge and went over Haystack, Basin, Saddleback and Gothic and returned that afternoon the same way. Here we had nine thousand feet of ascending and the same amount of descending.[3] But we had advantages over those who climb but one very high peak in a day. We got four different views, we were not so high up that the whole landscape was a blur, we did not have to bother about extreme cold or thin air, and we did not spend most of our time climbing over barren rocks and snow above the timberline but passed through delightful spruce forests.

The pleasure of standing on a lofty summit where only a few have ever stood before is easy to acquire in the Adirondacks. Of the forty-two high peaks only fourteen have trails up them. On certain summits, I have never seen any signs of man or heard of anyone being there. Probably some of these had never been climbed before, including Iroquois,[4] Allen,

Mount Marcy from Mount Skylight.

Street, Nye, Middle Dix,[5] Lower Wolf Jaw and South Dix. None of the others without trails is scaled oftener than once or twice a year.

In an endeavor to add to the knowledge concerning these mountains, and to encourage nature lovers to get out and climb them, I have attempted to give a brief description of the way up the forty-two high peaks and the view obtainable from them. In this article I have arranged the mountains in the order of their elevation. In the conclusion I give a rating of them as regards beauty. This, I believe, is the first complete rating of this kind ever made of all the mountains over four thousand feet. So far as I know, no one else has ever climbed them all.

MOUNT MARCY (Tahawus) 5,344 feet • Rating 9

This is the highest, most famous and possibly most often climbed of the Adirondack peaks. So far as is known, it was the first of the four-thousand-footers ever ascended, having been climbed as early as 1837.[6]

There are six important trails up it. Some of these join. The oldest starts at Tahawus Club, runs up Calamity Brook, by the Henderson Monument, to the Flowed Lands and Lake Colden. Here it branches at right angles to the former course and follows the Opalescent River and Feldspar Brook to the highest source of the Hudson, Lake Tear of the Clouds. Just beyond another trail crosses it at right angles. The lefthand or northeast branch leads directly on to Marcy. Straight ahead is the Marcy

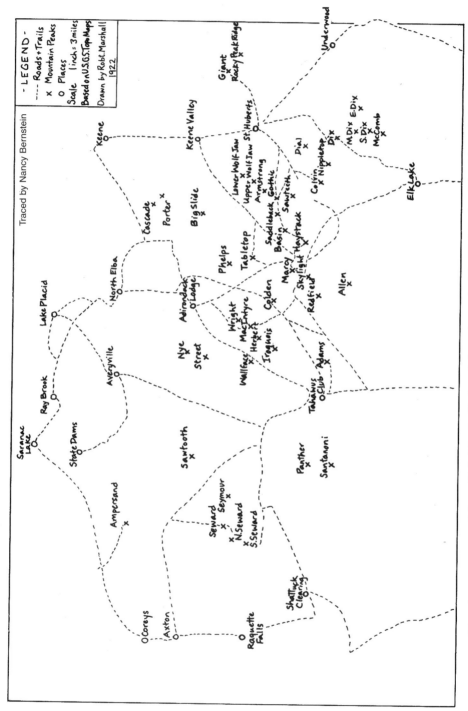

The above was traced from Bob Marshall's hand-drawn map in *The High Peaks of the Adirondacks*.

trail which comes up from Upper Ausable Lake. This cuts across Bartlett Ridge and then follows Marcy Brook. It can be reached by two ways. One is from St. Huberts via Lower Ausable Lake; the other from Elk Lake via Railroad Notch. Another trail up the mountain runs from Lake Sanford through the pass between Redfield and Cliff mountains and joins the Opalescent at Uphill Brook.[7] One of the most often used trails runs up the Johns Brook valley from Keene Valley and strikes onto the mountain proper from the head of the brook. From the north there is also a trail, very muddy and running mostly through a slash. It can be reached from either Heart Pond[8] or South Meadows. The trails I like best are from Tahawus Club and Ausable Lake.

The view from Marcy is not so fine as from several lower peaks, yet it is beautiful enough to suit the most exacting. The view I like best is over the Lake Tear notch toward those three magnificently wooded mountains Allen, Skylight and Redfield. The views over the Gothics, down Johns Brook valley and toward MacIntyre, merely to list them, are also very fine.

Marcy is the only mountain in the Adirondacks from which all the four-thousand-foot peaks can be seen.

MacIntyre 5,112 feet [5,114][†] • Rating 5

There are two trails up MacIntyre. The one most frequently used starts at Heart Pond and follows the Marcy trail a short way but then turns off for the mountain. It follows MacIntyre Brook a way and then, swinging around the base of Wright Peak, ascends gradually to the summit. About halfway up is a fifteen-foot waterfall, furnishing the last sure water. There is much slash on either side up to here. By this trail I consider MacIntyre the easiest of any of the high mountains to climb. The other trail starts at Lake Colden, ascends through the hollow between Herbert[9] and the main peak and then strikes onto the mountain from the southwest.

Though lower and much less often climbed, I think the prospect from MacIntyre far surpasses that from Marcy. At first it is hard to say which of the many views is most desirable. Mount Colden, with its great slides, backed by the dark and towering Marcy, attracts the attention perhaps most. But then on the other side is Wallface and the Scott Pond country, and it is hard to turn long from this view. Unfortunately dur-

† Numbers in brackets indicate measurements of more recent surveys. The figures are taken from Adirondack Mountain Club's *Adirondack Trails: High Peaks Region*, 2004.

Panther Gorge, with Haystack on the right.

ing the last few years lumbering has greatly marred this section. Between these opposite views one sees Placid, South Meadows surrounded by lofty mountains, the Gothics, Skylight and Redfield, and Santanoni, all most delightful and inspiring to view. When on top of MacIntyre it is hard to believe that any mountain can surpass it in beauty of view.

SKYLIGHT 4,920 feet [4,924] • Rating 13

At the four corners referred to in the Marcy paragraphs one of the four trails, that which leads to the southwest, was not mentioned. It takes a person, after an easy quarter-hour climb, to the top of Skylight, third-highest mountain in the state.

The view from Skylight is cut off rather abruptly to the northeast by a great wall formed by Marcy and Haystack. Yet I consider this wall in itself the finest part of the entire Skylight view. It is all heavily timbered, except near the top, where timber is crushed out by the high elevation. In the center between Haystack and Marcy is a great gash in the wall, Panther Gorge. This gorge, with the surrounding mountains, forms a bit of scenery which nature has wrought to perfection. Other fine views are towards MacIntyre, Santanoni and the valley of Skylight Brook.

HAYSTACK 4,918 feet [4,960] • Rating 1

Everyone has his favorite mountain. My favorite is Haystack. Primarily because in the whole vast panorama visible from the mountain there is virtually not a sign of civilization. Whichever way you look, save toward a small burned section near the Giant, there are the forests, the mountains, the ponds, just as they were before white man had ever set foot on America. It's a great thing these days to leave civilization for a while and return to nature. From Haystack you can look over thousands and thousands of acres, unblemished by the works of man, perfect as made by nature.

Of course there are individual views of overwhelming beauty. I know of no two finer prospects than the one over Panther Gorge toward Marcy and the one over the rocky Gothics. But it is the sense of being in the center of a great wilderness which gives the greatest charm.

The main trail up Haystack leaves the Ausable Lake-Marcy trail at the foot of Panther Gorge and ascends the hollow between Haystack and Bartlett Ridge. In the center of the hollow it is joined by another trail from Upper Ausable, which keeps the other side of Bartlett Ridge. From where these two trails join is a very steep forty-minute climb to the summit. Another trail up Haystack leads over the whole Gothic Range and ascends Haystack from the northeast.

WHITEFACE 4,872 feet [4,867] • Rating 23

There are three good trails up Whiteface, each starting at a readily accessible point. As a result, Whiteface is climbed more often than any other high mountain, with the possible exception of Marcy. One of the trails starts at the head of Lake Placid and runs up rather steeply to the summit. Another easier but somewhat longer way is from Wilmington. This trail runs over Marble Mountain and ascends Whiteface proper from the hollow between it and Esther. The third trail starts from French's old hotel near Franklin Falls and follows the general course of French's Brook.[10]

The view from Whiteface is one of the broadest in the Adirondacks. Both the St. Lawrence and Lake Champlain can be seen. To the south most of the high mountains are visible, while to the west stretches a vast extent of flat lake country. The view over Placid and the one toward the Great Range are very fine, yet they do not excel the average views from many other mountains. They contain none of that wildness that adds so much to some peaks.

HERBERT (Clinton, Border) 4,855 feet [4,840] • Rating 4

Somebody once cut a trail from MacIntyre to Herbert, but it is now virtually gone. To get to this peak you must tug, tussle, push and batter

your way through as dense a mass of mountain balsam as ever grew.
Progress is measured by inches. If you are strong and persevering you
may finally get through what as the bird flies is only a mile but as man
travels seems like ten.

The view which rewards you for your effort is much like that from
the main peak but even finer. Substituted for the view toward Placid
and the burned lands toward the Cascade Lakes, least pretty of any of
the MacIntyre scenery, is as beautiful and wild a valley as could exist,
backed by heavily wooded Iroquois.[11] It is a view which alone is worth
climbing a mountain. But in addition, being nearer the center, you get
a better view of both Indian and Avalanche Passes. That is why I like
this very rarely climbed mountain even better than MacIntyre.

DIX 4,842 feet [4,857] • Rating 8

There are two trails up Dix. The one now most often traveled starts
at St. Huberts, runs between Noonmark and Round Mountains, crosses the very slashy valley of the Bouquet and then ascends the mountain
proper. It is poorly cut out and is, all in all, the hardest mountain trail
I know of in the Adirondacks. The other trail, too, which starts at Elk
Lake, has not been cut out lately. I have never taken it all the way, having struck up on it from Middle Dix,[12] but I understand it follows up
the East Inlet a long way and then runs up the shoulder of Dix.

The view from Dix is very broad. One can see from Whiteface down
almost to the very southernmost mountains. Lake Champlain and
Vermont seem quite near, and virtually all the of the high mountains are
visible. Perhaps the finest view, one which could hardly be improved on,
is looking down toward the wooded valley of Elk Lake, with the island-
studded lakes standing out among the light-green trees. Since the valley
has been lumbered for softwood, all the darker growth is gone. The view
toward the Great Range is another very impressive sight. From Nippletop,
directly in front, to MacIntyre in the extreme distance, from Allen on the
left to the Wolf Jaws on the right, are many lofty peaks, all over four thousand feet, virtually unmarred by man, a most majestic-looking range.
Unfortunately, the Dix view is considerably spoiled by fire slash which
runs in a semicircle from Nippletop clear around to East Dix.

BASIN 4,825 feet [4,827] • Rating 6

This peak is really the central point on the Gothic Range trail. It can, therefore, be approached from two sides, northeast and southwest. From either way the trail is very steep and difficult, and one must proceed with great care. At one place is an almost perpendicular slide up which you can only ascend by the aid of a rope which has been stretched the length of the slide. The course of the Gothic Range trail (All Summit), which will be referred to again, may as well be described here. It starts on the road from St. Huberts to the Ausable Lakes, runs up over the Gothics, then over Saddleback, Basin, Little Haystack and Haystack, and finally meets the Marcy trail at the foot of Panther Gorge. A person traveling this trail in the direction mentioned would have approximately 6,500 feet of ascending and 5,000 feet of descending.

What most impresses one from Basin are the three great valleys which surround the mountain: Panther Gorge with its great cliffs, the broad Johns Brook valley and the great wooded basin to the south, which so impressed Colvin when in 1875 he first climbed this mountain that he named it after the basin.[13] No words can describe a person's feeling as he looks over this enormous hollow and gets perhaps the finest view now possible of the type of forest which once covered all of the North Woods region. Basin, situated as it is right in the center of the great mountains, affords a very fine view of them, and this, added to the valley views, makes it rank high.

GOTHIC   4,783 feet [4,736] • Rating 15

There are four trails up Gothic. One, already described, comes over the range and ascends the west side. In the hollow between Gothic and Saddleback it is joined by a trail which follows up Ore Bed Brook. From the east it is approached by the most often used trail, which starts, as already mentioned, on the Ausable Lake road. An old trail starts at the foot of Lower Ausable and follows a brook for some distance; then it strikes the mountain and picks its way among the great slides to the top. Still another trail starts at Upper Ausable Lake.

Looking back toward Marcy is one of the finest views imaginable of deep gorges, rocky precipices and virgin forests, mixed together and displayed on a great scale. Toward Dix is another delightful view looking over the Colvin and Nippletop ranges. Down toward Keene Valley fertile fields and houses can be seen. The views over Johns Brook valley and to the south are also beautiful.

Marshall Collection, Saranac Lake Free Library

Trap Dike on Mount Colden, rising from Avalanche Lake.

COLDEN 4,713 feet [4,714] • Rating 19

There is no trail up Colden. We climbed it from the north approach to Avalanche Pass. We left the Avalanche trail about half a mile from the center of the pass and followed old logging roads and flumes to the end of a very bad slash which extended well up the mountain. For a short way came fine woods, but near the top was as bad a stretch of mountain balsams as I have ever seen. We had a long mile of tugging through this growth.

Situated as it is between Marcy and MacIntyre, the view from Colden is very restricted. Yet there is much of beauty in it. I like best the view toward the Gothic, but it is also very beautiful looking over Colden[14] and the Flowed Lands. The Opalescent valley should be the finest view of all, but lumbering has considerably marred it. Fortunately it was stopped before the valley was entirely ruined. Perhaps the most sensational view is looking down the great slides. Lower down they are so steep that just a corner of Avalanche Lake is visible. Looking still farther, the long MacIntyre Range can be seen, badly burned at the north end. A very good view can be had of the great Elba valley.

GIANT 4,622 feet [4,627] • Rating 21

This was one of the first of the high Adirondack peaks to be climbed[15] and is still one of the most frequently ascended summits. The trail up it starts near the St. Huberts ballgrounds and rises gradually to the top. It is an excellent trail. There was formally a trail from New Russia, but I have been told that this is virtually obliterated.[16]

The Giant view is more or less of the same type as the Whiteface one, though in a very different section. It is situated at one edge of the mountain region. Thus there is a very good general view of the great ranges to the west. But they are too far off for their individual merits to stand out. To the east many farmlands are visible, both in New York and Vermont. North are some lower ranges. To the south is a very fine sight, Hunter Pass, with its two great walls, the Dix and Nippletop ranges. Were this view unmarred by fire scars there could not be a more beautiful one. Directly to the west is the valley in which St. Huberts lies, as pretty a hollow as can be. There is nothing in the whole prospect I like better.

SANTANONI 4,621 feet [4,607] • Rating 2

There is no trail up this mountain, although lumber roads run well up it from the Tahawus side. We climbed it from the dam on Cold River and from this direction found it to be the hardest mountain we ever attempted. First came a very, very long lumbered area. We followed roads a way, but as they persisted in going the wrong way, we soon had to leave them and take to the brush. After four hours of steady climbing came a great flat which seemed to be at the top of everything. By mounting a tree we found Panther Peak, and a thirty-minute desperate struggle with the mountain balsam brought us to the summit. We dreaded the mile and a half of balsam between us and Santanoni, but somebody had cut a rough trail between the two peaks, which made the going less difficult.

The view from Santanoni was worth far more than it cost us to reach the top—worth any trouble, in fact, for only Haystack do I consider finer. Whichever way you look, it is very impressive. Santanoni is in the heart of the wilderness, dividing the mountain from the lake region. Thus the view is very varied, with a magnificent panorama to the east of virtually every one of the four-thousand-foot peaks and to the west a heavily wooded wilderness, broken many times by shining lakes and ponds. To the north is the Cold River country, backed by the great Seward Range. Lumbering has affected this somewhat, but fortunately fire has not as yet touched it. One of the finest parts of the mountain view is the excellent profile of many of the famous passes. Through the notch of Indian Pass, far in the distance, is the notch made by Cascade. It seems almost like looking through the sights of a gun. Directly below to the east are four dark bodies of water, unusually attractive Henderson, Sanford, Bradley and Andrew. Santanoni indeed furnishes many sorts of beautiful scenery.

NIPPLETOP 4,620 feet • Rating 3

We climbed this mountain from Hunter Pass. We had taken the Dix trail as far as the big slide, where we cut into the second growth and struggled across the badly slashed valley. Once across it, where the great fire of 1903 had not touched, we found the going easier. We ascended the very steep mountainside to the Dial and then followed a ridge over two or three intervening, unimportant peaks to Nippletop.

The view as a whole could hardly be excelled. If it were not for the fire which destroyed so much land from Giant all the way to Dix, no peak in the state would be more commanding. But one can forget this desolation as he looks over all the remainder of the horizon. The finest two views are over the two passes which bound the mountain. Over Hunter Pass lies Dix, a mighty precipice for most of its height. Over Elk Pass one sees range upon range of unspoiled mountains. First comes Colvin, with several great cliffs showing among the virgin timber, then Sawteeth, the Gothic Range, Marcy and finally MacIntyre. To the south is the Elk Lake country and to the east the farmlands and mountains of Vermont seem very close.

We descended into Elk Pass, following a recent surveyor's line. We reached the pass just south of the divide and followed it north to the Colvin trail. We found this course most beautiful, and as the timber was all first growth it was a much easier way than that which we took up the mountain.

REDFIELD 4,606 feet • Rating 7

This is another mountain without a trail. In fact none of the remaining mountains, unless specifically mentioned, has one. We left the

Marshall Collection, Saranac Lake Free Library

Giant Mountain from the Ausable Club.

Opalescent trail and followed Uphill Brook for about a mile to where it branched, passing some good-sized falls on the way. We took the right-hand fork and followed it almost to the summit of the mountain. As we tramped along through the glorious, unmarred woods which covered the mountain, we certainly felt grateful to the state for having purchased this land just in time to save it from the lumbering operations.[17]

The top of the mountain was very flat and heavily timbered, the highest timbered mountain in the state. We had to do considerable searching to see anything but finally found three places which gave us a complete view. From the first we could see all the way from Marcy to Blue Mountain. The day was the clearest I ever had on a mountain, and I don't know when I ever saw so many peaks. We could see Hamilton Mountain[18] at the extreme southern border of the Adirondacks and hundreds of peaks between it and us. In the direction of Vermont there seemed to be so many ranges of mountains we thought the farthest ones must be in New Hampshire. But finest of all was what lay immediately before us, the deep valley of Skylight Brook, backed by Allen, North River Mountain and farther still the Boreas Range, all heavily wooded. This view we got from a high rock. From a windfall we could look over the Santanoni and Seward country and the intervening woods, while from another rock we got a magnificent view of MacIntyre, Colden and Marcy.

WRIGHT (North MacIntyre) 4,585 feet [4,580] • Rating 20

We climbed this peak from the MacIntyre trail where it crosses a ravine three-quarters of the way up. It was a relatively easy mountain to climb, a half-hour's struggle through some scrubby balsam and ten minutes on bare rock bringing us to the top. We came down a different way, cutting directly for the waterfall halfway up the MacIntyre trail. By this route we dodged all the balsam.

The view was similar to that from the main peak and therefore very fine. However, it was neither as broad nor wild as the prospect from MacIntyre. The only thing it had which the main peak lacked was the view of MacIntyre towering above.

SADDLEBACK 4,530 feet [4,515] • Rating 24

The Gothic Range trail, already described, runs directly over this mountain. Thus it can be approached from two sides. The view is somewhat like that from Gothic and Basin, but these two lofty summits cut off a great deal of scenery. Though on the sixteenth-highest peak in the state, one feels on Saddleback as though he were in a hollow, so many higher mountains surround him. The top is not entirely bare, which naturally detracts somewhat. What I liked best about the view is the Great Basin and the massive rocky sides of Gothic.

ARMSTRONG 4,455 feet [4,400] • Rating 18

Where the Gothic trail comes out at the edge of a big precipice shortly below the summit, we headed into the mountain balsam covering the Armstrong ridge. Half an hour of a tussling climb brought us to the summit of this mountain. It was mostly covered with balsam, but there was one big, bare ledge which afforded us a magnificent view back over a wild country of lofty mountains, great slides and awe-inspiring gorges. It was much like the view toward Marcy and MacIntyre from its next-door neighbor but had the advantage of including the Gothic as well. Through the trees one could see toward Dix, Big Slide and the Wolf Jaws. But it is that one great view toward Marcy and MacIntyre which makes Armstrong rank high among the sightly mountains of the state.

PANTHER 4,448 feet [4,442] • Rating 10

The route by which we went up Panther has already been mentioned in the Santanoni description. Being so near that peak, the view is of necessity much like it. However, Santanoni cuts off many of those ponds which add so much to the view from the higher summit. The passes do not stand out so well from Panther either. However, you can see three peaks from Panther which are invisible from Santanoni, and you get a better view of the upper part of Cold River.

TABLETOP 4,440 feet [4,427] • Rating 39

About six miles from Keene Valley the trail up Marcy divides. One part keeps to Johns Brook. The other leaves it and gradually works its way up Tabletop and from there goes to Marcy, joining the Heart Pond trail.[19]

Tabletop, as its name implies, is very flat and in addition is heavily wooded on top. As a result, one can see almost nothing from it. About the only worthwhile view can be had from just off the trail a short way below the summit. Here one can look down the Johns Brook valley to Keene Valley.

MACOMB 4,425 feet [4,405] • Rating 14

We climbed Macomb from Elk Lake. There were logging roads well up the mountain, and these we followed out of the lumberman's slash. Then we cut over to the left to a big slide, which we followed to the height of land of the mountain. Then a half-hour's tramp through mountain balsam brought us to the summit.

Macomb, being at the southern end of the Dix Range, presents a view very much like that from Dix. However, being much nearer Elk Lake, the view over its great valley is even finer. As on Dix one gets a magnificent view of the great unmarred ranges of mountains, stretching from Allen to Wolf Jaws. The east side of the summit is not bare, and one can only get views by peering through the trees. To the north is a rather unpleasant-looking slash.

IROQUOIS (South MacIntyre) 4,411 feet [4,360] • Rating 12

This is probably the wildest mountain in the Adirondacks.[20] It is all densely wooded. On the whole mountain we could not see a single trace of the presence of any human being, not even an old blaze on a tree.

We climbed it from Herbert, descending between precipices to Algonquin Pass, and then ascending the most luxuriant woods I have ever seen. From the very summit nothing was visible, but we walked around, finding ledges from which we procured surprisingly good views.

From one we could look back at the cliffs of Herbert; from another we saw the Scott Pond plateau; from a third we got a bird's-eye glimpse of Wallface from almost directly above it; from still another we could look over miles of forest-covered hills toward Santanoni. But the best view of all was from the southwest side of the mountain where a panorama stretching from Marcy to Mount Adams spread out. In it all there was not a sign to show that man had ever been there. First came a great mountainside of magnificent timber, then the valley of the Flowed Lands and Calamity Brook, back of which rose the great Marcy Range.

We descended toward the foot of Algonquin Pass, almost as remarkable as Indian, and came out from there into the latter pass.

SEWARD 4,404 feet [4,361] • Rating 11

There is an old trail up Seward from near Ampersand Pond. We climbed the mountain from the Cold River side, following lumber roads to the edge of the slash, and found it an easy climb.

The view of the lake country is most remarkable from this peak. Long Lake, Lila, Tupper, the Saranacs and Lake Clear can be seen plainly. On the other side the whole range of high mountains is in view, too far off for their individual beauty to stand out but very alluring en masse. Lumbering operations scar the view toward Cold River. The most attractive part of the outlook I think is over Big Ampersand Pond.[21]

MIDDLE DIX (Little Dix) 4,404 feet [4,400] • Rating 32

We climbed this peak[22] from the head of the South Bouquet. We descended what closely approaches a 1,500-foot sheer precipice on the Hunter Pass side.

The view, so far as one may be obtained, is very much like that from the main peak, but there is much which the mountain balsam and Dix cut off. The only extra view you get is toward Dix itself. The mountain is by no means worth the trouble of climbing.

ROCKY PEAK RIDGE (Giant's Wife) 4,375 feet [4,420] • Rating 30

We climbed this mountain directly from Giant. If one is not to be defeated by dense, hard slash, this route is to be recommended, for fire has burned all the territory between the two mountains. In fact, it has burned completely over and around Rocky Peak Ridge.

The view from this mountain is much like that from the Giant but more slashy. Of course the entire scenery toward the St. Huberts valley is cut off. To the southwest a better view can be had. The slides on the Giant are a great addition to the view. What catches the eye most is a little pond just to the east of the summit, almost up to the four-thousand-foot mark.[23] All in all, the prospect is not so fine as that from the Giant and hardly worth the trouble to obtain.[24]

ALLEN 4,345 feet [4,340] • Rating 17

This is in great contrast to the last mountain, being wooded with virgin timber and showing no trace of human interference. We climbed it from Redfield, crossing the broad south valley of the Opalescent, from where there was an easy ascent to the wooded summit.

This is quite pointed, but unfortunately there are not many ledges. However, we found two spots from which we got good views. From the one we could see a semicircle of forested mountains and valleys from Marcy to Boreas. What I liked best about the view was the profile of Panther Gorge, looking near the bottom like a bucket, so straight were the sides. The view of the Gothic Range was also very fine. From the other spot we could see only one view, but it was worth the whole climb. It was of the Opalescent valley, backed by dark-green Redfield.

ESTHER 4,270 feet [4,240] • Rating 38

We cut up this mountain through some very bad slash from the Wilmington trail up Whiteface. The view in no way compensated us for the trouble. We could see slash toward Bloomingdale, slash toward the Wilmington Range, slash toward the open fields along the Ausable. We could see some of the high mountains in the distance to the south. The best part of the view was Whiteface, towering up directly to the southwest.

BIG SLIDE 4,255 feet [4,240] • Rating 27

I understand there is a trail up this mountain from Keene Valley. We climbed it through a primeval forest from the head of South Meadows Brook. Even if there had been no view, the woods alone were worth the climb.

The top of the mountain has been only partially cleared. One gets a very fine, uninterrupted view toward the Gothic Range, just across Johns Brook valley, and Marcy, Colden and MacIntyre. On the other side through the trees there are glimpses of the view toward Placid.

West Branch of the Ausable River, with Sentinel Range beyond.

UPPER WOLF JAW 4,255 feet [4,185] • Rating 33

We ascended this mountain from Armstrong. The descent from the latter was quite precipitous, and we had frequently to work our way along narrow ledges over high cliffs. The climb up Wolf Jaws was quite steep but through very fine woods.

Though the summit was covered with timber, we found some outlook. The best view was back over the range, but it was not so fine as the similar one from Armstrong and Gothic. We could also catch glimpses toward Dix, the precipitous shoulder of Armstrong and the Johns Brook valley.

STREET 4,216 feet [4,166] • Rating 41

We ascended this mountain from the tote road leading to Indian Pass. The climb was long, but there were no very steep places. The top is flat, and for the last half-hour we hardly rose at all. The summit is also heavily wooded so that, aside from glimpses toward Nye, Heart Pond and MacIntyre, we saw nothing.

NORTH SEWARD 4,215 feet [4,140] • Rating 26

Thirty-five minutes' push through the mountain balsam from Seward brought us to this peak.[25] The view was much like that from the main peak but not so broad. Only toward Big Ampersand was it better.

Lower Wolf Jaw 4,175 feet • Rating 25

The descent from Upper Wolf Jaw was almost as steep as that from Armstrong. Both the descent and the climb up the lower peak were made through very fine woods. The only signs of civilization we saw from Armstrong to the Lower Wolf Jaw was a surveyor's line.

The sight from the Lower Wolf Jaw is, I think, better than from the Upper. The view over the range is much the same, but in addition there is a view toward Giant and Keene Valley and another toward Dix. This latter I consider one of the great individual views of the Adirondacks.

Phelps (Little Tabletop, North Tabletop) 4,175 feet [4,161] • Rating 40

I climbed this mountain one dark afternoon from South Meadows. I never enjoyed climbing a mountain so little. There were hours of pushing through terrible fire slash, working up slides and walking logs. Fortunately, old lumber roads led up as far as South Meadows Mountain.

A view over miles of ugly slash toward Heart Pond and a glimpse through the second growth toward Marcy Brook are all one can see from the summit.[26]

Nye 4,160 feet [3,895] • Rating 42

This is quite an easy climb, or rather mostly descent, through pleasant woods from Street. It is so heavily wooded on top that one can see nothing except the forest he is in.

In descending directly to Indian Pass from here one encounters the worst possible slash. Once through it to the base of the mountain, there is a broad flat to cross before reaching the road.

South Seward 4,139 feet [4,040] • Rating 35

Three-quarters of an hour of travel through the thick mountain growth brought us from North Seward to this peak.[27] It is quite heavily wooded on top; hence little can be seen. However, there is a better view toward Upper Saranac and Tupper than from either of the two Sewards.

Sawteeth 4,139 feet [4,100] • Rating 16

We followed the old Gothic trail by Rainbow Falls to where it crossed the first big slide on Sawteeth. We followed this up a way and then cut directly for the summit.

We had been told that Sawteeth was so heavily wooded on top a person was a fool to climb it. The first part of the statement was certainly true, but there were also ledges. From these on the way up we got two superb views, one toward wooded Armstrong, the other toward bare Gothic. But the best view was reserved for the summit. This was looking over the Great Basin, finest stretch of primeval forest in the state, toward Allen, Skylight, Haystack, Marcy and Basin, all heavily wooded save where some great slide had left a white streak. If I were asked to name the most beautiful single view in the Adirondacks, I would be inclined to place this grand prospect first.

SOUTH DIX 4,135 feet [4,060] • Rating 37

We climbed this mountain from Macomb, descending and ascending through terrible slash. We left it by heading through the slash toward East Dix. This is one of the most desolate views I know of—nothing but burned, wasted land on all sides. A few fine mountains in the distance could not seem beautiful when seen over the dreary foreground.

SEYMOUR 4,120 feet • Rating 28

We climbed this mountain very easily from our camp at its base on the Cold River side. Old roads took us out of the lumber slash and from there on there were fine woods to the summit.

A big bare rock enables one to get a great view toward the Saranacs, Ampersand Pond, the Sawtooth Range and Ampersand Pass. From the other side through the trees one can get a good view of the high mountain section. Looking over Ouluska Pass, the Seward Range is prominent.

CASCADE 4,092 feet [4,098] • Rating 29

There used to be a trail up this mountain from Cascade Lake, but like many other Adirondack trails shown on the map, it is no more. We followed the general course of the old trail but saw no trace of it. Lower down the going was very steep, and we had to crawl and pull ourselves along the rocks. Higher up this steepness largely disappeared, and a fire slash was substituted.

The view is quite varied. To the west are the fertile farmlands of North Elba, with Round Pond standing out; north is bare and burned Pitchoff; east and southeast is a most unpleasant-looking fire slash, culminating in Porter; to the south and southwest are the big mountains.

COLVIN (Sabele)[28] 4,074 feet [4,057] • Rating 22

There is a good trail up this mountain, starting on the road from St. Huberts to Ausable Lake. It is above the average trail in beauty. The summit of the mountain is only partially cleared. However, some very desirable views can be obtained from it. The best, and in fact one of the best I have gotten, is across Lower Ausable toward the virgin wooded mountains to the west. Not one of those peaks in the Gothic Range has ever been lumbered. We could see far down the valley of the Ausable and over St. Huberts toward the Giant. Nippletop cut off the view to the east, though in itself it was well worthwhile seeing.

PORTER 4,070 feet [4,059] • Rating 36

It was an easy half-hour's journey, with little climbing, from the top of Cascade to Porter. Fire had burned up most of the slash, which helped to make the going easy. We descended a better way than we had come up Cascade, striking down to the valley which runs between Cascade and Porter to the west. However, it was by no means easy going.

The view was very much like that from Cascade but even slashier. It was rather sickening to see the burned land on all sides. The view toward the Gothic Range and Marcy, with Big Slide in the foreground, was better than the similar view from the neighboring peaks.

DIAL 4,023 feet [4,020] • Rating 31

The way we climbed this mountain has already been described in the Nippletop paragraphs. The view resembled the one from that peak to a considerable extent, but aside from the fact that trees blocked off much scenery, it was considerably less enticing.

EAST DIX 4,020 feet [4,012] • Rating 34

We climbed this mountain through very bad slash from South Dix. We followed back the same way for a while and then cut into the south valley of the Bouquet for Middle Dix.

The view was interesting and very different from any other but badly marred by fire. The part I liked best was looking across the deep valley of the Bouquet toward the side of Dix. Other interesting views were toward the ponds to the east and Macomb to the south.

CONCLUSION AND RATING

In conclusion I give a rating of these mountains as regards beauty. It is a composite of the ratings of my brother George, Herb Clark, a great Adirondack guide, and myself. We three climbed all these mountains together during the past two years and so have had a good opportunity to judge their merits. Of course I realize that ranking mountains is, at best, uncertain and subject to criticism. Nevertheless, I am offering this rating for what it is worth:[29]

1. Haystack	15. Gothic	29. Cascade
2. Santanoni	16. Sawteeth	30. Rocky Peak Ridge
3. Nippletop	17. Allen	31. Dial
4. Herbert	18. Armstrong	32. Middle Dix
5. MacIntyre	19. Colden	33. Upper Wolf Jaw
6. Basin	20. Wright	34. East Dix
7. Redfield	21. Giant	35. South Seward
8. Dix	22. Colvin	36. Porter
9. Marcy	23. Whiteface	37. South Dix
10. Panther	24. Saddleback	38. Esther
11. Seward	25. Lower Wolf Jaw	39. Tabletop
12. Iroquois	26. North Seward	40. Phelps
13. Skylight	27. Big Slide	41. Street
14. Macomb	28. Seymour	42. Nye

NOTES

1 Actually, the three later learned that they had mistaken the summit of Donaldson (then called North Seward) for Emmons (then called South Seward). They returned to climb the real Emmons in 1925 (George Marshall, 1951).

2 The four are Blake Peak (3,960 feet), Cliff Mountain (3,960), Nye Mountain (3,895) and Couchsachraga Peak (3,820). Modern surveys also revealed that a 47th peak, MacNaughton Mountain, tops four thousand feet (Goodwin 2004, 270).

3 See "A Day on the Gothics," p. 41.

4 The peak Marshall believed was Iroquois was later renamed Mount Marshall. The real Iroquois Peak lies northeast of Marshall. See Philip G. Terrie's article in this volume, p. 285.

5 Known as Hough Peak since 1935. Franklin B. Hough was a proponent of scientific forestry.

6 Russell Carson says Marcy was the fifth of the High Peaks to be climbed (Carson 1927, 261).

7 Of the six trails, this is the only one that no longer exists.

8 That is, Heart Lake at Adirondak Loj.

9 Iroquois Peak. The Marshall brothers mistakenly thought that Iroquois was nameless and so named it after their guide. See "Herbert Peak," p. 37.

10 This trail no longer exists.

11 Now known as Mount Marshall.

12 Hough Peak.

13 The Adirondack surveyor Verplanck Colvin. Russell Carson credits Old Mountain Phelps, the Keene Valley guide, with naming Basin in 1857 (Carson 1927, 114).

14 Lake Colden.

15 Carson says Giant was the first of the High Peaks to be climbed. He gives the honor to Charles Broadhead and his survey party, who ascended the peak on June 2, 1797 (Carson 1927, 261).

16 There is today a maintained trail from New Russia to Rocky Peak Ridge and Giant.

17 The state purchased 12,250 acres on Redfield, Allen, Dix and Marcy from the Ausable Club in 1922 (Brown 1985, 30).

18 Located near the hamlet of Wells about 65 miles away.

19 This trail to Table Top (it's two words on modern maps) no longer exists.

20 Appropriately enough, this peak is now called Mount Marshall. See p. 285.

21 Apparently, "Ampersand Pond" and "Big Ampersand Pond" both refer to Ampersand Lake.

22 Now called Hough Peak.

23 Mary Louise Pond. Its elevation is about 3,900 feet.

24 The forest has recovered since Marshall's day. Tony Goodwin, editor of *Adirondack Trails: High Peaks Region*, regards the trek to Rocky Peak Ridge from New Russia as one of the most scenic hikes in the Adirondacks, especially in fall.

25 Now called Mount Donaldson after Alfred Donaldson, an Adirondack historian.

26 Marshall's low opinion of the view from Phelps is puzzling, for there is a clear view of Mount Marcy and other High Peaks from open ledges on the summit.

27 Now called Mount Emmons after Ebenezer Emmons, a scientist who led the first expedition up Mount Marcy in 1837.

28 Carson says Old Mountain Phelps named the peak Sabele in the 1800s, after an Abenaki Indian who came to the Adirondacks in 1762 (Carson 1927, 36 & 178). The hamlet of Sabael on Indian Lake is named after him (the different spelling notwithstanding).

29 These ratings differ somewhat from those in *Peaks and People of the Adirondacks*. In the most dramatic change, the Marshalls upgraded Table Top from thirty-ninth to twenty-sixth in the rankings. (Carson 1927, 259.)

Lake Placid from the summit of Whiteface Mountain.

Whiteface Mountain

The Marshall brothers and Herb Clark, accompanied by Carl Poser, climbed their first High Peak, Whiteface Mountain, on August 1, 1918, when Bob was seventeen. It was not an auspicious start for the future Forty-Sixers: Bob was somewhat disappointed in the view. This previously unpublished account is taken from a typewritten manuscript in the Bancroft Library of the University of California at Berkeley.

We left Knollwood at about half past seven and took the 8:40 train to Lake Placid. At Placid we walked about a mile to the lake itself. Here we paid four dollars to have a motorboat take us to the head of the lake, where the trail started. Thus we got a good idea of Lake Placid. It is a very pretty lake, but its beauty is somewhat spoiled by too many camps. The northwest side, with MacKenzie[1] Mountain rising back of it, is particularly beautiful.

Whiteface is one of the hardest peaks I have climbed. The trail is both long and steep and extremely rough. It is very wet, for not only numerous unbridged brooks cross it low down, but there are also several swamps and mud holes which it crosses, while high up springs kept the rocks constantly wet and slippery. There was much soggy moss, and our feet were very wet. At least we did not become thirsty. Low down the trail ran through nice woods. Almost all was virgin forest, there being very little second growth. Higher up only the low alpine vegetation grew. Taking all things into consideration, I think the trail was second only to the Ampersand trail in beauty, among the mountain trails I have traversed. With all the people who climb Whiteface annually, it is remarkable that the trail is kept in such poor condition.

The view from the top was beautiful, as all mountain views of necessity are. But we were somewhat disappointed, for it was not all it was cracked up to be by any means. We had been told that from it could be seen the prettiest view in the state. Although at the time we had climbed no very high peaks, still at least two mountains we had already climbed afforded finer views.

We had a very good day and could see into Canada, we were told. Lake Champlain and Vermont could be seen clearly to the east, and in front several low mountains, many villages and much farmland. South was the big range of mountains, and several ponds, while to the southwest Placid was the most noticeable feature. MacKenzie and Moose mountains blocked the view to the west.

We decided to walk all the way back to the station. Herb and I wanted to rush, for we wanted to make as early a train as possible, and besides we both enjoyed the foolish sport of running down a mountain. Carl and George wanted to go very slowly, so we made a sort of compromise. Herb and I would run and then wait. After getting off the mountain we took the trail by way of Connery Pond and came out on the Wilmington Notch road. Here Herb and I again hit up the pace, while the other two lagged. Fortunately for our chances of catching the train, an auto, running around fifty miles an hour, gave us a lift to town, and we reached the station in plenty of time.

NOTES

1 Spelled "McKenzie" on modern maps.

Dates of Ascents

The following table lists the High Peaks in the order that Bob Marshall climbed them. The dates of the first forty-one ascents are taken from Marshall's handwritten chart. The others come from a table compiled by George Marshall. Both documents are in the Adirondack Room of the Saranac Lake Free Library. The peak names are those used today.

PEAK	DATE CLIMBED	PEAK	DATE CLIMBED
1. Whiteface	Aug. 1, 1918	24. Nippletop	Aug. 9, 1921
2. Marcy	Aug. 27, 1918	25. Rocky Peak Ridge	Aug. 10, 1921
3. Algonquin	Aug. 28, 1918	26. Macomb	Aug. 13, 1921
4. Iroquois	Aug. 28, 1918	27. South Dix	Aug. 13, 1921
5. Phelps	Aug. 27, 1919	28. East Dix	Aug. 13, 1921
6. Giant	June 8, 1920	29. Armstrong	Aug. 15, 1921
7. Dix	June 9, 1920	30. Upper Wolf Jaw	Aug. 15, 1921
8. Hough	June 9, 1920[1]	31. Lower Wolf Jaw	Aug. 15, 1921
9. Colvin	June 10, 1920	32. Sawteeth	Aug. 16, 1921
10. Haystack	June 11, 1920	33. Table Top	Aug. 17, 1921
11. Colden	June 13, 1920	34. Redfield	Aug. 19, 1921
12. Skylight	Aug. 10, 1920	35. Allen	Aug. 19, 1921
13. Basin	Aug. 11, 1920	36. Seward	Aug. 23, 1921
14. Saddleback	Aug. 11, 1920	37. Donaldson	Aug. 23, 1921
15. Gothics	Aug. 11, 1920	38. Panther	Aug. 24, 1921
16. Cascade	June 20, 1921	39. Santanoni	Aug. 24, 1921
17. Porter	June 20, 1921	40. Seymour	Aug. 25, 1921
18. Big Slide	June 21, 1921	41. Wright	Sept. 1, 1921
19. Marshall	June 27, 1921	42. Couchsachraga	June 23, 1924
20. Street	June 28, 1921	43. Gray	June 26, 1924
21. Nye	June 28, 1921	44. Cliff	June 26, 1924
22. Esther	Aug. 2, 1921	45. Blake[2]	
23. Dial	Aug. 9, 1921	46. Emmons[3]	June 10, 1925

NOTES

1 The date of Hough is obscured by another date written in the same space, but he apparently climbed it the same day as Dix.

2 Blake was one of four peaks that the Marshalls overlooked when identifying all the peaks above 4,000 feet. The others were Couchsachraga, Gray and Cliff. It's uncertain when Bob climbed Blake, but he probably did so the same year he climbed the other three.

3 The Marshalls believed they had climbed Emmons on Aug. 23, 1921, but they later learned they had not reached the summit.

Mount Marcy, looking across Panther Gorge from Haystack.

Mount Marcy

On August 27, 1918, several weeks after climbing Whiteface, the Marshall brothers and Herb Clark bagged their second High Peak: Mount Marcy, the state's tallest mountain. Again they were accompanied by Carl Poser. They began the hike at the Fuller farm in South Meadow. The next day they climbed Algonquin and Iroquois. The previously unpublished account of the Marcy hike is taken from a typewritten manuscript in the Bancroft Library of the University of California at Berkeley.

We left Fuller's at 7:15. We cut across the pasture, climbing two fences, and picked up the trail on the south side of the Meadows. For a short ways it followed South Meadows Brook, but where the brook turned down toward the lower valley of the Ausable the trail cut up across the foothills of Tabletop.[1] For four miles it rose steadily. On the way Herb pointed out innumerable historical places where grizzlies, panthers, guides, wild cats, rugarues,[2] surveyors and the famous ox had thrilling adventures. As we proceeded the scenery became more and more beautiful. The trail was quite often [open][3] due to the great fire, so that we could see well on all sides. To the right were Jo and MacIntyre, to the left Tabletop, ahead of us Colden and Avalanche Pass. Now and then through a favorable opening we caught glimpses of the head of Marcy, towering above the high summits of Tabletop. On all sides were burned trees or the second growth of poplars, cherries, birch and scrubby maple which had grown during the fifteen years since the fire's destruction.

At the end of about four miles the trail crossed a brook, and we came to the second deserted lumber camp along the trail. This, Mr. Fuller told us, was the place where we were to branch off onto the main Marcy trail.[4] After a brief search we found the correct trail, which ran at right angles to the course we had been pursuing. It rose more sharply than the other trail, but at no place was it very steep. It led for several miles over a corduroy road, following the course of Marcy Brook. To the left Tabletop rose steeply, a rough mountain covered with fire slash. To the right rose Colden, a light-green mountain, despoiled of most of its trees by lumbering. Back of us lay one of the most beautiful views I have ever seen. MacIntyre rose up sharply from the valley of Marcy Brook. Two peaks could be seen, their bare tops reflecting the sunlight. Between them ran the dry bed of a former stream.

As we rose along the trail raspberries became abundant and our progress was somewhat checked by our desire to eat. These were the biggest berries of their kind I have ever seen. They were also most pro-fuse, stretching up the side of Colden as far as the eye could see. One could sit down in one place and keep eating for ten minutes without moving had he the desire.

After proceeding thus for about an hour a sudden change came about. We came to a flat, the site of a former lumber camp. Here the stream tumbled down twenty feet in one leap.[5] Beyond the flat the trail left the stream and plunged into the woods. Here we were no longer sur-rounded by second growth. Neither man's destruction nor fire had as yet ventured so far upon the mountain. MacIntyre faded from view as did all other mountains. We could see nothing but pine forest through which we were traveling.

The trail led along in such a manner for several miles. The elevation was becoming so high that the trees were all gnarled, not tall and state-ly. Chiefly we saw spruces, hemlock and mountain balsam. While not rising very steeply the trail certainly did something more than slope gradually. Now and then through the trees we caught glimpses of a mountain ahead and to the left. This at first we thought was Marcy. Actually I believe it was Haystack. There was now no water to be had, nor had there been any since we left the flat. The raspberries stopped there also so that we were now without any means of quenching our thirst.

We were traveling along the edge of a ridge when suddenly through

Lake Tear of the Clouds below Mount Marcy.

an opening in the trees to our right we saw a huge mountain rising from about our level. It was Marcy. All our traveling heretofore had been in getting over the foothills. And though we had already risen to a height attained by only sixteen peaks in all the Middle Atlantic states, now we had yet before us a mountain rising more above our present elevation than Baker does above the village.[6]

We followed the ridge for a short distance, then turned at right angles to our former course, cut across a small valley and started the ascent of the mountain proper. At this elevation the only trees that grew were mountain balsam. The path was cut right through them. They rose on both sides to a height of about six or eight feet. When we had about half finished our ascent we came to the trail from Keene.[7] Here we more or less separated. George and Carl dropped behind, stopping now and then to take in the view. Herb and I rushed ahead. It is always far more pleasure for me to wait until I have reached the extreme summit of a mountain before I take the view. I do not believe in spoiling it by peeping before the proper time. Then when I finally do get the view I can stop and admire it to my heart's content without the necessity of turning around and going further. Before me is spread out the whole wonderful panorama of lake and stream, hills and mountains, forest and clearing, and I can gaze at the miracle suddenly unfolded as long as I desire with pleasure and wonder unspoiled by any previous view.

Above the five-thousand-foot mark even the balsams disappeared, and nothing was left but the rocks, mountain blueberries and some small yellowish alpine flower whose name I do not know. We reached the crest of the mountain together and took turns standing on the extreme summit. When I first stood there, the highest person in the state, Herb remarked, "I congratulate you, Mr. Ferguson, for being the highest man in this great state of ours. Higher than Whitman and Roosevelt and all the other great men."

But we did not waste much time in such talk. Ten minutes later when Carl and George came up we were sufficiently recovered from the first wonder of the view to notice a few of the smaller details. To the northwest lay Colden separated by the Opalescent valley from Marcy itself. Over and beyond it rose MacIntyre, a mighty mountain but not nearly as beautiful as lower down on the trail. Due north the ridges of Tabletop sloped into a broad valley which finally culminated in distant Lake Placid. Beyond Placid rose lofty Whiteface, a peak isolated far above the neighboring mountains. To the east were great mountains, their tops bare and their sides streaked with landslides. These were of the massive stone range, Basin, Saddleback, Gothic and Armstrong. And far beyond these we caught the distant gleam of Lake Champlain. To the southeast across a finely wooded valley, rose Haystack, a giant mountain with a rounded top and a shape exactly fitting its name, the fourth-highest mountain in the state.[8] Far beyond and just to the left rose another great mountain, which looked to be even higher than the one on which we stood. It was Dix, seventh in size of all the mountains of the state.[9] To the south and southwest stretched a wild country covered with primeval forests and dotted here and there by lakes. As far as the eye could reach stretched the woods, with here and there a low mountain to break the monotony. Only in the extreme foreground rose very high mountains, Skylight, Redfield and Allen. We seemed to be raised on a sort of reviewing stand, high above the rest, while below stretched myr-iad hills and mountains and forests and lakes, exhibiting their wonders to whosoever might choose to mount the stand.

NOTES

1 The trail went along the base of Phelps Mountain, which Marshall elsewhere refers to as Little Tabletop or North Tabletop.

2 An imaginary monster (*Dictionary of American Regional English*, Vol. 4, 2002).

3 A word is missing in the typescript.

4 They probably were at Avalanche Camp. From there, they would have climbed to the east to Indian Falls, then turned south toward Marcy.

5 He apparently is describing Indian Falls.

6 Mount Baker rises nearly 900 feet above the village of Saranac Lake. Thus, at this point in the hike, the Marshalls should be somewhere below 4,444 feet.

7 Cut by Ed Phelps, son of the celebrated guide Old Mountain Phelps.

8 By today's measurements, Haystack is the state's third-highest mountain.

9 More recent surveys rank Dix as the sixth-highest mountain in the state.

View from Algonquin Peak of Boundary and Iroquois, with Wallface at far right.

Herbert Peak

While on Algonquin Peak on August 28, 1918, the Marshalls and Herb Clark decided to continue to the rarely visited Iroquois Peak. Because the brothers mistakenly thought the peak was unnamed, they dubbed it Herbert Peak after their guide.[1] This account is taken from a typewritten manuscript in the Bancroft Library. We pick up the narrative where the three begin their rugged bushwhack from the col between Algonquin and Iroquois.

We had not taken three steps off the trail when we were thankful that Herb had brought along the ax. We had come to an impassable thicket of balsam. From there on for about a quarter of a mile we had to progress through the balsam, pushing, chopping and tearing. Then we came to a rocky peak and found from here that there were two more valleys through which we had to pass before we would come to the peak we were aiming for. We called this first peak Robert. On the very top of it we found something which we had been looking for in various places for years. It was a Colvin nickel plate.[2]

We did not stop at this peak long, but having taken a picture, we once more plunged into the thicket. I will not weary you with a detailed account of our tussle to get through. We found an old trail which had not been used for years and followed it. But our walking in most places was just as hard as where there was no trail. It was probably cut by Verplanck Colvin thirty-five or forty-five years ago, and there was ample time for it to become overgrown.[3] We tore our clothing, we tore our skins, we got stuck fast in an extra-thick clump, we caught our feet in a root, we did everything uncomfortable but fall. This we could not do for the balsams were so thick that they held us up. We crossed the ridge between the two valleys and called it George Peak but did not stop to examine it. The last valley, while not as long as the first, was the most difficult. Added to the tussle against the balsam was the job of scaling at places almost perpendicular walls. At last, however, we reached the end of the balsams and had nothing left between us and our goal except an easy fifty-yard climb.

The view we got from this peak repaid us for all the effort we had in reaching it. It was even finer than the view from the main peak, though very much the same. We unanimously agreed that this was the finest view any of us had ever gotten. And since the view from the main peak of MacIntyre is generally considered by those who had done much climbing to be the finest mountain view in the Adirondacks, it is only fair to say that the view from this peak (which we christened Herbert), inasmuch as none of these experts probably ever climbed it, really is the finest in the Adirondacks.[4] As I above said, it is very much like the view from the main peak. You have substituted, however, in place of Clear Pond,[5] Mount Jo and South Meadows, the wild land lying to the south-west. Directly below us was as fair a valley as I have ever seen. On the other side rose the south peak of MacIntyre.[6] Through the bottom of this valley flowed a brook, five hundred feet below. At one place it formed quite a fair-sized pond. The sides of this valley were wooded by a primeval forest of huge pines and spruces and hemlocks. Only at one place was a natural mountain meadow far up the other peak. From Herbert Peak the view of both Indian and Avalanche passes was also better than from the main peak. A large-sized pond surrounded by a marsh and fringe of pines undiscernible from the other peak could plainly be seen from here. It was far up on the side of MacNaughton Mountain and higher than the top of Ampersand. It flowed into another, larger pond to the east and from there flowed down into Indian Pass and the headwaters of the St. Lawrence. Much of the burned and lumbered land which had detracted from the other view was invisible here, and in its place we saw only beautiful wild ponds and streams and primeval forests.

It is my firm opinion that not ten people have ever been fortunate enough to behold the finest of all Adirondack mountain views. ... We would have liked to remain on this wild, inaccessible and beautiful peak for a long time, but after twenty minutes' stay we had to leave.

NOTES

1 See Philip G. Terrie's article, p. 285.

2 He is referring to a survey bolt placed by Verplanck Colvin on what is now called Boundary Peak.

3 Carson (1927, 201) also says Colvin cut a trail to Iroquois during his survey work.

4 After he climbed all the High Peaks, Marshall bestowed this honor upon Mount Haystack.

5 Another name for Heart Lake at Adirondak Loj.

6 A reference to the peak now named after Marshall.

Courtesy of Roger Marshall

George Marshall and Herb Clark next to survey bolt on Boundary Peak.

Right to left: Gothics slides, Saddleback and Basin.

A Day on the Gothics

Marshall climbed Gothics with his brother George and guide Herb Clark on Aug. 11, 1920. Starting from their campsite in Panther Gorge, they climbed three other High Peaks—Haystack, Basin and Saddleback—and ascended about four thousand feet en route to Gothics. They then retraced their route back to camp. Bob, then nineteen, and George, sixteen, had trouble keeping up with the fifty-year-old Clark. Later, Bob rated this as his and George's third-hardest hike together in the Adirondacks.[1] He estimated that they hiked twenty miles and ascended 9,200 feet. Both figures are way off on the high side, but there's no doubt it was a tough day, for they had climbed the equivalent of seven High Peaks. The following article was published posthumously in High Spots, *the magazine of the Adirondack Mountain Club, in January 1942.*

When we awakened, things looked bad. A heavy fog hung low on the mountains, and while not raining, it looked as though we should be forced to spend the day in camp. Nevertheless, we wasted no time on sighing but started breakfast cooking. The dehydrated vegetables took less time than usual to cook, and three-quarters of an hour after arising we were eating a delicious meal. Shortly after eight the fog began to rise, blue appeared and, although it was by no means certain how the day would turn out, we decided to climb at least Haystack.

It was 8:23 when we started on what we hoped would be the big day of our trip—the traverse of the range.[2] The ascent to the forks of the trail in the flats between Haystack and Bartlett [Ridge] was a glorious climb through a magnificent coniferous forest, and because it continued to clear, the walk seemed even finer. At the forks, where the trail goes down to Upper Ausable, we turned at right angles toward the mountain itself. There followed thirty-five minutes during which we seemed to be going mostly in a vertical direction. However, our wind was good and we were fresh; so the climb did not bother us particularly. The two-thirds-way mark of the climb was at a cold, shallow spring back of a big rock. Then came that very steep climb over sharp rocks or soft footing where the mountain flora, particularly the beautiful Greenland sandwort and three-toothed cinquefoil, were growing. The trees had shrunk to insignificant size. We were conscious of a wonderful landscape unfolding, but we preferred to wait to look until we stopped just below the summit at a shoulder overlooking Panther Gorge.

The mist was rising, and Marcy had a halo about it. The sun was shining pleasantly and made Panther Gorge look less fierce than usual but possibly more beautiful. We sat there quite a while, gazing on the wild scenery and the rising clouds. Then we went to the summit and looked over on the heavily wooded valley and mountains on the other side. Our eyes rested on the range we were to traverse, and we realized far better than the map could indicate what a hard day lay before us. As we looked around us we realized that this was one of the few places east of the Rockies where a person could look over miles of territory without seeing civilization.

The question as to whether it would clear seeming to have been answered in the affirmative, we hastened to Little Haystack and after following the ridge a little farther descended rapidly toward the Great Basin, 1,900 feet below. We were soon in the woods, passing through as fine a cluster of ladies' tresses as I have ever seen. Always down, down we went as Herb set a rapid pace. Finally the dropping ceased, and we came to a cold fresh brook near the head of the Great Basin. After climbing over a little ridge and passing an old camp, the real climb of 1,900 feet to the summit of the Adirondacks' eighth peak commenced.[3] It was a bigger rise than to the summit of Haystack. Herb led a very fast pace, hardly resting at all. At one place he and George in the lead kicked up a hornet's nest, and one nipped me. I let out a howl and told my comrades what I thought of them, but they merely laughed. Herb cut away several small trees which blocked the trail. It was just eleven o'clock when, after emerging from the woods and traversing the rocky stretch near the top, we reached the summit. We had descended and then ascended 2,000 feet in an hour and three minutes.[4]

The view from Basin was almost as marvelous, as wild, as incomparable as from Haystack. The most impressive points were the three great, deep, wild valleys: the Basin, from which the mountain derives its name, a natural amphitheater, bounded by the precipitous walls of Sawteeth, Armstrong, Gothics, Saddleback, Basin, Haystack and Bartlett; Panther Gorge, that fiercest of all the wild places among the great mountains, besides which the celebrated canyons of Colorado look tame, and peaceful Johns Brook valley, a deep but gentler gash among the mountains. In the latter direction were some signs of slash, and the burnt area toward the Giant seemed more prominent than from Haystack. But on the whole the view was as unmarred as one could desire.

After fifteen minutes of extreme delight, we started on, hoping to spend a longer time on the way back. It was beginning to cloud up again, and as we were a little afraid of rain, we were anxious to hasten towards our destination.

An easy drop of about three hundred feet and another rise of a couple of hundred and we were ready for perhaps the steepest part of the whole trip. We could not go very fast, and even Herb continually cautioned us to go carefully. Although we went slowly, because of the very steepness, we dropped rapidly. Suddenly I heard George ahead exclaim, "Well, I've seen pretty many ways of traveling in the mountains but never this before." Looking over his shoulder I perceived a long rope stretched the length of a thirty-five- or forty-foot slide having a grade of at least 130 percent. Herb was just starting to let himself down. His feet acted slightly as brakes, but he depended mostly upon the rope for support. Had it broken he would have shot down the mountainside like a solid shot from a cannon. George and I followed, one at a time, for we were not anxious for this to happen. Shortly after, we came to the bottom of the mountain and crossed a beautiful, cool valley with the finest gentians and Indian poke I have ever seen. The former were particularly beautiful, literally covering the floor of the valley.

The climb up Saddleback was about 450 feet but not hard. When we reached the top we found that clouds had blotted out most of the scenery. However, the wonderfully wooded Basin, probably the finest big stretch of woodland I have ever seen, was visible and, together with the forest slopes of Saddleback and the neighboring mountains, afforded fine enough scenery to make anyone happy, even though all distant objects were obscured. Even this had its advantages, for no slash was thus visible, leaving only a world of forest and fog.

Soon we continued again along the trail, which led along the north side of the summit at the very edge of a very steep thousand-foot drop. Had a person fallen there would have been no stopping till the bottom was reached. There was a distance of about two hundred yards between the two peaks, and then began the last descent on the outward journey. While not as steep as the previous one, the four-hundred-foot drop was nonetheless rather sharp. Through the trees we could see the bold, sharp aspect of Gothics, with their awful precipices. The first peak looked like a needle pointing toward heaven.

We were beginning to grow thirsty. Realizing that the last chance to strike water would be in the valley, we searched for it. There was none in the saddle, but a short ways down on the Johns Brook side we struck a spring. We ate sandwiches and a little chocolate and washed them down with cold, clear water. Soon we were refreshed and started the final long climb for our goal.

The ascent was the rockiest we had ever encountered. It led along a steep slide. On mountains more often climbed and near civilization a ladder would have been considered imperative. Here it was impossible, and there was nothing to which to tie ropes. So we struggled up, taking care not to slip and cut ourselves on the sharp stone. We were thankful the way did not lead at the very edge of the worst precipice, over which Colvin's guide had so nearly plunged forty-five years before.[5] Those were the pioneering days, when the Gothics had rarely been scaled and many of the neighboring peaks were absolutely untraveled save by wild-cat and bear. For four million acres around, civilization was almost unknown just forty-five years before. Now we were in the heart of the wildest part left unscarred, an area tiny compared with the original one, yet we all were thankful that that much was left.

Finally we reached the first peak of the Gothics. It had once more cleared, although in the extreme distance, especially toward the east, things were invisible. Looking back toward Marcy, however, was one of the finest views imaginable of deep gorges, rocky precipices and virgin forest, piled together on a tremendous scale. We soon continued to the main peak, for we were anxious to reach our destination, and in a short time stood on the highest point, ten miles and 9,200 feet by up-and-down climbing from Panther Gorge. It was now 1:02. The journey had taken about four-and-a-half hours.

View from Haystack of (right to left) Basin, Saddleback and Gothics.

As we looked back on the wild land over which we had come, we could appreciate the pains with which we had traversed those deep hollows among the mountains, and we also appreciated the hardships before us on the return journey. Yet we did not spend much time on these thoughts for the view captivated us. Johns Brook Valley, although partly lumbered, was a lovely stretch of light green; Keene Valley, with the sun shining on the broad fields, looked very hospitable. The Giant appeared as the giant among the high mountains beyond, while directly east the Ausables, Colvin and Nippletop and the great Dix Range appeared as an endless barrier.

The clouds began to rise again, so I hastened down to a little cave where we had left the haversack. When I returned a couple of minutes later, I was amazed to find that the clouds had come up so rapidly that the entire landscape to the east was blotted out and the fog was rapidly surging beyond us to the west. Soon we stood on an island among the mist with just a few high peaks jutting above it. It was useless to remain longer, so after finishing our bread we started on the return journey at 1:42. Herb made several jocular predictions concerning our probable wetness before reaching camp, but as several rainstorms might come and go before then, there was no use hurrying. We were, however, anxious not to lose the poor trail in the fog, but with Herb's great skill we encountered no difficulty.

Despite the fact that there was no hurry, Herb proceeded to set a terrific pace down the very steep, rocky face of the Gothics, all the time admonishing George and myself to go slowly and carefully. We were not a bit bothered by his speed but decided to take our time, go as he would. Had he wanted, he could probably have been at Panther Gorge by the time we reached Basin. We noticed and admired his method. He never seemed to rush, and yet he never stopped or hesitated at the steepest place. It was steadiness that made his speed. George and I would stop every now and then at a bad place or sit down and gently slide, but never Herb. This sliding, incidentally, put two great big holes in my trousers.

In about half an hour we reached the valley where Herb stopped for us to catch up. The rise up Saddleback was a couple of hundred feet less than the descent we had just made, and less rocky, but nonetheless harder, for Herb now showed no sympathy, there being no danger of falling and hurting ourselves, but rushed and urged us on. We soon reached the first peak. The skirting of the precipice on the level summit seemed thrilling because we could not see the bottom. It seemed an endless drop.

The way over to Basin was not nearly as bad as we anticipated, despite the fact that we had to go over a very steep hill between and had almost one thousand feet of climbing.

When we reached the summit we found the most absolute blank I have ever seen. The fog had come down so thickly that we could not see more than ten yards away. There was nothing visible but the three of us and a little rock. We were, however, all in fine humor, and Herb made us laugh a great deal.

Near the top of Basin it was fully as steep and rocky as the Gothics. There were many places we had to let ourselves down with the most extreme care. At one place was a slide fully thirty feet in the center and about twenty-five at the side. Around was thick mountain balsam through which it was almost impossible to go. In the center there was a log about ten feet down, and if one could make that safely, the other twenty feet were comparatively easy, for it was not quite so steep below. Herb with his usual skill did this, but his weight so weakened the log that when I tried to use it, it almost snapped in two, so I had to return to the top or slide down twenty-five feet. I preferred the former course, particularly with my trousers seat in its precarious condition, and pulled myself back to safety by means of the Labrador tea, as Colvin's guide had done forty-five years before. George, however, was not so fortunate. He had taken the side way and had put his trust and weight on the trees which Herb had cut but not removed on the way out. I had just gotten once more to safety when I saw him shoot down fifteen to twenty feet like a cannonball. I thought surely he was hurt, but fortunately he received no injury. I followed his way, taking extreme care on what I used for support.

After this excitement the way was much less steep and the descent through the woods most pleasant. Yet I could not help but feel a dread for the 1,800-feet climb before us. Most people consider Ampersand a good climb, yet here was a climb before us even higher than Ampersand, fully as steep—after seven thousand feet of previous climbing. We crossed the head of the Basin at a rapid pace, and at the brook beyond the little hill we ate a little chocolate and took a brief rest preparatory to the hardest climb of the trip. Yet our expectations were far worse than the fact, and about when we thought we were half done we came out on the rocky ridge leading to Haystack. During the hour we had been below timberline it had cleared up a bit, but the fog was still very thick. As we struggled along the rocky ridge, George and I were frankly tired. Herb, however, seemed to rush. The journey from Basin had taken us just an hour and twenty minutes.

We remained on the summit of Haystack about a quarter of an hour. It was clearing up cold, and most of the landscape was unfolding before us. Mist was still around the tops of the highest mountains, but from all the valleys it had risen. With a crown of clouds the beauties of Marcy and the Gothics and Dix were only accentuated. We looked back over the course we had pursued with a feeling of deep satisfaction. Ahead of us was all downhill; the hard part was passed. We were merry, and Herb joked as he hammered the nails from the second heel I had lost that day. Yet a feeling of awe of the sublime was with us all the time, increased perhaps by the rolling clouds, the coolness and clearness of autumn, and the approaching night. It was not as beautiful as on a perfectly clear day with the sunlight streaming, yet in many respects it was the most impressive time I ever spent on the mountains.

We had to get to camp, so around a quarter past five we started the last descent. Haystack is perhaps the steepest big mountain of the Adirondacks, yet the steepness is rather evenly distributed and there are no very bad places. About halfway down to camp Herb cut down a good-sized dead tree and told me to carry it into camp. It was about twenty feet long and continually caught among the trees at the bends in the trail. I counted twenty-two other trees on the way to camp which would have done just as well for firewood and meant a lot less work for me, but we had good fun joking about me lugging a tree halfway down the mountain. Nearer camp George and Herb again brought one in, so we had plenty of wood for the rest of our stay. It was 6:04 when we returned from the hardest day of our lives. We had been gone nine hours and forty minutes.

We set to work immediately preparing for supper, and within fifty minutes it was ready. It was great. I have seldom eaten a better meal. The main course was that almost perfect dish of dehydrated beans and potatoes boiled together, with thick butter sauce. Of this there was more than we could eat despite our long tramp. Bread and jam was another thing which we ate in great quantities. Small portions of spaghetti, soup, coffee, cakes and the finest water that ever flowed rounded off the delightful meal. Its pleasure will live long after the joy of far fancier meals have died from my memory and stomach.

It was very pleasant sitting around the campfire after the labors of the day and very comfortable to dry out. We discussed the events of the day and calculated, with the aid of the map, how many feet we had climbed. We made the following chart of climbs, and of course for every foot of ascent there was a corresponding foot of descent:

OUT	MOUNTAIN	BACK
1,710	Haystack Mt.	320
100	Little Haystack	1,800
140	Ridge in Basin	160
1,900	Basin Mt.	400
300	Rope slide to hill	650
450	Saddleback Mt.	430
540	Little Gothic	100
200	Gothic	
5,340	TOTAL	3,860
3,860		
9,200	GRAND TOTAL	

Thus in one day we had climbed a fifth again as high as the climb up Pikes Peak from its base. Counting ascent and descent together, we had gone 18,400 feet, or more than three-and-a-half miles just up and down. Our total mileage for the day was about twenty miles.[6] We had seen no one outside our party in over twenty-four hours.

When the fire was nearly out we got ready for bed. Herb went into the tent first, and after walking up to the crossing, George and I followed. It was delightfully cool, and the clear stars shining through the piney canopy promised a great day for the morrow. As we laid our heads down on this wildest bed, it was the knowledge of having spent the hardest, the wildest and one of the very most enjoyable days of our lives.

NOTES

1   Descriptions of the two hardest hikes, a traverse of the Dix Range and a circuit of Whiteface Mountain, are found, respectively, on p. 53 and p. 79. Bob Marshall also rated the Gothics hike the third-best day he spent in the Adirondacks with his brother. The ratings are among George Marshall's papers in the Adirondack Room of the Saranac Lake Free Library.

2   That is, that portion of the Great Range from Haystack to Gothics.

3   More recent surveys rank 4,827-foot Basin at the state's ninth-highest peak.

4   For Marshall's estimates of the ascents and descents, see note 6.

5   Colvin encountered ice and snow on the summit when he climbed Gothics in October 1875. He writes that one of the guides "attempting to pass along below the crest, where some ice-clad stems of the Labrador tea (*Ledum latifolium*) alone offered assistance to the hand, was suddenly suspended over the edge of a cliff– where, a thousand feet below, the clouds were drifting–and rescued himself by the sheer strength of his muscular arms" (Schaefer 1997, 167).

6   Marshall's figures are off. The hike from Panther Gorge to Gothics is roughly 4.75 miles, making a 9.5-mile round trip. Topographical software reveals that the total ascent is about 3,850 feet on the way to Gothics and about 2,550 on the return trip. Thus, the total ascent was about 6,400 feet.

Photo by Lynda McIntyre

Nippletop and Dix mountains from Elk Lake.

Mountaineering
in the Adirondacks

In August 1921, the Marshalls and Herb Clark went on an arduous thirteen-day trek during which they climbed eighteen High Peaks. The following year, in an article he wrote for the New York Evening Post, *Bob Marshall estimated that they had hiked more than three hundred miles and ascended fifty thousand feet. On one of the days, the threesome started in Elk Lake, climbed five High Peaks in the Dix Range and straggled into a boardinghouse in St. Huberts fifteen hours later. Marshall regarded this as the toughest hike he and his brother did together.[1] Back then, most of the Dix Range lacked trails. Nowadays, trails and herd paths connect all five summits, making it much easier to bag them all on one hike. The following account of the entire thirteen-day expedition is taken from the* Evening Post. *The original article contained introductory material that later appeared in* The High Peaks of the Adirondacks. *Since that booklet is reprinted elsewhere in this volume, nearly all of that material has been omitted here. Our title is the one Marshall used in his handwritten manuscript.*

There are forty-two peaks in the Adirondacks over 4,000 feet high, of which sixteen rise more than 4,500, while two surpass 5,000 feet.[2] These peaks are in the northeastern section of the Adirondacks. All except four lie in a region unpenetrated other than by lumber roads,[3] with an area of more than six hudred square miles. … Perhaps the best way to illustrate the possibilities of this region would be to mention a two-weeks trip on which, like almost all I have ever taken, I was accompanied by Herb Clark, the Saranac guide, and my brother George. The figures at the end of each paragraph refer to number of feet climbed in a day.

51

Herb Clark and Frank Hale.

August 8. We took train from Saranac to Placid and then carried our thirty-five-pound packs twenty-three miles along the road to Frank Hale's house at the foot of St. Huberts Hill. Took an evening walk to Chapel Pond. 1,800.

August 9. We followed the Dix trail to the slide at the foot of the mountain, then turned west and crossed the horribly slashed valley of the Bouquet. We ascended Dial and followed the narrow ridge to Nippletop, from which we got a remarkable view. We descended through a virgin forest to Elk Pass, along the route which Charles Dudley Warner had taken forty-five years before.[4] From here we journeyed directly home [i.e., the Hale residence]. 5,700.

August 10. Ascended Giant by trail in two hours. Descended the steep and rocky east side to Roaring Brook Pass and then climbed Rocky Peak Ridge, a badly burned and ragged mountain. Climbed down five hundred feet to a little pond at an elevation of three thousand feet, uncharted on the maps, probably the highest body of water of its size in the state.[5] We returned to St. Huberts a slightly different way,

Courtesy of Roger NMarshall

Herb Clark and Bob Marshall near Hunters Pass.

encountering as bad slash as I have ever experienced. For nine-and-a-half hours the only drinking water we had on this scorching day was the two quarts in our canteen. 6,100.

August 11. Came through seldom-traversed Hunter Pass to Elk Lake. There were some very high cliffs in the center, which appeared ready to topple over. The going was very rough on the north and in the center of the pass, but on the south side old lumber roads furnished fine traveling. 3,400.

August 12. It was raining in the morning so we were forced to take a day of rest at Elk Lake. We walked to Blue Ridge and back in the morning, fifteen miles. In the afternoon we climbed Boreas, from which we got an unusual rainy-day view. 3,300.

August 13. Came from Elk Lake to St. Huberts, climbing over McComb,[6] South Dix, East Dix, Middle Dix[7] and Dix. We climbed a total of 7,800 feet and descended about 8,400, covering over thirty miles, of which twenty miles had no trail.[8] For a couple of miles we followed a lumber road and then up a trail of the choppers, well up

McComb, cutting pulp and reached a slide which took us almost to the summit. We descended through a bad slash to the foot of South Dix, up which there was only a short climb.

Most of the way from South to East Dix we walked over down timber four to eight feet high. From East to Middle Dix we had to cross the burned Bouquet valley. Constant care had to be taken not to take a false step, for a broken leg or worse could easily have resulted. This would be serious with two high mountains intervening between the nearest settlement. The descent from Middle Dix was down what amounted to almost a sheer precipice of 1,500 feet. We had descended a short way when we came to a straight drop of twenty feet, below which was a three-foot ledge, but as Herb remarked, it was better to be a living coward than a dead hero. So we turned back and commenced a fresh descent.

Working our way among the mountain growth, crossing slides on cracks, using slender roots to support our weight, we finally reached the valley below Dix. Here lumbering operations had dried up the brooks, and we had the prospect of climbing the seventh mountain of the state [in height] after a hard day without water.[9] Luckily, we stumbled across a cold spring. The ascent, while not particularly rough woods, seemed interminable. After a while I felt sure we were damned to climbing that mountain forever. After a few centuries, however, we reached the summit, where we hastily ate a cold supper at seven o'clock.

The steep descent to the slide we made at top speed, for we wanted to get across the very rough valley of the Bouquet by night. Just across the slide we got off the trail and had to tear through the brush for forty minutes until we reached it again. There was enough daylight left to see our way across the bad places along the river, but when the trail left it and headed between Noonmark and Round, night had settled. Up to the divide the moon helped considerably, but when we reached the center it went behind the clouds, and we had to feel our way along the rocky path. Several times I thought I had stepped in an endless pit, but in every case the hole had a bottom, though I believe my leg had to frequently grow ten feet to reach it. I will never forget the joy I felt when I heard Herb, who was ahead, yell, "By goll! I guess we won't have to sleep out after all. There's a light ahead." In a few minutes we reached Hales' after fifteen hours of continuous travel. It made a very pleasant ending to a great day to find that Mrs. Hale very kindly had a dandy supper awaiting us. 7,800.

August 14. It rained from morning till night, so we recuperated from our previous day's exercise. Walked fourteen miles to Euba Mills and back in the afternoon. Had a delightful evening walk up the Ausable.[10] 2,100.

August 15. Having cleared up beautifully, we started off next morning along the Gothic trail. When near the top of that mountain we turned to the right and after a half-hour's struggle with mountain balsam reached the summit of Armstrong. We descended the very precipitous north side. We had to work our way along over one- or two-foot ledges, with drops of thirty or forty feet awaiting a misstep. It was no consolation to reflect that every few years a great landslide started on this range of mountains. We certainly were encouraging them, but they refused to start.

Reaching the hollow in safety, we commenced the ascent of Upper Wolf Jaw and soon reached the top. The descent from the mountain was steep but not as precipitous as Armstrong. Next we climbed Lower Wolf Jaw and descended from there to the Ausable, where we followed trails and the road home. All day we had passed through luxuriant virgin forest and had time to enjoy three different mountain views. Had we done our 5,300 feet of climbing all on one mountain, we undoubtedly would have found much less beauty and probably no more excitement. In the evening we walked to Keene Valley and back. 5,300.

August 16. We walked to the foot of Lower Ausable and after visiting Rainbow Falls started along Gothic trail. We were planning to climb Sawteeth, despite the fact that we had been told by an old guide that we were fools to attempt it, as it was all heavily timbered on top. After half an hour we left the trail and headed for the summit. From one ledge we got a fine view toward Armstrong and St. Huberts, while from another we got a remarkable view of the sides of Gothic. But from the very summit of this "worthless mountain" we got the finest view of all, as fine a single view as I have ever had, towards Haystack, Marcy and Basin. The descent to the valley between Sawteeth and Gothic was steep, but the ascent of the latter by the now seldom-used trail was steeper yet. Being a perfect day, there were more than twenty people on top of Gothic, which was in marked contrast to the summit we had just come from, on which not twenty people had ever stood. 5,700.

August 17. Taking up our packs for the first time in nine days, we said goodbye to Frank Hale and started for Keene Valley. We followed

Pyramid Peak on Gothics as seen from Sawteeth.

an excellent trail up Johns Brook Valley, over Tabletop and on to Marcy.[11] Although the weather was not very good, we met fifty-two people on or near the summit. Descended to the Opalescent River, where we stopped in a lean-to. 4,800.

August 18. It rained hard all day, so we stayed pretty close to camp. Built a much-needed bridge from the trail to the lean-to. 200.

August 19. I never knew of better weather than there was on this day. We followed Uphill Brook by some beautiful waterfalls and then, taking the right-hand branch of the brook, headed for the summit of Redfield. Here, by considerable searching, we got three magnificent views. Saw where someone, possibly a surveyor, had cut his way through from Skylight, but he stopped at the very summit, which is heavily wooded, and failed to get a view. This was the only sign of man we saw during the whole day's travel through this glorious wilderness.

We descended to the broad valley of Skylight Brook and then climbed Allen. Aside from the many large old trees which covered this region, a very thick second generation had also sprung up, which was very good from a forestry standpoint but very bad from an optical viewpoint, as they persisted in scratching the eyes. After cutting out quite a few branches we obtained a very enticing view from Allen. It was pleasant to feel that we were looking where man had very likely never looked before. We returned in much the same way as we went out. When we reached camp we calculated we had fallen in at least five hundred holes for the day. 5,200.

August 20. Getting an early start, we walked out to South Meadows in the morning, passing some of the most imposing scenery in the Adirondacks on the way, including the flumes on the Opalescent and Avalanche Lake. At the meadows we beheld human beings for the first time in two days. We had seen but three people in seventy hours, yet we were camping right along a main trail. Had we cared to go back a little way—to Skylight Brook, for instance—we could have gone all summer without seeing anyone. Walked out to Placid and took the train back to Saranac, ending a thirteen-day trip on which we walked over three hundred miles and climbed about fifty thousand feet, with the same descent. 400.

Such enjoyment is possible for anyone. If you get back in the woods your lodging is free and the cost of board is trifling. But you get amusement such as the most expensive tour can never furnish.

NOTES

1 The ratings are found among George Marshall's papers in the Adirondack Room of the Saranac Lake Free Library.

2 The most recent surveys found forty-three peaks over 4,000 feet and seventeen over 4,500 feet. Only Mount Marcy and Algonquin Peak top 5,000 feet.

3 The four exceptions are Whiteface, Esther and Giant mountains and Rocky Peak Ridge.

4 Charles Dudley Warner describes his ascent of Nippletop in his 1878 book *In the Wilderness*.

5 Mary Louise Pond, elevation about 3,900 feet.

6 The accepted spelling today is Macomb. See Carson 1927, 27.

7 Renamed Hough Peak in 1935. See Philip G. Terrie's article, p. 285.

8 Marshall's figures seem to be high. Retracing their route on mapping software shows that they hiked about fifteen miles and ascended less than six thousand feet.

9 Later measurements showed Dix to be the sixth-highest summit in the state.

10 The East Branch of the Ausable River flows through St. Huberts. Euba Mills is a small settlement on State Route 9.

11 The trail from the Johns Brook Valley to Table Top no longer exists.

Courtesy of Roger Marshall

Bob Marshall and Herb Clark rejoice at reaching the 300-mile mark in their multiday trek.

Algonquin Peak in winter.

A Winter Ascent
of MacIntyre

Winter climbs of the High Peaks are common these days, but they were still fair-
ly rare in Marshall's day. Here he describes an ascent of New York state's second-
highest mountain, 5,114-foot Algonquin Peak (also called MacIntyre), in
February 1923. Marshall reports that along the way Herb Clark came across the
track of a panther—a species supposedly wiped out in the Adirondacks in the late
1800s. The article is reproduced from a typescript in the Bancroft Library of the
University of California at Berkeley. A shorter version appeared in the New
York Evening Post *on Jan. 14, 1924.*

The literature of the Adirondacks contains several accounts of winter
ascents of Mount Marcy and Whiteface, but I know of no similar
account concerning MacIntyre. Yet I imagine that the latter has been
climbed in the snow as frequently as the other two. So I have prepared
this article about a trip Herb Clark, my brother George and I took up
the second-highest mountain in the state a few weeks ago.

As a preface to these remarks, I want to state that we were all greenhorns at winter mountaineering. Herb, though he had been more or less
brought up on snowshoes, was always too busy during the cold months
to scramble over the landscape in search of lofty elevations. I had used
snowshoes four or five times but always on the level, while George had
never had them on until two days before.

On Friday afternoon, February 23, we took the train from Saranac
to Placid and then walked out to Woods Farm. Here we spent a very
pleasant evening listening to some reminiscences of two of the pioneer

ladies of Essex County, who have lived for forty-two years on the edge
of civilization in the permanent dwelling closest to the big mountains.[1]
When we awoke next morning the sun was just rising, painting the summits of the mountains a beautiful purple. The atmosphere was unusually clear. The thermometer read eighteen below, and it had been six
degrees lower an hour earlier.

We started out for the Adirondack Lodge before eight. The snow
had been packed hard by a party that had gone into the lodge a few days
before. It seems very queer to see the places always associated with summer in such a different aspect. Here we had stopped last time to eat
strawberries, while at yonder drift was a bed of bluets. It took us an hour
and a quarter to cover the four miles.

At the lodge we put on our snowshoes and started along the red
trail. The bare woods seemed to have a supernatural stillness, with no
birds or insects or falling leaves. We found about four feet of snow on
the level. For perhaps a mile the going was easy, for the grade was slight,
but then we commenced to huff. It would have been a cinch in summer, but it was very different now. We panted along in silence, which
was finally broken by Herb, who despite his fifty-two years easily kept
ahead. "By goll!" he exclaimed. "These are the first panther tracks I've
seen in twenty-five years." We found him looking down at some large
holes in the snow, almost round and about five inches across. At the
bottom were the marks of four toes. The interesting fact, however, was
the mark of a long, dragging tail. The animal evidently was traveling
from Indian [Pass] toward Avalanche Pass. "Just follow him," said Herb,
"and he'll take you over all the high mountains you want." It might
have been a kangaroo track for all I knew, although I didn't doubt
Herb's word. However, I looked up about the panther's tracks when I
got home and found the book description to coincide perfectly with the
marks actually seen in the field.[2]

The burn looked even barer than in summer and the view from it
even better. The waterfall at the halfway point was of course a mass of
snow and ice. Occasionally we came to places where the slope was so
steep we could hardly make it, but we did not have to take off our snowshoes until just beyond the bald dome of West MacIntyre. Here we were
forced to pull ourselves up through the snow, which came above our
waists, by young trees. Once we crossed the ridge and came out on the
hillside above the pass separating Wright and MacIntyre, we put on our

Mount Colden and Mount Marcy (in distance) from Algonquin.

shoes again. Here we got our first view of the summit, and it surely looked a discouragingly long distance off. One thing that seemed especially strange was the sight of two yellow trail markers, which should have been on the level of eyes, just appearing above the snow. Higher up they were entirely buried.

Just beyond the three-quarters mark our real troubles commenced. For the grade became so steep that we had to take off our snowshoes for more than half the remaining distance. At one place we sank up to the chest in the soft snow. We didn't know how much was below that. Here it took us, or rather George and I, five minutes to make five yards. Herb kept out of sight ahead, so I don't know how he made it. As we worked higher we occasionally came to places where we were above the trail and had to push our way through the dense, snow-laden boughs of the dwarfed forest. Gradually the snow grew deeper and the trees smaller until finally we found ourselves treading above them.

Once timberline was reached we found the snow frozen so solidly that we no longer required any artificial support. At places where it had drifted we could walk right over cliffs twelve and fifteen feet high in summer. At other places the bare ledges showed. The surface of the snow was roughened by particles of ice. The cold wind blowing on our overheated bodies did not add any to our comfort. Each put on his extra coat, but without keeping warm. The gale was in a great hurry to get somewhere. It seemed to drive the way-below-zero air right through us. The beautiful morning had turned into an overcast day, though the atmosphere remained remarkably clear. At last, however, feeling half-frozen, we reached the very summit and gazed out upon a great frozen landscape.

The most impressive feature was the prospect toward Colden and Marcy, in which the great snow-clad slides on the former were particularly prominent. In the other direction, the cliff of Wallface stood out in its white setting. To the southwest Santanoni appeared about ten thousand feet high. To the south and southeast, where miles of virgin coniferous forests stretched, one would scarcely have known it was winter, except for the occasional frozen ponds. South Meadows and the Plains of Abraham looked desolate indeed. Giant to the east seemed like a great mound of solid snow, while across its shoulder, plainly visible, were frozen Champlain and the mountains of Vermont.

Photographing was an extreme hardship. To remove the gloves long enough to take one picture meant fingers frozen stiff. In fact I was in such a hurry to get my hands back in the gloves that I forgot to turn twice and took a triple exposure. Changing a film was out of the question. It was with great relief that we found protection from the wind beneath the massive summit. Here we drank some hot coffee brought up in thermos bottles, and it certainly felt great. Our appetites, however, were frozen. After quarter of an hour, the cold and the time of day alike warned us to leave. We took a farewell look over the heart of the snow-covered wilderness and started on the descent.

Going down the mountain was doubly easy, not only because it always takes less energy to go downhill than up, but also because the snowshoes were not continually slipping off. We had no more wading in fine snow up to our chests. We strode easily over the surface or sat on the backs of our raquettes and coasted down thirty or forty feet. We made good progress and reached the halfway point in a third of the time it took us to go up. For the last half of the return journey we went at a more moderate pace. George tried to get a picture of the panther tracks, but his whole film was lightstruck. As we approached the lodge the straps on our feet began to dig into the flesh, so we were mighty glad when we once more reached the road and could take off our snowshoes.

Mike Storey

Panther track.

The times we reached various points on our climb follow:

Leave lodge	9:25
MacIntyre trail	9:35
Halfway waterfall	10:37
Valley between Wright and MacIntyre	11:52
Summit	1:15-1:30
Valley	1:55
Waterfall	2:23-2:30
Lodge	3:18

While I have spent several considerably harder days, I confess I was pretty tired that night. Perhaps it might seem that the fleeting view we got from the summit was not worth the difficult climb. But there comes the blessing of a memory. Though we could only gaze on that superb panorama for fifteen minutes, the picture of what we saw will remain in our minds for a lifetime.

NOTES

1 George Marshall writes in "Approach to the Mountains" that on their journeys to the High Peaks the three hikers often stayed at the farm of Mrs. H.K. Wood and her daughter Hattie. George's article is reprinted in this volume, p. 263.

2 New York state wildlife biologists say panthers were eliminated from the Adirondacks by the late 1800s, but some people believe the cats have returned or never entirely left (see Jenkins 2004, 51). Al Hicks, a scientist with the state Department of Environmental Conservation, said it's likely that the track seen by Clark was made by a lynx or bobcat (personal conversation).

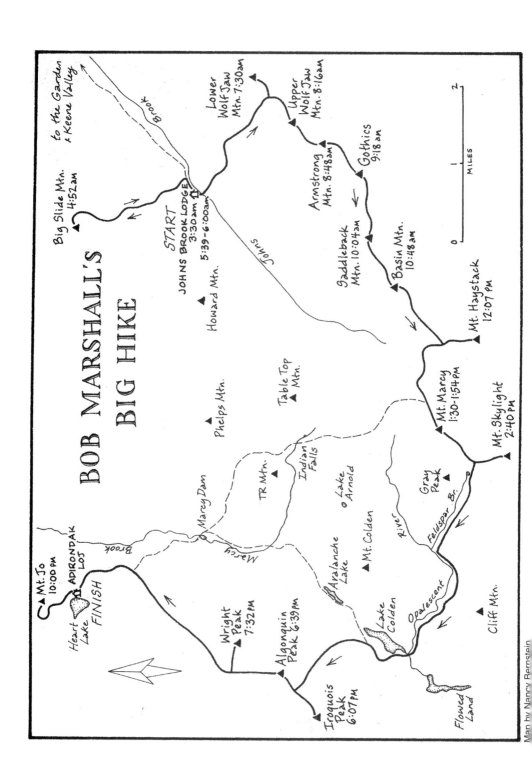

BOB MARSHALL'S BIG HIKE

to the Garden & Keene Valley

Big Slide Mtn. 4:52am

Lower Wolf Jaw Mtn. 7:30am

Upper Wolf Jaw Mtn. 8:16am

Armstrong Mtn. 8:48am

Gothics 9:18am

JOHNS BROOK LODGE 3:30am
START
5:39-6:00am

Howard Mtn.

Saddleback Mtn. 10:04am

Basin Mtn. 10:48am

Mt. Haystack 12:07 PM

Johns

Phelps Mtn.

Table Top Mtn.

Mt. Marcy 1:30-1:54 PM

Mt. Skylight 2:40 PM

Marcy Dam

TR Mtn.

Indian Falls

Lake Arnold

Gray Peak

Mt. Colden

Cliff Mtn.

Mt. Jo 10:00 PM

ADIRONDAK LOJ

Heart Lake FINISH

Wright Peak 7:32PM

Algonquin Peak 6:39PM

Avalanche Lake

Lake Colden

Opalescent

Flowed Land

Iroquois Peak 6:07PM

Feldspar Br.

River

Map by Nancy Bernstein

Adirondack Peaks

In 1930, Bob and George Marshall climbed nine High Peaks in a single day, breaking the record of six set thirty-six years earlier by Newell Martin. Their feat fostered a friendly competition among a coterie of marathon hikers who over the next several years would strive to outdo each other in the number of peaks climbed, feet ascended and miles hiked. A year after the Marshalls' trek, H.L. Malcolm climbed eleven High Peaks and ascended twelve thousand feet. It was this record that Bob Marshall set out to break on July 15, 1932. Starting at Johns Brook Lodge at 3:30 a.m., he climbed thirteen High Peaks and then capped off the day with a jaunt up Mount Jo overlooking Heart Lake, ascending a total of 13,600 feet. Coincidentally, the devoted Adirondack conservationist Paul Schaefer was on top of Mount Marcy when Marshall arrived on the summit about noon. Years later, Schaefer wrote about this chance meeting of like-minded champions of wilderness.[1] The day after his epic hike, Marshall wrote this article for High Spots, *the Adirondack Mountain Club magazine. For more on marathon hikes, see "A Short History of Adirondack Peak-Bagging" p. 291.*

July 16, 1932

Yesterday I ascended fourteen Adirondack peaks. The details of my climbing are shown in the following table:

PEAK OR PLACE	TIME	FEET ASCENDED
Leave Johns Brook Lodge	3:30	
1. Big Slide	4:42	1,900
Johns Brook Lodge (breakfast)	5:39-6:00	
2. Lower Wolf Jaw	7:30	1,900
3. Upper Wolf Jaw	8:16	600
4. Armstrong	8:48	500
5. Gothics	9:18	400
6. Saddleback	10:04	500
7. Basin	10:48	700
8. Haystack	12:07	1,000
9. Marcy (lunch)	1:30-1:54	1,200
10. Skylight	2:40	600
Lake Colden	4:04-4:10	
11. Iroquois	6:07	2,100
12. MacIntyre	6:39	400
13. Wright	7:32	400
Adirondack Lodge	9:15-9:30	
14. Jo	10:00-10:10	700
Adirondack Lodge (supper)	10:35	

Additional elevation gained on minor peaks, including Boundary, Little Haystack and the subsidiary summits of Upper Wolf Jaw, Armstrong, Gothics, Saddleback, Basin: 700.

Total: 13,600.

Thus I have carried a little farther the fantastic pastime of record climbing, adding three to Malcolm's total of eleven. Perhaps within a few weeks, surely as soon as a few more mountains in the vicinity of Mount Marcy have trails cut on to them, somebody will readily enough overtop my record.[2] Certainly it is a mark which any reasonably vigorous person in good physical condition can equal if he tries when there are long daylight hours. In fact, it would fit perfectly in a class with flagpolc sitting and marathon dancing as an entirely useless type of record, made only to be broken, were it not that I had such a thoroughly glorious time out of the entire day.

To begin with, the weather was absolutely perfect, one of those crystal-clear days such as only occur occasionally in an entire Adirondack summer. Furthermore, although I had already climbed each mountain from two to twelve times, the views seemed almost as fresh and exciting as on the first ascent, so splendid, in fact, that any one peak was worthy of a long and tedious journey. Finally, seeing the view from fourteen different mountains all in one day gave me an excellent opportunity to appreciate the distinctive character of these Adirondack mountains, which made each summit leave an entirely different effect of delight.

From Big Slide I was chiefly impressed by the rising sun playing on the summits of the Great Range across Johns Brook and then by the joy of running downhill at 5:00 in the morning through the dewy raspberry bushes and feeling how good it was to be young and able to feel sure you could climb fourteen mountains in a day.

The Lower Wolf Jaw showed the entire Johns Brook Valley bathed in the still-early-morning sunlight, looking so bright and cheerful that I couldn't help feeling a triumphant happiness.

On Upper Wolf Jaw I recall especially the trail which violates almost every proper trail standard and is delightful for this very quality. It shoots straight up cliffs, stumbles over all sorts of tree roots and skirts through narrow crevices among the rocks. All the time it shows the flora which at normal elevations is blooming a month earlier–goldthread, wood sorrel, twinflower, saxifrage–and the shady freshness of the mountaintop forest of spruce and balsam and paper birch.

On Armstrong it was pleasant to walk out on the same ledge Herb and George[3] and I had found eleven years ago before there was any trail on this mountain and see the same splendid horseshoe of high mountains which has remained in my mind ever since, with Armstrong and Big Slide at the two ends and the rocky cone of Marcy at the apex.

From Gothics I was particularly impressed yesterday by the two mountain masses, one of Giant and Rocky Peak Ridge, the other of four successive tiers of Sawteeth, Colvin, Nippletop and Dix, which frame a vista of the Champlain Valley, while the Green Mountains beyond appeared so close that I had the feeling that I ought to be able to skip over in a couple of hours.

From Saddleback, as always, there was the breathtaking sight of the overtowering rock needle of Gothics across Storrow Pass, with an almost sheer wall nearly a thousand feet high tumbling off on the south face of the peak.

The views of the three undefiled valleys of Shanty Brook, Haystack Brook and upper Johns Brook, all lying directly below me, gave the greatest exhilaration from Basin.

I had wondered whether, after three summers and a winter of exploration in Arctic Alaska, I could still recapture any of the sense of wildness I had always gotten from Haystack. Gloriously enough, I did. It was still possible to forget the automobiles and machinery of the present in the vista from this rocky summit from which only in the extreme distance could any sign of man's meddlesome ways be observed.

Marcy as always impressed me with the breadth of vision, encompassing as it does in its panorama practically the entire expanse of the Adirondacks except the extreme southern and western portions and being the only mountain from which all forty-six of the four-thousand-foot peaks are visible. But if this familiar delight was pleasant, it was exceedingly disconcerting to find the nearby slope of Mount Adams all scarred by logging operations, which I had supposed were ended in the high-mountain region, while a great fire streak extended up the slope of North River Mountain.

From Skylight a wall of virgin summits, extending from Iroquois to Dix and including all twelve of the highest peaks in the Adirondacks, filled the entire northern half of the panorama. It gave me an impression of massiveness which I do not recall from any other Adirondack mountain.

After Skylight there followed three splendid hours down Feldspar Brook and the Opalescent, around Lake Colden and up the steep grade to the height of land of the MacIntyre Range. All but half an hour of this journey was through the most inspiring sort of virgin spruce-slope forests.

Then came Iroquois, from which the magnificently wild country north of Wallface seemed even darker and less explored than usual when backed by the late-afternoon sun. In the middle of these black mountains the waters of Scott Pond and Upper Wallface were sparkling in the sunlight.

MacIntyre showed the rolling mountains which culminated in the Marcy-Skylight divide all light and cheerful as the setting sun shone directly on their western flanks. The usually dark streaks on Colden between the rock slides were just as bright as could be.

After a strenuous tussle with windfall and mountain balsam, the trailless summit of Wright was reached just as the sun was dipping behind the distant mountains north of Street, and the entire panorama, including the nearby slope of MacIntyre, the Marcy Range, the mountains back of South Meadows and the fields of North Elba, were tinted by a reddish-purple glow.

Mount Jo, ascended with the aid of flashlights, made an ideal climax.[4] Northward, Lake Placid was a host of lights twinkling beyond an extensive plain. Southward and westward towered the pitch-black mass of Marcy, Colden, MacIntyre, Wallface and Street, while right at our feet the almost full moon was reflected in the waters of Heart Lake. All around a heavy mist was rising from the streams and meadows, giving everything an appearance as unreal as this entire perfect day had been to the normal world of twentieth-century mechanization.

In concluding this account of a great day I want to mention that Herb Clark met me on top of Marcy with luncheon and his usual uproarious humor. In addition to Marcy, Herb also went over MacIntyre and Wright with me, which was quite a day's activity for a man of sixty-two. Eugene Untermyer accompanied me on the flashlight ascent of Mount Jo. When I got down from this last peak Jed Rossman gave me the kindest sort of reception, and Elise Untermyer had a most delicious supper awaiting, which tasted doubly excellent after nearly seventeen hours since my last warm food which Mrs. Hanmer[5] had served that morning at Johns Brook Lodge.

NOTES

1 See "Bob Marshall, Mount Marcy, and–the Wilderness," p. 277.

2 Before the year ended, Ernest Griffith surpassed Marshall's mark by ascending 16,930 feet, although his itinerary included only ten High Peaks (and three lesser summits). In 1936, H.L. Malcolm ascended 25,551 feet in climbing twelve High Peaks and Noonmark Mountain (four times). (Waterman 1989, 517-8.)

3 Marshall climbed Armstrong with his brother George and Herb Clark on August 15, 1921. See "Mountaineering in the Adirondacks," p. 55.

4 Mount Jo near Adirondack Loj is only 2,876 feet. Of Marshall's fourteen mountains, it alone is not a High Peak.

5 Mrs. Roy Hanmer was a caretaker of Johns Brook Lodge.

Photo by Phil Brown

Middle Saranac Lake seen from the top of Ampersand Mountain.

Night Trip
on Ampersand Mountain

*In 1919, a year after they had begun climbing the High Peaks, the Marshall broth-
ers returned to one of their favorite lower peaks: Ampersand Mountain, which
was visible from Knollwood, the family's camp on Lower Saranac Lake.
Situated between the high mountains and the lake belt, the 3,352-foot summit
affords one of the best panoramas in the Adirondacks. Bob and George wanted
to watch the sunset and sunrise from the mountaintop. They were then eighteen
and fifteen, respectively. Bob's account, taken from a manuscript in the possession of Roger Marshall, George's son, documents the brothers' camaraderie.*

George and I had decided some time before that we wanted to sleep
on top of Ampersand Mountain some night so that we might see
both sunrise and sunset from its summit. While Thursday, July 17th, was
not an ideal day for mountain climbing, due to a haze, we decided for
several reasons to ascend Ampersand. First, we thought, from several
different signs, that the haze would diminish rather than increase, as it
subsequently did. Second, being quite warm, we thought we would not
have to carry so many blankets as would otherwise have been necessary.
Thirdly, we knew that we would have to go to New York in a few days,
when Father would return, and we were anxious to get this little trip in
before leaving for the city. These were the reasons which determined us,
against what should have been our better judgment, to spend that night
on the heights of Ampersand.

As the *Geroruja* was out of order, we went up to the Round Lake beach by rowboat.[1] We left the house at 2:15, as Herb was anxious to get back home in plenty of time for supper. He went along so that we would have someone to take back the boat and also to save time in getting up to the beginning of the trail. He rowed us to the locks, and I pulled the oars from there on. My right eye, which I had scratched with a twig that morning, bothered me considerably on the way up to Middle Saranac, as it did the rest of the day. Herb was not particularly funny on the way,[2] and nothing out of the ordinary occurred. When we reached the beach, Herb stopped long enough to eat a couple of slices of bread and then started back again. We each shouldered a pack and started on the trail, which stretched for almost four miles to the summit, 1,800 feet above us.

Despite the fact that we were carrying twenty-four and eighteen pounds respectively, we made good time to Mr. Rice's camp.[3] We covered the three miles in less than an hour, reaching the camp shortly after five o'clock. No one was there yet, so we waited a little while before starting our supper, as we wanted to ask Mr. Rice if we could use a little of his wood. We were in no hurry, so it was pleasant to sit around the quiet camp. But when no one had come by half past five, we commenced to prepare our meal. We did take some of Rice's wood, and while one of us peeled the potatoes, the other split some kindling wood and started the fire. The potatoes were only half fried when Mr. Rice came into camp. He was very cordial and said that he was very glad we had made ourselves at home. He asked for Herb and Lloyd[4] and wanted to know how Knollwood was. He was surprised that we were the only guests up there at that late date. Then we talked about the Adirondacks in general, and certain parts in particular, until two more people came into camp from up the trail. They were a young man and a young woman, brother and sister. Shortly afterwards two more people came into camp from the direction of the lake with a four- or five-pound pickerel. We had seen them going towards the lake shortly after we started. The older of the two was a lady who looked to be about forty-five or fifty years of age. We soon found out that she was the aunt of the other two. Her companion was a young man of about twenty-five, the son of Mr. Rice, Seaver. The other three had come from Boston to visit him and were spending their ten days' visit in camp with Mr. Rice. What a fine way to spend a vacation! There are not many city people, and particularly women, who, even if they had the chance, would spend their

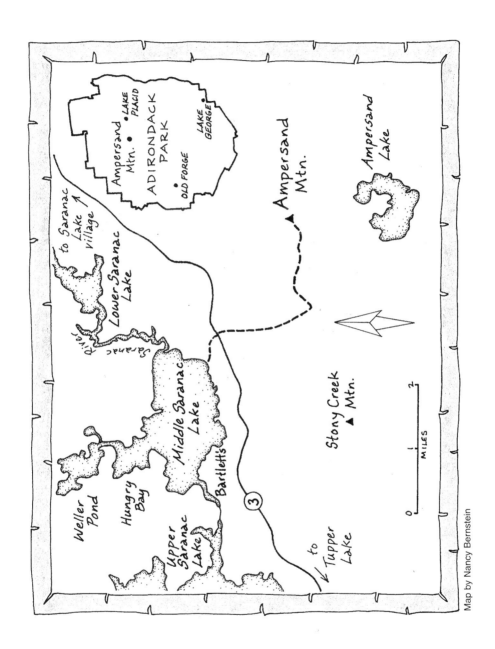

vacations on a mountain, six to seven miles from the nearest habitation. All seemed to be very nice. They were all jolly, particularly the elderly lady, who evidently thought nothing of a five-mile walk to work up an appetite for supper. They were all greatly interested in our cooking set and particularly the frying pan. Mr. Rice, meanwhile, was cooking their supper. After finishing our meal and washing the dishes, which we did in a leisurely way, we lifted our packs, said goodbye and started up the last long, three-quarter-mile climb to the top.

We did not go at all fast, as we now carried a load both outside and in. Besides, the trail rises very steeply beyond the camp, and this small section of the trail causes people more bother than all the rest of the trail put together. We were not bothered, as we took our time. At the last spring we filled two cans with water for the night. We tried to imagine the last quarter-mile as the distance from Sixty-Seventh Street to Seventy-Second Street and Madison Avenue, a distance often traversed by us. Now, for once, distance in the woods seemed longer than distance in the city. Though we were not at all tired, we were not sorry when we had climbed the last ladder, squeezed between the last trees and stood on the highest point of the rocky crest of Ampersand.

The sunset was a great failure. Though we reached the mountaintop an hour before the time set for the disappearance of the sun, we only saw the center of the solar system about ten minutes. It was a big red ball, and it made the waters of Hungry Bay and Weller Pond[5] look blood red for a short time. But when it was still many minutes above the horizon it disappeared, hidden by the gray haze. Thereafter we saw no very pretty sight until sometime after we had gone to bed.

We did not want to bed down too soon, for we thought the night would probably be very long, as we did not expect to sleep well. We made elaborate plans for the night and rehearsed several times the retreat from our beds to the house in case it should start to rain.[6] We feared that it might get too dark to see our way. For our beds we chose a spot just east of the house and covered with alpine flora. It was protected from the wind, which had shifted to the southwest, by a steep wall of rock eight or ten feet high. Therefore, while the wind was raging at most places on top of the mountain, our beds were as quiet and protected as if we were home.

It was very cool so high above the surrounding country, and each of us wrapped a blanket around himself, in the best Indian manner, as shown by cigar-store advertisements or dime-novel illustrations. Consequently George called me Chief Cavort, and I responded by christening him Little Mudjikammis. Then we made up an Indian dance, in order to keep warm, which was accompanied by the tuneful chanting of our names. Fortunately we were isolated from the rest of the world, so no one suffered.

Steadily the haze grew thicker, while added to this was the evening mist. Rapidly mountain and pond were blotted out until, just at dark, everything was blotted out except our mountain. Even Round Lake and Ampersand Pond[7] were invisible. But then we got a new interest: looking for lights. First we would see one twinkle a minute, then the haze would obscure it. Over where we knew the village to be was a bright glow. At Bartletts were the most consistent lights. At one time we could make out fourteen, and several showed through the haze almost always. But the most interesting of all was to watch the moving lights of autos on the old state road. They puzzled us a good deal for a while, for we did not think there were any people in that section. But when we saw that they moved we solved the mystery.

Finally we concluded that it was time to retire. It was already 10:30. We resolved to get up every hour and a half so we would miss no sights and also so we would not get too stiff. We each wrapped ourselves up in a blanket and spread the third blanket over both of us, curling up as close together as possible. Though it was cold, we managed to keep warm through the night.

The first time we awoke was at midnight. We got up and walked and danced a bit to get the stiffness, caused by lying in one position so long, out of our bones. We felt particularly stiff in the shoulders. The haze was as thick as when we went to bed, and consequently we could see nothing. We went back to bed in five or ten minutes, resolved to get another hour and a half of sleep. We were very much surprised that we had rested so well the first hour and a half.

The second time we awoke a beautiful sight met our eyes. A silver half-moon shone above us. We arose and looked over the whole vast landscape visible from our perch. The mist and haze had risen, and lakes and forests and streams and distant mountains were illuminated by the pale light. Just enough were they made visible that their outlines might be distinguished; not enough were they visible to distinguish the details in the black night. We looked silently at the wonderful spectacle, unable

State archives/Courtesy of Wray Rominger

The old stone hut on Ampersand's summit.

to express in words our feelings for the weird beauty of the scene. But it was cold, so we decided to go in the house for a short time. There was no room to lie down, so we sat. I struck a match and found it was a quarter to two. We stayed about ten minutes longer in the house. Then, taking one more look at the night-enshrouded country, we lay down again for another sleep in the absolutely pure air of the mountaintop.

At half past three we awoke again, and the same joys which we experienced at the previous awakening were repeated. The same quiet beauty covered the whole vast panorama. We stayed [awake] for about ten minutes and then lay down again for our final sleep of the night, feeling strangely happy.

The next time we awoke there was a reddish glow in the eastern sky. We threw off our blankets and jumped up to see the beauty of the far-famed mountain sunrise. Soon, however, we put the blankets on again, for it was very cool. We sat at the eastern end of the summit and watched the sky get brighter and brighter. Otherwise there was not much of exceptional beauty to be seen, for mist and haze once more so covered the landscape that it once more became very indistinct. George and I had hoped, after sunrise, to study some geography from the maps, but the brighter it became, the more indistinct were the other mountains and lakes. The mist rising from Ampersand Pond did look very red. We took several pictures, none of which turned out very well. George lost my Ingersoll watch, and we spent quite a lot of time looking for it, but without success. We were thus left without a timepiece and therefore had to guess when it was time to leave the top. After a while we ate our breakfast, consisting of an orange for each and bread and butter. We enjoyed it very much. It is surely a fact that sleeping in the open gives a person a good appetite. After breakfast we looked some more at the landscape, rapidly growing hazier. Despite the poorness of the atmospheric conditions, it was very pleasant on top of the mountain, so far from people and the rest of the country, and we both felt a trifle sorry that we had not determined to return in the afternoon instead of in the morning. But we saw by the sun that it was time to leave, so we loaded our packbaskets on our shoulders and started the descent.

NOTES

1 The *Geroruja* was the family's wooden launch. Its name is an amalgam of the first two letters of the names of the four Marshall children: George, Robert, Ruth, James. Round Lake is an old name for Middle Saranac Lake.

2 Herb Clark, their genial guide, often entertained the boys with tall tales and humorous songs.

3 Walter Channing Rice was the fire observer on Ampersand from 1915 to 1922. A plaque on the summit pays tribute to him.

4 Lloyd was Herb Clark's nephew.

5 Hungry Bay and Weller Pond are large inlets on the north side of Middle Saranac Lake.

6 Walter Channing Rice built a stone hut on Ampersand's summit. Two years after the Marshalls' hike, the state erected a fire tower. Given the summit's wide-open vistas, a tower had not been deemed necessary when fire observers were first assigned to Ampersand in 1911. Both the hut and the tower are gone. (Podskoch 2005, 26-8.)

7 Now called Ampersand Lake, it lies just south of the mountain.

Photo by Carl Heilman II

Whiteface Mountain from Little Cherrypatch Pond on State Route 86.

Wilmington Walk
Aug. 31, 1920

When they weren't climbing mountains, the Marshall brothers explored the rural roads around Saranac Lake. One day they walked fifty-four miles. In the expedition described below, they set out to surpass that mark by making a circuit of Whiteface Mountain. It took them nearly nineteen hours, much of it in a chilly rain. No wonder that Bob ranked this as his second-hardest hike with George— harder, even, than their traverse a few weeks earlier of the Great Range from Haystack to Gothics and back.[1] Yet the brothers refused to let fatigue, cold and dampness get the best of them. They fended off misery with songs, jokes and bonhomie. The following article, never before published, exhibits the closeness of the two teenage brothers.

At 4:40 A.M. the alarm clock sounded, and we immediately got up to prepare for what we hoped would be our record-breaking walking. I speedily went down to the kitchen and started the water for our eggs to boil. It did not take us long to dress, and we were soon eating breakfast, which consisted of orange, cereal, eggs, milk, and bread and butter. Breakfast over, we hurriedly got our haversack packed and filled the canteens. Herb, entering the kitchen at that time, kindly offered to wash the dishes and helped us with a few odds and ends. He prophesied the weather would be the best in seven years, and indeed the outlook was very good for fine weather. It was just 5:40 that George shouldered one canteen, and I took the other and the haversack and started out along the Knollwood Road.[2]

79

There was just a streak of light when we started, but by the time we reached the gate it was considerably lighter. Coming down toward Fish Creek a nail worked thru George's shoe, and we had to stop at Fish Creek to hammer it out with a stone. This was certainly a gloomy omen in the very first mile of our long journey. Stuffing a piece of paper in to be sure the nail would not work through again we continued, and George was not bothered again. It was certainly careless of him to not have taken a good pair, but he had no other. I also was careless in that I was wearing a pair of shoes for the second time, but just luckily they needed no breaking in. Slightly grouchy feelings about the delay were soon dispelled by the beautiful weather. There was just a single pink, feathery cloud in the whole sky. As we kept going the day became brighter and brighter, till finally, just beyond the Van Dorrien, we saw the sun rising.

The walk through the village was very pleasant at that time of day. There were few people on the street as yet, and everything was very quiet. Passing by the Boepre house we called out, "Good morning, Shon," though we knew John would not hear us. We took a shortcut out to the Bloomingdale Road, passing by the station. At the crossing beyond we saw Herb's brother, Andy, but he did not know us. However, he remarked, "Fine day, boys." Despite all delays we reached the Bloomingdale road, five miles from home, in an hour and a quarter. So at least we were starting out at good pace.

Before we reached Trudeau[3] we noticed several dark clouds coming up from the south. This worried us a bit. However, as we were walking towards the north we did not notice them so much. After a while, though, they had overspread the whole sky, except for a bit toward the east, where the sun was. But before we were halfway to Bloomingdale the sky was all covered with thick, dark clouds. Soon the first drops began to fall. The weather certainly had a depressing effect on us, and we felt very gloomy. It looked as if our chances for breaking the record were about gone. The question was, What to do? It was still early, and we had three alternatives, it being obvious that we were in for all-day rain. We might return home by the Paul Smith Road in plenty of time for lunch; we might explore the Vermontville Roads and be home for a warm supper, or we might continue despite rain with our original plans, cross the mountain to Wilmington and come home via Placid. To this later alternative there was the possible variation of stopping at the end of about 40 miles at the Notch House, where we were sure of a warm welcome and supper from the Fullers.[4]

We thought the matter over and decided to make our decision at a big red barn, a short ways this side of Bloomingdale. As we hustled along the half-mile straightway before it we each became anxious in regard to what the other would decide. It certainly seemed a long way down that straightway, with a driving rain blowing against our necks. But finally the moment for deciding came, and together we shouted, "Keep on!" Soon after that we reached the beginning of Bloomingdale. It was only about half past eight but seemed much later to us. At the Widest Street in the World we turned off the road we had been following. Under a shed we looked at the maps while the water from our soaking caps dripped on them. We were thinking of sending home a postcard from here, but it was too wet. We continued on but soon had to leave the macadam and take to the mud road to Franklin Falls. This we did with a sigh, fearing it would be a long time till we struck solid ground again.

There were few houses along the road we were now following. For a while we could look back and see Bloomingdale, but after that human beings and their homes were very rare. The road was an unusually pretty one. Second-growth pines grew on either side and partly overhung the road, though not enough to keep off any rain. They grew very straight and right up to the edge of the road, which was only wide enough for one vehicle. In addition this road was dirt and not much traveled, so we had almost the sensation of walking on a broad trail. Along here we saw our first harebells and were much delighted with these beautiful flowers. But there were also parts about the road that were not delightful. The rapidly falling rain turned it into a mud hole, and every step we sank into the ooze. This made the walking very hard indeed. The sky kept growing blacker and blacker and the rain falling harder and harder, and we naturally started to sing "Darkness and Hardship," but we were never able to get beyond the words "will night never end," for there were no "faint gleams of daylight breaking through the cloudbanks." To our right was the river, which we could now and then see through the trees and when not in sight hear, because for several miles the Pyramid Rapids extended and made a loud noise.[5] We were able to trace our progress on the way by the various roads and trails which branch off from the one we were following. After a while, how-

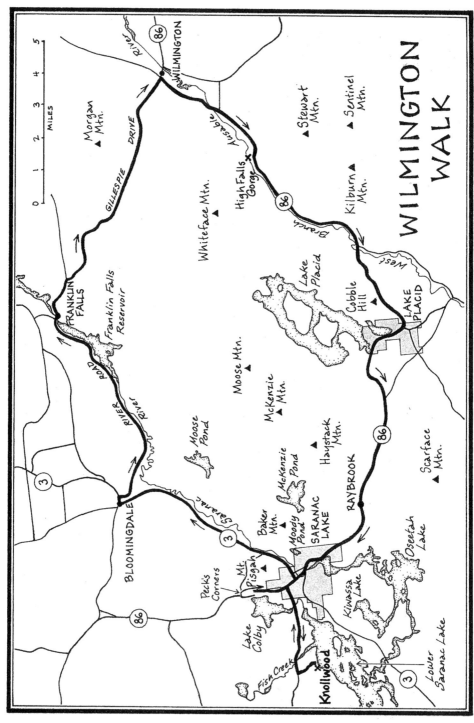

Map by Nancy Bernstein

ever, we lost ourselves as it were. The map showed us to be on the right side of the river, while we knew perfectly well we were on the left. We had seen no decent road cross the river, and on the other hand we certainly were on a road. We saw by signs when we had crossed from Essex into Franklin County, but here our road should have stopped. We worried a bit and heartily wished for Franklin Falls. It now seemed we had been floundering through the mud for an age. The way was no longer pretty; the pines were gone. So were the harebells. To the right was a river, no longer running rapidly but a dead-looking pond filled with old dead trees, the result of Franklin Falls dam. At last some dwellings came into sight, and through the gloom we saw a little settlement, in the center of which was a big flagpole. We hastened our steps through the mud and soon crossed the river. From the bridge we took a few pictures, despite the weather. Then we entered the settlement of Franklin Falls.

There were so many roads branching here, and our map had been so far behind time on the road we had just been following, that we thought we had better ask the way. So we knocked on the door of a ramshackled boardinghouse. An old lady, who looked ready to die at any moment, came to the door and with great difficulty understood and answered our question. We continued down the road, which led along the river, passing the falls, or rather what should have been the falls. But not a drop was falling over them. The company had temporarily turned the water in a side channel while repairing the big cement dam, and the falls were gone. We were greatly disappointed, not so much because the water was turned off, as because of the lowness and artificiality of the falls. We had heard so much about them.

The road followed the river about three-quarters of a mile and then turned off to the east. It continued this way almost a mile when we came to a road intersecting it at right angles, with a birdcage to one side. This was our landmark, and we took the new road. But in a short distance another road intersected it, running east again, so we thought this must be the one we wanted. There being a house at the corner, we stopped to inquire the way, and a woman prompted by a man sitting at the stove gave directions. But they seemed to think we must have been crazy to be striking across the mountain for Wilmington on such a day. Had we mentioned where we were from and where we expected to return they would have been sure we had just escaped from an asylum.

Looking ahead on the new road, we saw it cross a meadow and enter a hole among the trees as black as the mouth of a cave. In all my walking I have never seen along road or trail such a black-looking hole. It was almost enough to fill a fellow with terror. Upon entering the hole we found it not quite as dark as it looked from without, but it was certainly gloomy. We mounted a small hill, and just over the ridge we found a fork in the road. The right-hand branch appeared the natural one to take, but we were cautioned against it. It led to Lake Placid. We were now walking mostly through meadowland in a hollow. After another mile we came to a road branching to the left. It had a sign saying Rosman Lane. Just beyond was a deserted homestead. We stopped at a branch here to look at the maps. To our great joy we noticed that the clouds were breaking up a bit, and it was getting considerably brighter, so we said, "Faint gleams of daylight break through the cloud-banks, night's fears will fade away, dispelled by the hope of the dawn." We could get no further, however, and pretty soon we were back to "darkness and hardship." On a fine day the view from this valley must be superb. As it was, to our right we could see Esther, Whiteface and McKenzie mountains and to our left the Wilmington Range, though some of the peaks were mist-capped. Due north was a most singular-looking, bold, rock peak, and very steep. It was Catamount and appeared to be well-named. We could see several high passes crossing this long range in front of us, but it seemed like an awfully high, steep climb to ours. And indeed it was, as we soon learned. Just across the meadow the climb began. The road was very rough and rose 650 feet in two-and-a-half miles. Of course this would have ordinarily meant nothing to us, but after walking two dozen miles without food or rest, with three dozen lying before us, it became a noticeable climb. Aside from a brook which tumbled rapidly down to the left of the road there was nothing of beauty, for around the road was mostly second growth. It was now very muddy, and this added to the difficulties. Despite the rain and cold we even perspired a bit. But finally we reached the long, level floor of the pass. Here we saw a lot of harebells, more than we had ever seen before. It began to rain quite hard, and we were anxious to find a place where we could eat lunch without getting the food drenched. We had only seen one shelter since starting on this road.

In the very center of the pass, or perhaps a little beyond, the sides were very steep, making it seem as a pass should. To the north was a cliff rising quite straight for a couple of hundred feet. George called it

Mouseface. To the south Esther rose in more gradual slope but much higher. Yet there was little beauty up here, aside from harebells—only a cold, drenching rain. The mountainside had been slashed by lumbermen and fire. Just beyond the center we saw an old dam, which had evidently held up quite a good-sized pond for the lumbering operations. A short way beyond was a large, deserted wooden house, the old lumber camp. Here we gladly stopped for lunch.

The house we entered was two-storied. The entire bottom floor was a large dining room and kitchen. There was a great deal of old junk such as nails, matches, kettles and tacks. But the place was nice and clean. We took off our light loads for the first time in seven-and-a-half hours and started to eat our lunch. This consisted of a couple of sandwiches and hard-boiled eggs apiece, with an orange. While we were eating and resting, we had to keep punching each other so that we would not get cold or stiff, for it was very chilly sitting around on the cold day in soaking clothes. We also wiggled our legs so the muscles there would not get stiff, but we did not walk around, that we might rest our feet. George for fun suggested that somebody might be upstairs. We did not think it worthwhile to take the trouble to look. Cold as it was in the house we hated to go out in the pouring rain again. We had just gotten a little bit dry, but there was no help to it, so saying goodbye to the house which had made lunch possible, we stepped out into the heavy rain.

The next ten minutes were about the chilliest of my life. The house had not been very warm, but at least it had sheltered us from the cold rain and wind. But out here we got both with full force. In addition after sitting around half an hour our blood was not in such good circulation. We thought we would freeze right on the highway before we had time to get down from this high elevation.[6] It was certainly a wild spot, and had we frozen it might have been days before we were found, so far as we could judge, for we had not seen a soul on the road since leaving the house where we inquired the way. Odd to say, despite the great discomfort, we laughed and joked about the matter, and George's notions to get warm were certainly very funny. We ran a bit, which made our blood circulate, and as we got lower down the temperature was warmer so we had no discomfort. To our right was a flume[7] which followed the road a ways but later cut off through the woods, straight for the Ausable. It was in great disrepair. Now the rain stopped falling, and to our amazement and joy the sun almost came out, but not quite. We sang vigorously, hoping to encourage it, but it would come no further. Anyway, we began to dry out a bit, and this and the bright harebells made us feel gayer than we had been all during the trip. It was just forty minutes after starting that we reached the first house and saw people again for the first time in two-and-three-quarters hours. We had been walking along a highway all that time, crossing from the Saranac to Ausable watershed, yet we had not seen a soul. Shortly beyond the first house was the Whiteface trail.[8] This was the way Father had climbed the mountain thirty-five years before. We had hoped to get a nice view of the valley from here, but the clouds began to gather again, and we got little view. We could see the town of Wilmington, though. At 2:41 we stepped on the macadam road which leads to Placid. It was a great moment. After seventeen miles and six hours of floundering through mud we were at last on solid ground. An auto whizzed by us. It was the first we had seen since leaving the Bloomingdale Road. After reading the signs we headed for Placid, thirteen miles away, and commenced on the backstretch of our journey.

Once on good, firm footing we hit up our pace from about three to four miles an hour. It was certainly fine to be able to touch bottom at each step. The road was fine and wide, which was dandy for autos and in this case for us also, because it did not seem so gloomy and cold. There were nice woods to either side. The clouds kept growing thicker and thicker, and soon it was raining hard, and we were once more drenched. But by now we were used to this and only sang our old standby. After a couple of miles the road crossed the river on a narrow bridge, making a very sharp double bend. This place was notorious for accidents, just a short time before three people having been killed here. It was also famous for its scenery, and with good cause. The river fairly boiled through its narrow, rocky channel, with several drops of fifteen or twenty feet. On either side was a pine forest. It was a view well worthwhile.[9]

There were several big signs along the road informing people that this was the Adirondack Park, and also several auto-camping grounds. Once we stopped for a drink at a cold spring, though we had not as yet taken more than a swallow or two from our canteens. It was too wet outside. The rain kept falling intermittently, which was more unpleasant than if it had fallen steadily, for we would just start to dry out a little when we would be soaked again. We had hopes every time it stopped that it might at last clear up, but always we were doomed to disappointment. Once, just before we got to High Falls, the clouds broke apart more than they had all day. Suddenly, over the steep shoulder of Whiteface a corner of the sun appeared. That was enough, and at last we shouted together:

> Shout mountains and hilltops, valleys and cornfields,
> All earth is gold with morn's glorious light.

Jubilantly we pulled up at the house at the entrance to High Falls. These are private property and all fenced in. We found they soaked fifty cents apiece to see them, so we bought some chocolate bars and looked through the fence instead.[10] We saw all we cared or had time to see that way. We were just leaving when a man in an auto, about to start from there, offered us a lift. It was the first we had been offered in thirty-three miles. When we declined he asked us if we were Boy Scouts. I guess he thought that Boy Scouts were the only people who walked. We had to tell him where we were from and where bound. He was greatly surprised. He told us the distance to Placid, and thanking him, we continued on our way.

It was now definitely clearing up. The clouds slipped back of Whiteface and Sentinel, and the sky became almost blue. These two mountains, the one to the right and the other to the left, kept growing steeper and steeper. We were entering the famous Wilmington Notch. Now the river became very rapid and babbled and foamed. There was a great precipice on the Sentinel side, while on thickly wooded Whiteface were several cliffs. This was the finest scenery of the whole walk. Yet I must confess I was a bit disappointed. I had heard so much about the Notch I expected something finer, something which would leave a fellow more breathless. Street had called this one of the four finest gorges in the Adirondacks. I certainly could agree with that [sic].[11] I wondered what was the matter, until about eight months later in an old book I chanced to see a drawing of the notch in the early days. It certainly appeared most charming, much more than actually was the case. Yet the cliffs were not exaggerated, the narrowness not intensified. Then I saw the answer. Here was no broad macadam road to make the wilderness tame, no trees cut away to "improve" the view. Just a narrow sand road and the forest. Then it was almost in a state of nature; now it was civilized, and the change was all to the bad.

Bob Marshall, Herb Clark and Ed Young.

As we drew nearer and nearer to the Notch House, we became drier and drier and more ambitious, and we definitely decided to go all the way. Yet we were anxious to see the Fullers, and as we had been on our feet for four hours we thought we might as well stop and rest there in a dry place a few minutes, for the ground had not dried out yet. As we drew near, Mr. Fuller recognized us and called to us a pleasant greeting. We sat down in the kitchen and were cordially received by Mrs. Fuller, Charlie and Ed Young. They wanted us to stay overnight or at least for supper, but we told them of our walk, so they understood. Ed wanted to know about Lost Pond pictures. He said not a soul had been there since we were there, for he had not even gone.[12] The Rogers Co. at last had gotten their drive down to the Forks. It was good to see the Fullers again.

They had had great crops and were then putting up for the winter. I don't know how many bushels of peas and beans. The potato crop was also great. But they did not like the place as much as the Meadows and wished they were back there. They had gone fishing a few times. They all particularly asked for Herb. After twenty very pleasant minutes we left.

The rest greatly refreshed us, and though a little stiff for the first few strides, we soon fell into a four-mile-an-hour pace, which was pretty fast after having covered thirty-seven miles already. We read the interesting U.S. Rubber Co. historical sign about old Indian encampments. Soon we were to the forks where the road goes directly to Placid and the other to North Elba. The latter route would have been three miles longer, making our total if we reached home sixty-one miles, while the short way would be only fifty-eight. But we decided, as the sun was sinking close to the mountains and the clouds were coming up, to take the short way and then if we had a little extra time nearer home to walk a couple of miles more. Just beyond the forks was a bridge, and here we each stopped for an orange. Then we continued at a rapid pace for Placid. We for fun suggested visiting Connery and Cherry Patch Pond or maybe climbing Cobble Hill. But we kept straight along the road. After a while we came to the clearing where the Lake Placid Club golf links are. We stopped and looked back and got a beautiful view. The setting sun was shining on the great Sentinel Range, which was beautifully draped with clouds, the whole mass being a composite of pink and green blended in a way that only the sunset can do.

We now struck the first houses and presently were in the incorporated town of Lake Placid. We stopped at a store and bought some ginger-snaps and chocolate. Then we continued to the center of town. Here was the forty-two-mile mark, and it was very cheering to feel that we had completed seventy percent of our journey. It was not very cheerful, however, to look into the warm houses and smell the warm meals cooking and know that eighteen long miles lay before us before we should know these joys. This feeling was perhaps increased by the fact that clouds were beginning to overspread the sky again and a few drops fell. However, they did not amount to anything. We raced people through the streets of Placid who had not gone one-fortieth as far as we had, and we had no trouble beating them. When we reached the end of town we realized it would be several hours and well after dark before we reached the shelter of another village. Ten long miles of lonely road lay before us first.

Just outside Placid we stopped on top of a high sandbank overlooking the road for supper. The place was rather wet, but by sitting on a rock we managed to keep tolerably dry. It was pleasant to rest again, and the meal of eggs, sandwiches and chocolate was very enjoyable. A few evening strollers and several autos passed, but few noticed us on our high perch. After twenty-five minutes we continued.

We started before we had really finished our supper, because we were afraid we would get stiff sitting too long in that damp place. So the first ten minutes were very pleasantly spent eating gingersnaps. There were several strollers out, but by the time we had finished the crackers they were all left behind. Then the long, dull pull for Ray Brook began in earnest. At first a few autos offered us lifts, but as it grew darker they stopped doing this, doubtless fearing tramps. Then we realized that whatever the mishap there was no relief that would be offered till Saranac. If one of us was to sprain his ankle he would have to hobble many painful miles or sit on the roadside till morning. By the time we reached the Whiteface Inn Road it was perfectly dark. Just now and then a star shone among the shifting clouds.

The next three miles to Ray Brook[13] were the hardest three I have ever walked. We had now reached a stage where the effects of fifteen hours of almost steady walking were beginning to tell. In addition it was hard and unpleasant to walk in the almost total darkness. But what was far worse was the great quantity of autos with glaring headlights that went whizzing by. For every one driver who slowed up because of the darkness, two put on gas. I think I can appreciate how it feels to a deer when he is jacked.[14] It was certainly benumbing to have all the glaring searchlights flashed in our eyes, and when they were gone the darkness seemed more intense. And yet these searchlights weren't the worst part of the autos. It was the bother of having to continually look out for them, continually keep turning around, continually keep our sleepy senses on edge that was most unpleasant. At first whenever one passed we stopped and stepped off the road, but we found that if we stopped for each one we would never get anywhere, so we kept on walking at the edge of the road, where it was very rough. It was certainly a wonder neither of us sprained an ankle. But despite all the autos we did not see a soul all the while, for the bright lights cut them out. It was like walking through a wilderness with fierce, fiery monsters dashing by continually out of whose path we had to keep or court death. After all these hours of dampness our clothes and shoes began to chafe us at every step unmercifully. And the monotony was terrible. Every step was about the same. There was no scenery to view, nothing to see but the black road and the speeding autos. But I almost forgot. There was one thing alone that did seem interesting. It was the appearance in the sky long after darkness had settled of several balloon-shaped patches of light. We could never account for them, but these blimps did us a good turn in breaking the awful monotony. After several centuries we began to look out for the Cameron House, which we knew marked the beginning of Ray Brook. We had just about fully adopted this faith when the longed-for Cameron House at last appeared.

That was something even though five long, black miles yet stretched between us and Saranac. Now we turned sharply to the left, determining to follow the state road through to Saranac. For some time before reaching Ray Brook we were able to watch the auto lights as they approached from far away, for the low marsh in the concave side offered no obstructions to a distant view. Out on the boulevard between us and Scarface[15] were several twinkling lights, which looked to be right on the mountain. George for fun suggested climbing it, and the very thought of venturing on that awful mountain at this time gave us a good laugh. Where the road crossed Ray Brook we sat down on the wooden fence to rest. An auto passing must have thought it a strange seat at that time of night. Soon we heard a sharp train whistle from behind and started on. As the train drew closer we stopped to watch it approach. We sighed as we realized that in two short weeks it would be carrying us away from the section we loved. It approached slowly with loud noise, seemingly a giant reproduction of the monsters that had been passing us. Suddenly we jumped almost out of our skins, for the great light in front flashed full upon us, and the reflection of the wires overhead on the ground made it appear as though we were standing right on the tracks. This supermonster passed on, and we continued. Passing through the sanatorium grounds we hoped that no one would mistake us for cons and stop us.[16] At the very end of the ground on top of the hill is a store, and here were a lot of people buying soft drinks and talking. At last the spell of strange monsters was broken, for here were the first human beings we had seen since dark.

Coming over the crest of the hill we commenced eating some chocolate, determining to make it last till we came to the crossing of the tracks. Thus the next mile passed with the munching breaking the monotony. Just beyond the tracks at Birch Pond[17] we sat for five minutes on another fence. Then we continued, determined not to rest again till the village was passed. We expected the distance into town to seem very long, but actually it was not nearly as bad as before. Soon we came to the first house, and shortly after the sidewalk started. This made matters much easier. True it was a long ways down Lake Flower Avenue, but with street light and houses it did not seem nearly as long as it had along the pitch-dark road. In addition the moon had come out from among the clouds, and this helped. I don't mean to say the four miles from Ray Brook to River Street weren't long and hard, but they were not as long and hard as we expected.

We turned in on Church Street and headed straight for the center of town. On the way we met Harley McDougal. It was quarter past ten that we reached the center of town, which was indeed the latest we had ever been there. At Vincents Pharmacy we stopped to get some water, buying adhesive tape as an excuse to ask for a drink. On the way from there to Ampersand Avenue we raced and beat several people, though we had gone fifty-three miles and they not one fifteenth as far. Late as it was we decided to walk out a mile towards Pecks Corners[18] and back so as to make sixty miles on the walk.

The crossing at the D&H tracks marked the fifty-four-mile point in our journey. So as soon as we had gotten across we set up a loud cheer, for we had broken our old record, come what would. We were now once more walking in the dark, but it was not nearly so hard as before, both because we realized we had only a mile to go in this direction and because the moon was out. Taking our rate of speed for the last ten miles, we walked out for eighteen minutes, till we came to a big maple by a white house. Here we turned. Later we found this was slightly more than a mile. Coming back the walking was even easier for we had the lights of the village to walk toward. It was 11:05 that we turned into Ampersand Avenue and started on the last leg of our journey.

Just four-and-a-half miles more. It was nothing compared with sixty, but it seemed like quite a bit before us. Yet we were cheerful as we stroke along and called out, "Good night, Shon," as gaily as we had shouted the opposite sixteen-and-a-half hours before. That time now seemed almost like a different summer. It was well-nigh impossible to think of it as the same day. The three-quarters of a mile to the Van Dorrien passed rapidly enough, and then as we turned into the Forest Home Road we realized that we had seen our last house or man till we reached home.

At the fence on Jack-the-Tie-Walker bend[19] we sat down for a well-earned rest, the first in six miles. But after five minutes we continued again, determined not to stop till we reached Fish Creek. We each now took out a chocolate bar and started to slowly munch, deciding to make them last till Limburg's garden. This was something to pass the time away. At each of the eighth way marks we made mental notes of joy; yet the seventeen posts between seemed now to be double in number.[20] We finished our chocolate, per schedule, and rejoiced that we had covered two-thirds of the distance to the next rest. Three-quarters of a mile is not far, but it certainly seemed so now. However, we reached the bridge and sank down for our last rest. We felt like staying there all night and going right to sleep. For aside from being tired from the long exercise we were sleepy from having been up nineteen-and-a-half hours. But we realized it was utterly impracticable to spend the night there, so after five short minutes we rose and commenced the last long mile.

We dreaded the hills that lay before us; we couldn't see how we could possibly get up them. Yet almost before we realized it the first had been passed. When we reached the Knollwood gate, I looked at my watch. It was 12:05 a.m. "Good morning!" I yelled, and George answered, "Merry September." Then we became silent and headed for the big hill, climbing it several times in imagination before we really reached it. Then, as the imagination had done little good, we grit our teeth and started the steep ascent. When about halfway up George commenced singing with much fervor:

> I saw two way-worn travelers in tattered garments clad,
> They were struggling up the mountain, and it seemed that they were sad.
> Their backs were heavy-laden, their strength was almost gone,
> But they shouted as they journeyed, "Deliverance shall come."

Now I joined in the chorus and was about to begin the second verse when George reminded me it was not quite time yet. Then I understood the object of his singing and the appropriateness of the song. So when we had almost reached the crest we began:

> I saw them in the midnight, the moon was bending low,
> They overtopped the mountain, and reached the vale below;
> They saw the golden city, their everlasting home,
> And shouted loud, "Huzzanah, deliverance has come."

Then palms of victory, crowns of glory,
Palms of victory I shall wear

Now we commenced the downward road to home and triumph, and those last three joyful minutes of knowledge of success were worth much of the pain that made it possible. It was just 12:20 that we reached the back door. We had covered sixty miles in twelve hours and forty minutes.[21] We had set a new record for ourselves.

NOTES

1   Bob rated the Great Range hike (described on p. 41) third in difficulty. Their hardest hike took them over five High Peaks in the Dix Range (p. 53). Evidently, however, the ratings were made before 1930, when the Marshalls climbed nine High Peaks in a single day. The ratings are among George Marshall's papers in the Saranac Lake Free Library.

2   The long driveway leading to Knollwood, the family's summer residence on Lower Saranac Lake.

3   The Trudeau Sanatorium, which treated tuberculosis patients till its closing in 1954.

4   Abe Fuller and his family used to live at South Meadow, where the Marshalls would visit them en route to the High Peaks.

5   He apparently is referring to the Permanent Rapids on the Saranac.

6   The height of land is roughly 2,400 feet.

7   Built to float logs to the Ausable River.

8   The 1898 topographical map shows a trail that parallels White Brook awhile and then turns west to ascend a ridge to the Whiteface summit. Today's trail starting at the Wilmington reservoir ascends the same ridge, but it follows a different route in the beginning.

9   He is describing the Ausable Flume, a chasm a few miles west of downtown Wilmington.

10   High Falls Gorge on the Ausable is still a commercial attraction.

11   In *The Indian Pass*, Alfred Billings Street extols as "peerless in majesty" Indian Pass, Panther Gorge, Hunters Pass and Wilmington Notch, which he calls "the Clove or Notch of Whiteface" (Street 1869, 3). Marshall must have meant to say he could not agree with this assessment.

12   The Marshalls, Herb Clark and Ed Young, a lumberjack and hunter, had hiked to Lost Pond, south of Street Mountain, a few months earlier. George Marshall wrote about the outing twenty-one years later. See p. 273.

13   A hamlet between the villages of Lake Placid and Saranac Lake. Also the name of a stream that runs through it.

14 Deer jackers would shine a light, such as a lantern or flashlight, in a deer's eyes. The deer would freeze, as if in a trance, creating an easy target for the hunter.

15 A 3,088-foot mountain near Ray Brook.

16 The state built a tuberculosis sanatorium in Ray Brook in the early 1900s.

17 He seems to be referring to Turtle Pond.

18 Located at intersection of Trudeau Road and what is now Old Lake Colby Road (Harrietstown Town Historian Mary Hotaling, personal communication).

19 This may have been one of the whimsical names that the boys gave to features of the landscape around Knollwood.

20 Apparently he is referring to posts placed every eighth of a mile.

21 As they left Knollwood at 5:40 a.m., they had been gone from home eighteen hours and forty minutes.

Bob Marshall took this photo of Saranac Lake in 1919.

Courtesy of the Adirondack Room, Saranac Lake Free Library

The State Forestry College Summer Camp at Cranberry Lake, about 1920.

Bob Marshall (lower left) in Forestry College yearbook.

Part Two

POND
HOPPER

*"The forest outlined against the rising moon,
the deer drinking in the rippling brook,
the cool wind from the west were all as they had been
when the first pioneer trapper spread his blankets
in the untrammeled country."*

– Bob Marshall, NICKS POND

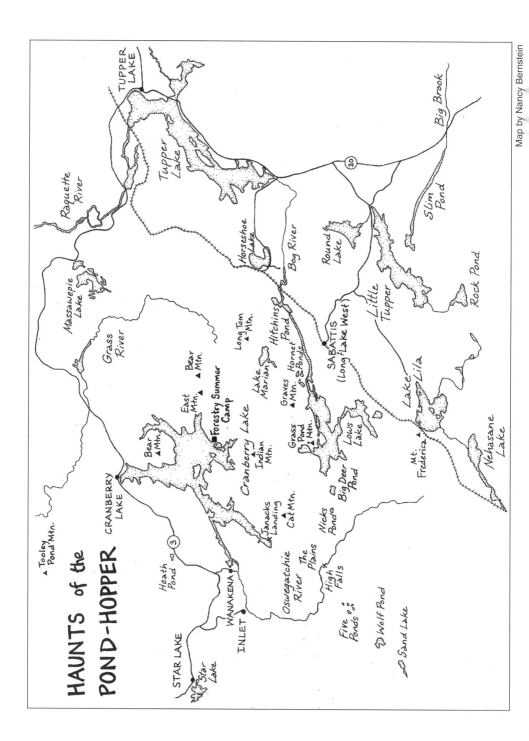

HAUNTS of the POND-HOPPER

Map by Nancy Bernstein

Week-End Trips in the Cranberry Lake Region (Summer 1922)

In 1922, Marshall and the other sophomores at the New York State College of Forestry spent two and a half months at the college's Summer Camp on the east side of Cranberry Lake. Their life was regimented in quasi-military fashion. They slept, ate and attended classes in large canvas tents. They awoke to reveille in the morning and retired to taps at night. In between, they took classes in silviculture, entomology and other subjects, went on field trips and performed chores around the camp. Marshall and his classmates built the camp's first permanent structure, a log cabin used as an administrative office. On the weekends, the students were given liberty. Marshall spent his free time on long hikes in the woods, visiting as many ponds and mountains as he could in the Cranberry Lake environs. On one solo hike, he estimated he covered forty miles in a single day. Over eleven week-ends, he saw ninety-four ponds and climbed ten mountains and, as usual, compiled lists rating their scenic beauty. In his senior year, the college yearbook described him as "the Champion Pond Hound of all time, a lad with a mania for statistics and shinnying mountain peaks." Some years ago, the New York State College of Environmental Science and Forestry published the accounts of Marshall's hikes serially in its alumni magazine, but this is the first time they have been reprinted in one volume and made available to a wider audience.

Horseshoe Circle
June 4

The first Saturday of camp was so rainy that I decided not to go out overnight, but contented myself with walking to Curtis Pond in the afternoon. Going out by way of Sucker Brook and back by East Inlet made a pleasant little stroll for a wet day.[1]

Next morning it had cleared up, so Bill Osborn[2] and I set out along the Sucker Brook trail. Our object was to follow it to the old Usher Farm Road and then return by way of Lake Marian, making a good long day's trip. All went well until we reached Proulx's First Camp,[3] but here there were so many diverging roads that we took a wrong one. After half an hour's pleasant wandering in the lumber slash, we struck the correct road near Irish Pond. From here we had no trouble following it through the Second Camp, by Center Pond, which at the time we thought was Dog, and beyond. We heard the song of the three-toed woodpecker, which Bill said was uncommon, though he could have told me it was an Australian cuckoo, for all I knew to the contrary.[4] In the cabin near Center Pond we found a very large hedgehog making himself at home.

Beyond the pond the trail became worse, and as only part of it was shown on the map, we were afraid it was going to end abruptly. However, we soon came to posted property, which was encouraging. But we had ahead of us a long walk through an unpleasant slash during the hottest part of the day. We ate lunch in one of the few shady places we could find. There were a number of branching roads along here, but by always taking the right-hand fork we had no difficulty. Finally, around two o'clock, we reached a good dirt road and telephone wires. Our map indicated that by following it to the right we would come to Horseshoe,[5] while our compass told us it would take us to Lake Marian. We believed the latter.

The four miles to Lake Marian were uneventful but pleasant. The person who doesn't enjoy a walk in the fresh woods of early June, after nine months in the city, must indeed be hard to please. We were a little disappointed in the area around the lake, which had been ruined by fire, but more so when upon approaching the houses where we hoped to get information on the return trail, we were greeted only by a couple of ferocious-looking dogs. Fortunately not being devoured, we set out to find the trail. This was easier said than done. We spent almost an

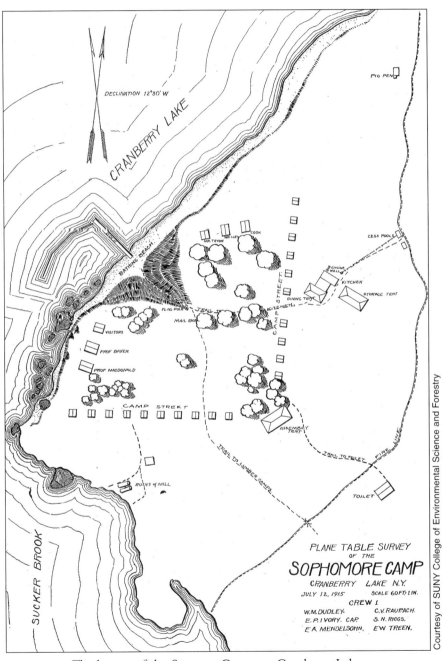

The layout of the Summer Camp on Cranberry Lake.

hour following half a dozen different wrong trails and seeing in the meantime Panther Pond.

For almost two hours we hurried rapidly through the dense thicket of second growth, which, fortunately, was not very bad underfoot, while the sun, which we kept to the front and left, sank lower and lower. About the only thing of particular interest we saw was a little spotted fawn which scampered away from almost under our feet. The entire country being strange to us, we were anxious to come out on the Sucker Brook trail before it began to get dark. Therefore, it was with considerable delight that upon descending some steep rocks, we came out on a corduroy road, which we realized must lead into some main highway. Sure enough, in ten minutes we came out at Proulx's Second Camp. After a little discussion, we started west along the road. Following it in a different direction than before made it appear a little unfamiliar, and it was not till we reached the bridges at the foot of Irish Pond that we were absolutely sure of ourselves. Here in the dusk of evening we saw a very pretty sight. A deer was quietly drinking, backed by the dark-green shores of the pond and a brilliant sunset sky. Soon she heard us and in a few great leaps was out of sight.

The stars were rapidly increasing in numbers as we reached camp, and the sunset had mostly faded from the sky. We were a little afraid we might have to go to bed hungry, but the dandy supper which Sandy got for us was a fitting finish to a very pleasant June day.

NOTES

1   Sucker Brook empties into Cranberry Lake at Barber Point, the site of the Summer Camp.

2   Bill Osborn was a forestry student from Tarrytown, N.Y., who accompanied Marshall on five of his weekend hikes.

3   Oliva Proulx's lumberjacks cut the woods east of Cranberry Lake.

4   The bird could have been either a black-backed three-toed woodpecker or northern three-toed woodpecker.

5   Horseshoe was a stop on the New York Central Railroad just west of Horseshoe Lake.

Bog River
June 10-11

Early Saturday afternoon I got started along the Chair Rock Creek trail with my packbasket, having a rather indefinite plan of climbing Graves Mountain and visiting the Bog River country. As the trail of the creek was good and from there to Darning Needle Pond was a first-rate road, though perhaps a bit confusing due to many other branching roads, I was soon at the foot of Darning Needle. Almost directly beyond the head of this pond my first objective seemed to rise, but I was soon to relearn the fact that no distance is short through a slash.

An old lumber road led to the east of Darning Needle for half its length and then followed up a brook to Little Fish Pond, one of the ugliest bodies of water it has ever been my misfortune to see.[1] I had been told there was a good trail around this slashy waterhole. I guess the trail was good enough, but the water came well above my knees. Beyond the pond lay a number of burned, rolling hills, the highest of which gave a good view toward Cranberry to the north and Scott Pond and Graves Mountain immediately to the south. Unfortunately, somewhere on this hill I lost my map, which fact I did not notice until I had gotten all the way to the other side of the pond. This was decidedly inconvenient but could not be remedied without a big waste of time.

The ascent of Graves Mountain from Scott Pond was neither steep nor difficult, even though the brush was thick and the pack beginning to feel heavy. I had chosen a good route, striking for a rocky ledge which led to the summit. Suddenly, when about three-quarters of the way up, I noticed my camera was missing. Then I recalled that at the base of the mountain I had rested and tightened my belt. It must have been here that I left the camera. Leaving my pack on the ledge, I tried to retrace my trailless journey, feeling that I did not have one chance in a hundred to find what I lost, but luck was with me, and soon I noticed a mountain ash in blossom, which appeared to be the same as one I had admired while resting.[2] Taking my bearings from it, I soon found the missing camera.

As I reascended I noticed heavy clouds were rolling up from the southwest. I hastened upward and by 5:30 stood on the peak whose rocky summit had so attracted the early explorers.[3]

What a wild view lay spread out before me! Vast areas of lowland

Graves Mountain summit, circa 1907.

stretched on all sides, partly covered by virgin forest, but mostly by second growth, and open spaces with only grass and ferns. Southeast lies a great barrier of water, stretching for miles, Bog River. Due to the construction of a dam, the river overflows much of the lowland around and is really much broader than the map indicates. Under the influence of the heavy clouds and the approaching evening, it was not hard to understand why the early writers called this the gloomiest region in the Adirondacks. There is not a sign of house or road in the entire prospect, except miles away, at Long Lake West.[4] But what is that moving column of smoke over there to the east? A railroad train as sure I live. It is no use trying to dream of the olden days, for that train has blotted them out.

After forty minutes I commenced the descent of the steep south side. I was amazed at two things. First, I saw many ripe strawberries under the shade of the ferns, which formed the principal vegetation of the mountains. This was the earliest I had ever seen this delicious fruit in the Adirondacks. Second, I found white pine reproducing high upon the steep mountain, where the soil was very shallow, and no seed trees were in sight.

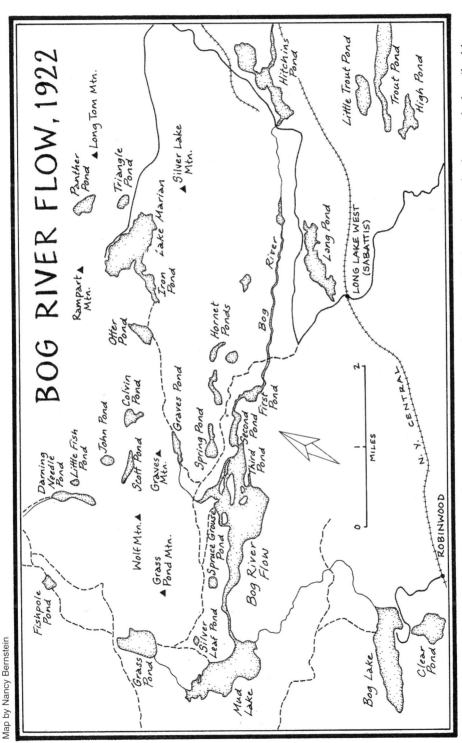

Map by Nancy Bernstein

The map shows the Bog River Flow as it existed during Bob Marshall's day. Mud Lake and several other ponds described by Marshall were flooded when the flow's dam, located just above Hitchins Pond, was raised in the 1930s.

I came out at the foot of Graves Pond and followed down the outlet until I came to a place which was suitable for camping. Darkness was rapidly approaching, and before I had entirely finished supper night had entirely set in. The wild spot, ten miles from the nearest occupied house, the cold brook close at hand and the soft bed of ferns under the open sky make a pleasant campsite. It was not long before I wrapped myself in my blankets and fell to sleep.

I was awakened around two in the morning by rain, which was not unexpected. So I ducked my head under the covers and fell to sleep again, hoping that the blankets would not wet through before morning.

It was not yet five when I recommenced my journey, after a light breakfast hastily gotten in the rain. Following down the right bank of the brook, I soon came upon a very large buck taking a drink. He stared at me for some time, as if wondering why anyone should want to enter his private slash.

Soon I reached the slough of the Third Pond,[5] where the brook enters into Bog River. Beyond was a plateau, about fifty feet above the surrounding lowland, treeless and covered mainly by ferns. It was a strange, open country, different from any I had ever seen before, and looked to be an ideal place for game. I walked over to the southern edge of the flat to get a look over the Bog River country and was greatly delighted to see three deer calmly feeding at the pond below. Two were on the opposite shore, while one was standing on a very peculiar island consisting merely of a complete outer ring about twenty-five feet wide surrounding a pool of water perhaps two hundred feet in diameter. I was intently watching this interesting display of wildlife when I was startled by a loud snort almost directly in back of me and wheeled around to see a doe within fifty feet of me, stamping her foot as if in great anger at my intrusion. While I was looking at her a snort on the other side caused me to turn around in time to see another doe go plunging through the high ferns. I waited around more than half an hour at this interesting deer resort and saw two more appear on the opposite shore. Finally, with considerable reluctance, I set out through the ferns for Spruce Grouse Pond,[6] seeing two more deer on the way. The country was, literally speaking, all cut up by runways. I now began to comprehend why some of my Saranac Lake friends regarded this burned, barren country as a hunter's paradise.

My next objective was Grass Pond,[7] and as I had lost my map and was not sure just where it lay, I calculated that the best and most inter-

Lows Lake from Grass Pond Mountain.

esting way to reach it would be to go right over the top of Grass Pond Mountain. The climb was only about seven hundred feet, but it was quite steep and very slashy and my pack with the rain-soaked blankets was heavy, so despite the cold, damp morning, I perspired considerably before reaching the bare summit.

The view was superb. The low, fast-moving clouds added an element of wildness on a perfect day. The entire length of the Bog River could be seen, from Grass Pond to Hitchings.[8] While the view toward Cranberry was not as good as from Graves Mountain, the prospect toward Mud Lake, Grass Pond, and the virgin woods to the southwest more than made up for this shortcoming.[9] Neither the cold nor a sudden, violent hailstorm could drive me away, and it was a most delightful hour I spent enjoying for the first time the finest mountain view in the Cranberry region.

When I finally left the sun had broken through the clouds. I made a steep descent to Grass Pond and frogged[10] the shoreline to the houses on the upper end. The houses were deserted, but not so the lake. Two loons made the bare side of the mountain vibrate with their shrill cry and indicated why the pond was called by some Echo. A beaver was swimming about two hundred yards away, while slightly further a deer was feeding. It was certainly a pleasant spot, and I resolved to return before long.

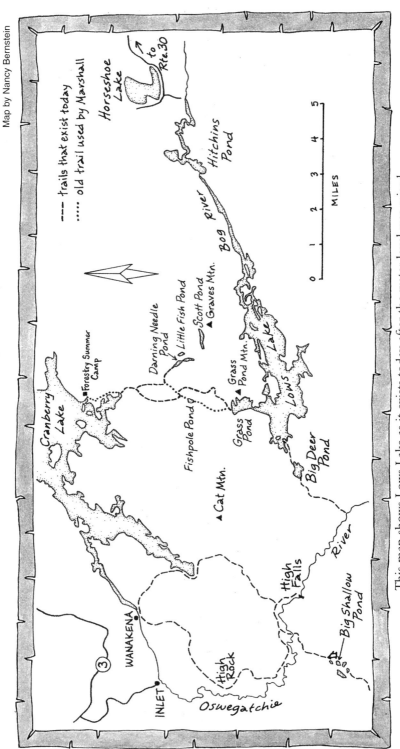

Map by Nancy Bernstein

This map shows Lows Lake as it exists today after the water level was raised.

I took the low road back to Fishpole Pond.[11] This is the poorer and harder to follow of the two old tote roads leading between the two ponds. The big swamp I am told is a favorite place for hunters to get lost. Certainly there are enough side roads and trails to confuse anyone.

Fishpole is a low pond, but it has a shoreline unmarred by fire or ax, which makes it prettier than most of the other ponds in the region. I followed along the shore until I came to the road which leads to Bushee's deserted camp, a few hundred feet away, and from there right down the west side of the Fishpole outlet to the Darning Needle trail. From here I had a leisurely and uneventful hour's journey to camp.

NOTES

1 Marshall visited ninety-four ponds in the region and ranked them in order of scenic beauty. Little Fish Pond was last on the list.

2 E.H. Ketchledge writes of the mountain ash in *Forests and Trees of the Adirondack High Peaks Region*: "Each June it has the most beautiful panoply of flowers of any Adirondack hardwood, bright clusters of snow-white flowers 6-8 inches across."

3 Marshall probably has in mind the Adirondack surveyor Verplanck Colvin, who took measurements from Graves in October 1873.

4 Long Lake West was the stop along the New York Central Railroad for the hamlet of Long Lake. Also called Sabattis.

5 Several ponds described by Marshall on this trip, including Third Pond, were inundated when a dam at the foot of the Bog River Flow was raised in the mid-1930s (Tupper Lake Historian Bill Frenette, personal communication). The flow is now usually referred to as Lows Lake.

6 Spruce Grouse Pond also was flooded by Lows Lake.

7 Once a separate waterbody, Grass Pond is now a large inlet of Lows Lake.

8 Hitchins Pond lies just below the Lows Lake dam. Marshall's variant spelling also appears in Wallace 1894, 455.

9 Mud Lake lay three-quarters of a mile due south of Grass Pond. It disappeared with the expansion of Lows Lake. The largest tract of virgin timber in the Northeast begins a few miles southwest of Grass Pond Mountain.

10 Marshall uses this curious term in several of his trip accounts. According to the *Dictionary of American Regional English*, one definition of the verb *frog* is "To cross a swampy place by jumping like a frog from hummock to hummock."

11 Topographical maps from Marshall's day show two trails leading north from Grass Pond back to the Chair Rock Creek trail. The western route would have taken Marshall to the shore of Fishpole Pond. The eastern route, sticking to higher ground, came within a quarter-mile of the pond. This route is now a state-marked trail.

State Forestry College students making the cut.

Tupper Lake
June 18-19

As the entire class was going to Turner[1] on Monday for Utilization, Neil Hosley,[2] Bill Osborn and I decided to leave Saturday and walk all the way. So, shortly after lunch, at 1:15, we lifted our packs and started along the East Inlet trail. The weather was very threatening when we started but didn't remain so for long. It was soon pouring, and consequently in a short time we were soaked to the skin.

Our plans were to follow up East Creek to the divide and then descend the other side of the pass to Burntbridge Pond and Grasse River Club. We were hoping to find lumber roads which would help us out. As soon as we reached the inlet we struck one, which went just right for a ways but suddenly made up its mind to strike for the summit of East Mountain. After giving it a fair chance to mend its way, we struck off into the bushes toward the lowlands.

Traveling in a second-growth slash is never a great pleasure. With a pack on one's shoulders it is decidedly undesirable. But in a pouring rainstorm, with the thick branches just loaded with water, ready to swat you in the face, or trickle down your back, it is punishment fit only for the most terrible criminal. So our descent to the valley was not exactly an unblemished joy.

When we reached the valley we found an old corduroy road leading through the swamp. While very far from an elegant highway, and very wet, it was a luxury compared with what we had been going through. But the best part was that after quarter of an hour it led into a good tote road, over which a wagon could well be drawn. We hoped it would lead right through to Burntbridge Pond and pass on the way the hunting cabin which we had been told was somewhere in the valley. As the afternoon wore on and the rain beat down on us as hard as ever, we began to become particularly desirous about it, for we were not anxious to sleep out in the open under existing conditions. It was, therefore, with great delight that upon crossing a brook we entered a deserted lumber camp and found one of the houses the longed-for one. It made a very cozy place to spend the night, with the storm raging outside, miles though it was from civilization.

We took off our soaking clothes and prepared a delicious supper. After it was finished we uncautiously ventured outside and in two minutes were pretty nearly devoured by gnats. Hastening inside, we wrapped ourselves in blankets, after which a scratching bee ensued for more than two hours. To try to forget the burning itch we sang songs till well into the night. It was a long time before we finally fell to sleep.

Next morning, as it was still raining and the woods were reeking wet, we determined to follow the tote road, lead where it would, rather than plunge for miles through the second growth. Our only anxiety was that the road might end abruptly. It climbed rather steeply for a ways and became worse. After crossing the height of land between the two halves of Bear Mountain,[3] however, it became better. This was very consoling. We were not sure just where we were headed for, as the road was not shown on any maps. We came after a while to a fork and chose the left-hand branch. The right, we later learned, ran right back to camp. After a while we reached Center Pond, which I immediately recognized. We examined it for quite a while and then continued on along the Horseshoe trail. We wanted to come out at Usher Farm, so we bore to the left at every fork. We plodded steadily ahead, crossing several floating bridges, due to high water, and passing the Little Mountain cabin, a rather uninviting place to stop. By ten o'clock we came out on what we supposed from the map would be a good road but was really a very poor and sandy one. Here was the beginning of Usher Farm.

Usher Farm was another surprise. We expected a large, prosperous, fertile place and instead found only barren and deserted meadows. Instead of good crops were weeds, while the forest was gradually filling in. We later learned the farm, which had been operated by the Potsdam Lumber Company, was deserted about twenty-five years before.

We proceeded along the road through the farm, offering various hypotheses for its desertion, none of which happened to be right. There was an abundance of large, dusty strawberries, which filled our stomachs for more than a mile. A short ways beyond was the old farmhouse, renovated by the Grasse River Club for their own use. It was deserted, save for two large hedgehogs which were trying desperately to enter the cellar.

Beyond the house was a long, interesting stretch of road. We saw one deer and several old logging railroads. Just before the Grasse River Railroad[4] we cooked lunch. Shortly after crossing the tracks interest was revived by the appearance of the first pond, Deer, lying east of the road. Climbing a narrow ridge to the west, we got a fine view over the Grasse River country, with Town Line Pond lying just below us. Both were very pretty ponds, while several others equally fine followed in the next two miles, including Boot Tree, Horseshoe, Massawepie and Long. They were so close to the road it generally took only a minute or less to reach the shore. These were all part of the Childwold Preserve,[5] which had fortunately protected the beauty of these ponds from the lumberman. Incidentally, they must also have protected the game, if the large number of deer tracks could be taken as an indication.

But aside from the natural pleasure which the place afforded, man had furnished an additional one. Just after Deer Pond, in a very wild spot, was a stalled auto, in which was a scared-looking woman, while a man's footprints led away. Many solutions of the mystery were offered, but we never definitely found out the true one.

Massawepie was an especially beautiful pond, or rather lake, only marred by the rotting remnants of the former summer colony located there. The main hotel, which has been deserted since 1908, looked like a good spot for ghosts. Across the road we purchased supplies for supper. This farmhouse is the only occupied place at what, from the map, one would judge is the thriving town of Massawepie.

Following the road for half a mile more, as it took a broad bend through the open fields, we soon reached its end and stepped out on the main highway from Potsdam to Tupper. Here was a little settlement called Gale. We met the son of the first settler, Henry Gale, who came there way back in 1864, when a wilderness stretched on all sides. We bought a loaf of bread which was probably baked shortly after he arrived.

We would have liked to stop and talk with this interesting pioneer, but Tupper Lake was still thirteen miles away and we wanted to cover most of that distance before dark. So we started to pound along the macadam. Many autos passed us, but none deigned to offer us a lift. Personally, I was rather glad, as a walk on an unknown road is always a great pleasure to me, even with dull scenery and a heavy pack. We caught occasional glimpses of the Racquette River, but that was about the only thing of interest that we saw. We covered the six miles to Piercefield in an hour and a half.

The sixth town of the Adirondacks held no particular interest for us, and we passed right through without stopping and crossed Piercefield Flow. A couple of miles beyond, where a little brook crossed the road, we stopped to cook supper.

After supper, as it looked like a night of rain, we became anxious for some barn or old house under which we might sleep. It took half an hour's walking before we found such a place, the barn of William Jarvis. He kindly gave us permission to spend the night there and took our socks to the house to dry. After a game of ball with young Harlin Jarvis, we climbed up to the loft, and though the floor was hard, we slept soundly ten hours.

We left our kind friends next morning around seven o'clock and, after an uneventful half-hour's walk, reached Tupper Lake Junction, where we got a good breakfast.

Here we really ended the trip. However, it might be appropriate to mention a couple of short journeys we took during the day while waiting for the rest of the class, who were delayed, to arrive.

In the evening we set out for Follansbee Pond, where Emerson, Lowell, Agassiz and Judge Hoar, among others, had camped as early as 1858.[6] We had gotten halfway when we were unceremoniously stopped and told we were trespassing on private property. After lunch we walked three miles to Moody and from there climbed Mount Morris. The walk was very pleasant, but the view was like the legs of a snake. It didn't exist. A heavy fog had settled down on the mountain while we were climbing, and we could not see ten yards.

Thus bad weather followed us the entire trip. Nevertheless, it was very enjoyable and a great success.

NOTES

1   An apparent reference to the Turner Tract north of Tupper Lake, where there was an old lumber camp used by forestry students (Gove, 2005, 198).

2   Neil Hosley was a student from Arkport, N.Y. A few years later, he and Marshall roomed together at the Harvard Forest in Massachusetts, where they studied for master's degrees in forestry (Glover 1986, 61).

3   This small peak lies about three and a half miles southeast from the better-known Bear Mountain that rises above the east shore of Cranberry Lake.

4   The sixteen-mile Grasse River Railroad was built to assist logging east of Cranberry Lake, but it also carried passengers, freight and mail (Fowler 1959, 131-6).

5   A 9,800-acre private preserve created in the late 1800s. The palatial Childwold Park Hotel entertained such influential guests as Grover Cleveland and Theodore Roosevelt (McMartin 2004, 45).

6   Ralph Waldo Emerson and nine other intellectual luminaries camped at Follensby Pond in July 1858. The artist William James Stillman commemorated the gathering in a painting and in an essay, both titled "The Philosophers' Camp." Like Marshall, Stillman used the spelling "Follansbee," but modern maps use "Follensby." (Donaldson 1977, vol. I, 172-189.)

Locomotive on the Grasse River Railroad.

Courtesy of Susan Smeby

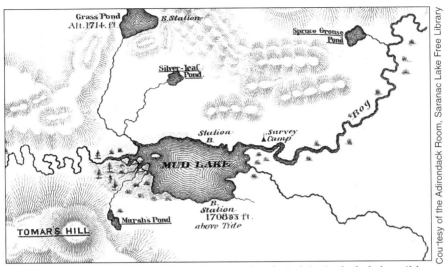

The 1873 map of Adirondack surveyor Verplanck Colvin included the wild, remote Mud Lake, which has since been flooded by Lows Lake.

Grass Pond Mountain
Trail-Cutting Expedition
June 23-25

Immediately after the final exam in Utilization on Friday afternoon, the crew that volunteered to cut out the Grass Pond Mountain trail prepared for their two days' trip to Grass Pond, where they were going to stop while working on the job. At 5:30, loaded with packs and carrying their various trail-cutting implements, the party set out for their destination, seven miles away. The personnel consisted of Sid Smith, Sam Forebell, Wilmer Lewis, Bill Osborn, Neil Hosley and Bob Marshall.[1] After two and a half hours, when night was drawing close, they pulled up at the cabins at Grass Pond. The place was deserted, as expected, and the main building was locked, but the other cabin furnished ample space for all of them to stop. They were preparing a late supper, when suddenly from the inside of the padlocked house floated the strains of some ghost-like song. They were dumbfounded for a moment and almost thought the house was haunted but soon found out the truth. Sam had found the back door open, walked in and started the phonograph.

Next morning, immediately after breakfast, four of us set out to start the trail, leaving two to clean up the house, which was very dirty, cut wood and prepare lunch. We made good progress. I went ahead to pick the route and mark it; Neil followed with the ax, and Sam and Sid brought up the rear with brush hooks. In the afternoon, with six working, progress was even more rapid, and by seven o'clock we reached the summit, having cut out one mile of good trail. It is to be hoped that future classes will make use of it and obtain the best view in the region.

Sunday morning, as our task was all completed, I rowed across Grass Pond and took the trail to Mud Lake.[2] I knew of this sluggish body of water from the accounts of all the early writers. They were unanimous in calling it the wildest and gloomiest place in the Adirondacks. So I let my imagination carry me back sixty years to the days when the tread of wolf, moose and panther were of daily occurrence, while man was almost unknown in the region. The lake was not particularly beautiful, but with thoughts of the past in mind, the visit was very enjoyable.

After lunch we set out for camp, traveling leisurely. We returned by way of Darning Needle instead of Fishpole. When we reached Cranberry we had gone forty-seven hours without seeing anyone outside our own party.

NOTES

1 It's unclear why Marshall refers to himself in the third person. He first climbed Grass Pond Mountain two weeks earlier. The trail they cut is no longer in use.

2 Mud Lake now lies under Lows Lake.

Heath Pond
July 9-10

This trip stands out as a good example of one not to take. Perhaps I should have had enough sense to omit it, for Mr. Bancroft warned me I would encounter much slash. But Heath Pond's position on the map, miles from any real highway, looked very attractive, and besides, I had never penetrated the section west of the lake.[1]

As Entomology continued over Saturday, I had to make this a one-day trip. Bill Osborn and Altpeter[2] kindly ferried me across Cranberry, leaving me at the point opposite Birch Island. I followed the shoreline around to the bay and then struck off through the saddle for the upper end of Peavine Swamp. Here were fresh indications of the lumbermen, but as it was Sunday, no one was around. The lumber roads were help-ful in crossing the swamp, but beyond they were only misleading. I soon crossed a ridge and found myself in another swamp of great size, in which Heath Pond occupied a very inconspicuous position. How to find it in all that vast area of flat land, much greater than shown on the map, was indeed a problem. In the dense swamp growth I could pass within a few rods of it, without ever seeing it, and might perhaps con-tinue in the same direction almost to Benson Mines.

I determined to ascend State Ridge, which I was anxious to climb anyway, and try to spot the pond. I encountered much slash and found a view by no means commensurate with the trouble it took to attain. True, Cranberry could be seen and some of the mountains to the south and east, which did look fine, especially in the perfectly clear weather of this day. But their effect was much marred by the slash on all sides. Trees on the top of the ridge prevented any continuous view. But what inter-ested me most was the sight of Heath Pond, surrounded by burnt and waste lands, lying about a mile southwest. After twenty-five minutes of very rough traveling I stood on its shore, or rather, as near as I could get to it, for, because of beaver, the water was knee high far inland among the alders. The pond was one of the most unattractive I ever saw and, as a main object of the trip, a terrible failure.

My next objective was Muskrat Pond, lying about three-quarters of a mile northwest. I had to cross an open plateau, which, fortunately, was free from a jungle of second growth but was so flat that I could not see the pond until within a few rods of it. On a little hill to the east I ate lunch, marveling at the clarity of the air, which made the tower on Cat Mountain[3] to the south appear only about a mile away, while in reality it was seven, and which made the smoke of Newton Falls seem just beyond the next ridge, while actually four ranges of hills and a broad swamp intervened.

Beyond Muskrat Pond, according to the map, there should have been a secondary road, which I expected to follow over Twin Mountain back to Cranberry village. But not even a dim trail, still less a road, exist-ed. So I resolved to cut out to the main highway by the shortest possi-ble route. Taking out my compass, I headed due north.

No need to go into details about the slash encountered the next two miles, nor the difficulties in crossing the foot of Chaumont Swamp. I fol-lowed for quite a ways along the edge of a long series of cliffs east of

Chaumont Pond, from which a good view of the swamp, as well as the hills to the northwest, could be obtained. These cliffs gradually broke away into lower ground, and the last mile to the Oswegatchie was decidedly damp.

When I came to the river I found it about fifty feet wide and much too deep to ford. I did not want to swim for fear of losing my camera, and I knew I would have to frog a very rough shoreline two miles in the direction I didn't want to go to get to the nearest bridge. Fortunately, there were a few logs left stranded in the river. By [getting][4] on the end of one I managed, with considerable labor and loss of time, to get across the river and still keep my camera dry.

It was but a few steps to the road, along which I hastened toward Cranberry, gradually drying out as I progressed. The walk was, indeed, enjoyable and only marred by the sight of the rapidly setting sun, which warned that I would have a hard time reaching camp before dark.

At Cranberry I met Emmett Hurst, who got someone to show me where the path to Summer Camp started. It was 7:20 when I got going, with thirteen miles over an unknown trail to camp. It almost seemed foolish thus to set out, for I had no blankets, having planned to make this a day's trip. But it seemed the only possible way of getting back by eight o'clock next morning, unless I hired a boat, which for several reasons I did not care to do. While daylight lasted I made good speed over the trail, or rather road, but as night drew on the way was somewhat less plain, and I had to slow up. So it was nine o'clock before I had covered the six and half miles to Brandy Brook, and the daylight was entirely gone.

Around here so many branch roads led off that it was impossible to find the right one in the darkness, and I realized it was useless to go further until morning. There were two parties of fishermen around, one of whom invited me to their fire. Here were a couple of elderly men, Messrs. Callard and Thorne, and a pleasant young fellow, Blackford King. The other party, composed of a city man and his guide, was considerably more than half seas over. They went out in a boat and started a long chain of uncomplimentary remarks about Thorne, which really sounded very humorous to a distinguished bystander. When they finally landed, Thorne, who was an actor, knocked them both in the brook and then began a very grandiloquent conversation with them, which sounded as if he was quoting from one of his plays. The chief offender seemed to have reached that stage in his intoxication where he had to make a long, staggering speech about the most matter-of-fact affair, so between the two it was really better than a circus. The drunks apologized and were very humble thereafter, but it was past midnight before matters had quieted down enough to sleep. The night was decidedly chilly, but King very kindly gave me one of his blankets, and by rolling up close to the fire I slept well until two o'clock, when all arose because of the cold. At the first streaks of dawn Thorne and Callard went out on the brook, and not much later, at 3:45, I said goodbye and set out on the last leg of my journey.

The trail was very confusing, due to recent lumbering operations, and I was thankful I had not tried to follow it during the night. As it was, I soon got off it, but as I knew the direction I wanted to go, this was not disconcerting. As I had now plenty of time to reach camp for the opening of Pathology, I determined to go right over the top of Hedgehog Mountain, which was not much out of my way. The view was very poor, due to the fact that the summit was covered with timber. But the walk was very pleasant. In fact, this entire early-morning tramp was most enjoyable, even though made on a stomach which had only received three sandwiches and a piece of cake in the past twenty-four hours, for the woods were fresh and, though lumbered, not very badly slashed. There was also an abundance of game, for I started up five deer, as well as many smaller animals.

I reached camp just in time to find out that I was in charge of the wood-chopping detail, when recall was blown.[5]

NOTES

1 Heath Pond, located about three miles west of Cranberry Lake, is no longer "miles from any real highway." State Route 3 is only an eighth of a mile away.

2 Leland Stanford Alpeter and Osborn were fellow students.

3 The state built a fire tower on Cat Mountain in 1909. It was removed in the 1970s (Smeby 2002, 57).

4 The word in the manuscript is "tissint," an obvious but puzzling typographical error.

5 In military lingo, a recall is the signal to cease work duties. At Summer Camp, this would have been 7:10 a.m. (*Camp Log* 1922, 7).

Nicks Pond
July 15-16

Shortly after lunch, on a pleasant afternoon in July, I set out with the main objective to find the corner where St. Lawrence, Hamilton and Herkimer counties come together. I paddled leisurely to the Cat Mountain landing with Clark and Joslyn, who were going fishing.[1] It took us nearly two hours to cover the seven miles. We then started along the Cat Mountain trail. At Glasby Pond the trail forked. We took the right-hand branch, which did not go up the mountain. Soon we reached a maze of crossing trails, one of which we followed to Cat Mountain Pond. This must certainly have been a beauty before the lumbermen and fire ever entered the region. Cat Mountain rises directly from the shore. It almost seems as if one could throw a stone up to the tower.

I left my two companions here, and after a slight search continued along the trail. Soon it crossed the outlet of Bassout Pond. Here I left my pack and headed up brook. Lumber roads helped considerably, but there was a good deal of pushing through brambles and bushes before I reached the pond. It was a distinct disappointment, to which it was not worth paying respects. Once back on the path, it did not take long to reach the junction above Cowhorn Pond, where trails from four different places come together.[2] The one which led in the direction I wanted was considerably overgrown and was evidently used much less than the others. It was an old lumber road. I passed one old camp in a hollow and after skirting the foot of a hill reached the lower end of Clear Pond. This body of water was less marred by man than the others passed so far, but the beaver had killed much timber. No wonder! Just below the pond were four dams.

As the day was well advanced, and the prospect of seeing some interesting animals enhancing, I determined to camp on a meadow near the lower dam. Some old bark shanties had once graced this spot. There was plenty of firewood, fine water and a good place to sleep, which made up for the lack of beautiful scenery. While supper was cooking I saw two beaver but failed to get a good picture.

By the time I had finished a dandy supper, washed the utensils, spread my blankets and gathered wood for the morning, darkness was pretty well at hand. Sitting by the dying fire, it seemed hardly possible

Courtesy of Susan Smeby

John Janack, the longtime Cat Mountain fire observer, in 1914.

that I was in the crowded Empire State of today. Not a house nor a soul was within miles. Probably none had passed or would pass along the trail for days. The gathering darkness blotted out the unpleasant signs of man. The forest outlined against the rising moon, the deer drinking in the rippling brook, the cool wind from the west were all as they had been when the first pioneer trapper spread his blankets in the untrammeled country, termed Couchsachrage,[3] the dismal wilderness.

After a light breakfast next morning I followed down the brook. There was more or less of a trail, but principally less. The lumbermen had left an unpleasant slash. It was not only unpleasant to see but, loaded as the weeds and reproduction were with dew, very wet to feel. Soon I came to a queer-looking, long, narrow ridge, at the base of which the outlet of Big Deer joined the brook. It was not far beyond here that the boundary between St. Lawrence and Herkimer counties was reached. It was plainly visible not only by the witness trees but especially by the distinct line of demarcation between the lumbered lands to the north and the virgin timber to the south.[4]

It was fine to get into the shade of the primeval forest, the first of any great extent that I had encountered in the entire region. After a few minutes I came out on the shores of Nicks Pond, as delightful a body of water as could be imagined, with high, unmarred banks. A deer was calmly feeding along the shore a few rods away. The day was young, the sun just rising above the trees, and the pond before me seemed as wild as when Colvin first placed it on the map.[5] I could not seem to be able to tear myself away from it and must have remained for more than an hour. It was time well spent too, for in the entire Cranberry region this was the most beautiful pond I saw.[6]

When I left I half imagined I was back in the days of Colvin. It gave added pleasure to the task which lay before me, finding the great corner where the three counties met. I walked to the nearby boundary between St. Lawrence and Herkimer, found a couple of iron markers and started east along it. The climb up the razorback was very steep, particularly with a packbasket. At the crest I got a good bird's-eye view of the neighboring country and could pick out the approximate location of the corner on the next hill east. Crossing the valley, I soon reached the approximate spot. But to find the exact one was another matter. A lane about thirty yards wide had been cut east and west, but the north-south line was not readily visible.[7] Old witness trees were as common as old ladies at a sewing circle, but they all seemed to indicate a different point. Finally, after more than an hour, I found a mouldering old post, half buried, at a spot I had passed half a dozen times.[8] It was the long-desired corner. Of course I had to stand in three counties at once and do equally foolish things, but behind it all there was a keen sense of gratification that I had realized an old ambition.

I now struck due east for Big Deer Pond, concerning which there had been much discussion in the early days, some claiming that it did not exist. For years it was regarded as a lost pond.[9] It pretty nearly was a lost pond to me. The country was so flat that there were no landmarks to go by. It was covered with meadows of grass and fern and second growth. Deer trails were numerous and so well beaten that I was afraid I might not be able to distinguish the Long Lake West trail if I crossed it. It seemed a very long ways across this tableland, and I was beginning to fear that I had overrun the pond when suddenly loud laughter a short distance away startled me. I came out in a clearing, which I subsequently learned was made by old Fide Scott.[10] A party of men were just eating breakfast. I guess they were even more surprised to see me stalking out of the bush than I was to be awakened from my dreams of Colvin

Courtesy of Susan Smeby

SLIDING ROCK FALLS.

Sliding Rock Falls on Sixmile Creek.

Land. We exchanged the greetings proper for a chance meeting in the woods. They told me they had seen sixteen deer at the pond a few rods down the hill and had taken several pictures. Leaving my pack, I soon hastened down the trail and soon reached Big Deer. Only one of the animals after which it was named remained. However, it was well worth seeing for its beauty. It is the biggest pond in the section, exclusive of those on the main chain of the Bog River.[11]

Returning to the clearing, I took up my pack and, declining a kind invitation to eat some pancakes, started along the trail to Cowhorn. The sun was by this time well up toward the zenith, and the scant vegetation left by the fire afforded little protection.[12] It was indeed a scorching walk, and I felt more pepless than at any other time all summer. The trail led close by three ponds, and I walked down to the shore of each. They were all unattractive. Tamarack had been badly marred by beaver. An interesting thing about this pond is that it flows into the Racquette River system, while Big Deer and Slender, very near it on either side, swell the waters of the Oswegatchie.[13] Beyond Slender, Cat Mountain stood out as a lighthouse, showing proper course. It was pleasant to have something stand out in that uninteresting country.

At the Cowhorn Corners I took the trail running north. It led along a ridge just west of the pond, which was prettier than most in the vicinity, and then followed in a general way the course of Six Mile Brook.[14] The path was very good, and the lookout station telephone line made a fine trail marker. There is little to remark about the journey to South Bay except that it was very hot. I took one side trip to Indian Mountain Pond, following up the outlet which crossed the trail. A pleasant rest at Sliding Rock Falls is the only other thing which stands out in memory.

From here on the journey was cooler. I reached the lake and then followed the trail along the hillside to the rear of Indian Mountain Club. From here the trail swung around the base of Indian Mountain to Chair Rock Creek, from which place I followed the familiar course to camp.

NOTES

1   Today the Cat Mountain landing is called Janacks Landing, after John Janack, who manned the fire tower on Cat Mountain for twenty-three years, starting in 1909. He lived at the landing with his wife and eleven children. (Smeby 2002, 57, and Fowler 1959, 56-7.)

2   At the junction, Marshall had the choice of taking trails south to Clear and Nicks ponds, southeast to Big Deer Pond or north along Sixmile Creek to Cranberry Lake. Only the last is still maintained.

3   The name Couchsachrage appears on a 1776 map. It has been translated as "the dismal wilderness" and "the beaver hunting grounds." Marshall and his brother George gave the name Couchsachraga to one of the forty-six High Peaks. (Donaldson 1921, vol. I, 12-13; Carson 1927, 240-1.)

4   In 1896, the state purchased a large tract of virgin forest from William Seward Webb that extended north from Stillwater Reservoir to the boundary between Herkimer and St. Lawrence counties. Witness trees are used by surveyors to locate corner boundaries.

5   The surveyor Verplanck Colvin explored the region in 1873.

6   Nicks Pond indeed is rated first for scenic beauty in his ranking of the 94 ponds he visited that summer. See p. 148.

7   The north-south line is the boundary between Herkimer and Hamilton counties.

8   A year later, two other students at the College of Forestry Summer Camp were unable to find the post. One of them, William Harlow, wrote: " 'Bob' had described it as 'mouldering,' and at the end of half an hour we decided that it must have mouldered away" (Harlow 1923, 48).

9   Verplanck Colvin refers to the pond as "Lost Lake" in his report for 1873: "My inquiries of the guides as to the location of such a lake had for years been met either with incredulity or professions of ignorance" (Colvin 1874, 55).

10 Philo "Fide" Scott was a hermit who lived at Big Deer Pond. The hero of Irving Bacheller's 1906 novel *Silas Strong: Emperor of the Woods* was inspired by Scott. (See Paul Jamieson's note in Keith 1976, 162.)

11 These ponds were flooded during the creation of Lows Lake. Nowadays, the only maintained trail to Big Deer is a canoe carry leading from the west end of Lows Lake to the headwaters of the Oswegatchie River.

12 An apparent reference to a large fire in 1908 that started at Long Lake West.

13 Big Deer's outlet does flow into the Oswegatchie River, but Slender Pond's outlet flows into Tamarack Pond, whose outlet feeds Lows Lake (and eventually the Raquette River).

14 It's "Sixmile Creek" on modern maps.

Star Lake
July 22-23

I left camp right after lunch on the mail boat. George had a big load, with the baseball team, the rooters and a platoon of old maids. As a result the *Gray Dawn*[1] broke down a couple of times, and it was two o'clock before we reached Wanakena.

I set out along the back road to Benson Mines, preferring that to the main one as I would see a couple of extra ponds. Three and a half miles of very hot and dull walking brought me to the Inlet Road. Here was a dandy spring. After drinking, I proceeded north. This whole territory had been lumbered and burned, and there was hardly a big tree left. So it was not very pleasant walking. Luckily, I had only a haversack. When I judged by the map that I was opposite Nicks Pond I cut through the woods and soon stood on its desolate shore.[2] I think I counted thirteen decent trees around the entire body of water. Sunny Pond could be seen from the road. It certainly was well named. Nearby was a sad-looking farm with the pretentious name of Sunny Pond Ranch. The next point of interest along this road was the cemetery. It had very novel flowers planted on all the graves, pigweed.

The 1920 census gave Benson Mines a population of 950. So I expected to see a thriving town; but it was absolutely dead. The mill had shut down, and the only indication that the town had ever known any industry was a mountain of yellow gravel back of the mill.

It didn't take long to see the town, and soon I set out along the upper road to Star Lake. As it was getting late and there was much territory to be covered before dark, I accepted a lift into Star Lake in a bakery auto. The driver showed astonishing honesty by deliberately going out of his way to pay for a chicken he ran over.

Star Lake was a thriving summer resort, fancy hotels, white duck pants and shirts abounded, so after a couple of journeys down to the lake at different points, I hastened away. Soon I left the macadam road to Oswegatchie and branched off on the dirt road running through the Twin Pond Preserve. The ponds were only of mediocre beauty and hardly worth leaving the road to see. From here the thoroughfare ran over and around rolling hills covered with meadow land and second growth. There were a few deserted houses along the road. I followed the railroad tracks to Oswegatchie, a small town, and then followed down the fertile valley to Lower Oswegatchie, which consisted of only a few houses. Here I turned my back on the setting sun and headed for Newton Falls.

The scenery until I had crossed the Twin Pond Road was typically rural, with several farms. But from here on for four miles the road passed only one house. It was very pleasant to be traveling in the quiet of evening along this back road, even though there was no beautiful scenery.

As I had no pack, I planned to spend the night somewhere in Newton Falls. But there wasn't a place to be had in the whole town. The paper mill was cutting to capacity, and then some, and so the town had more people than houses, very different than at Benson Mines. I saw a couple of men who were even sleeping in remodeled chicken coops. With the prospect of tramping the highway all night, I set out on the Cranberry Road. After a while, just before the road crossed the Oswegatchie, I came to the house of the blacksmith. This kindhearted man gave me a supper and permission to sleep in his barn. Shortly after the rain came pouring down, so I shall be ever grateful to John J. Carlin for rescuing me from a mighty unpleasant night.

My host, a typical Irishman, regaled me with many interesting stories of his experiences in the woods around the beginning of this century. Fulton Chain of about 1900 he described as the toughest town in the world. He seemed particularly to delight in telling of getting lost in the woods. But at history he was at his best.

"Did you know that John Brown cut the road which starts just twenty rods back of the house?" he asked.

"No," I replied, thinking I had discovered some great new historical fact.

"Yes," replied Carlin. "He was at work on that road when the Rebels captured and hung him!"

"What started the Civil War anyway," I asked, trying to draw him out.

"Why, Abe Lincoln objected to the Southerners having slaves, and Jeff Davis didn't want the Northerners to build roads!"

This was history with a vengeance. How few realize that the great war which cost almost a million lives, $5 trillion and untold suffering was all caused by the building of an obscure road fifty miles from civilization! But I wanted to get more historical data, so I asked: "Are you any relative of Major General William P. Carlin, hero of the battle of Perryville?"[3]

"Sure and it must be my uncle. He was a captain or sergeant, or some high officer like that in the Utica Police!"

Next morning, after bidding my kind friend goodbye, I returned to Newton Falls. There I got a dandy breakfast and then set out along the bed of the old logging railroad to Newbridge. Crossing the trestle at the head of Newton Falls Pond was made difficult by 454 logs which had been stranded on it in high water. The woods on both sides of the railroad bed had been lumbered, and quite a bit had been burned. The country was mostly flat and monotonous, especially as the rain precluded the possibility of seeing more than a hundred yards. After an hour of slow walking, a lumber road led off to the right. Taking a chance it might go to Moosehead Pond, I followed it and soon reached virgin timber and saw my objective through the trees.

Moosehead Pond is one of the very most beautiful bodies of water in the region. Surrounded as it is by virgin timber, with its irregular shoreline, two pretty islands and background of Tooley Pond Mountain, it cannot fail to delight anyone. After passing so much desolate, lumbered land, it seemed particularly fine. I followed around the shoreline until the lumber road was reached again and then returned to the railroad grade, passing Little Moosehead, a small pond with some fine white pines.

It was a wet, weary hour's tramp before I came to the next point of interest, a large clearing with scattered deserted houses and what looked like a freight yard. For a moment I thought it might be Newbridge, but I had thought of it as a bustling little town and had been told the railroad ended there, so I realized it could not be my goal. I continued along the grade but soon—to my dismay—came out upon a big river which I was sure must be the Grasse. Then I knew I had overrun Newbridge. A spur line soon crossed the river on a high, decaying trestle, and along this I found a precarious way to the Clifton Falls road.

The twelve-mile walk back to Cranberry was uneventful. The chief recollections I retain are drenching rain and mud. Three ponds were passed–Tooley, Cook and Dillon. I had planned to climb Tooley Pond Mountain,[4] but the rain made a such a project useless. Near Cooks Corners I passed the windfall of 1845, now once more a forest.[5] The Oswegatchie was full of logs, drifting down to Newton Falls. It was about 3:30 when I reached Cranberry, drenched to the skin.

Here I met the drunken guide of Brandy Brook.[6] He was just going up the lake to call for a fishing party with his launch and offered to take me to camp for fifty cents. As the regular price was two dollars, and the alternative to riding a long, wet walk and a good chance of sleeping out in the rain without blankets, it did not take me long to accept his offer.

NOTES

1 Because of a typographical error, the name of the boat appears as "Gray Dwan" in the manuscript. An alternate interpretation would be "Gray Swan."

2 This is not the Nicks Pond he visited the previous weekend. Both are named after Nick Glasby, one of the region's early hunters and trappers.

3 Marshall was a Civil War buff. He once ranked the top two hundred military leaders of the war and sent his list to several of the generals then still living for their reaction (Glover 1986, 39).

4 In Marshall's day, a fire tower stood on Tooley Pond Mountain. The New York State Ranger School dismantled the tower, starting in the 1980s, and eventually reconstructed it at Cathedral Rock near Wanakena (Laskey 2003, 41).

5 The 1845 tornado leveled trees in a half-mile swath from just north of Cranberry Lake to the vicinity of Upper Saranac Lake (Fowler 1959; 9, 63).

6 See account of Heath Pond, p. 118.

Hornet Pond
July 30

It was a beautiful July morning that Roy Sahm, Bill Osborn and I started for Grass Pond Mountain. We followed the well-known trail to Grass Pond, about seven miles in the length. This leads first to Pigs Ear Flow,[1] then to Chair Rock Creek, where it leaves the bay just beyond the high bridge and turns off to the left. From here it follows Chair Rock Creek in a general way to a point where a lumber road crosses the brook to the right. Here we nailed up one of Bill's signs. This road brings you out, after two miles, at Bushee's old lumber camp, where you strike another road. Taking it to the right brings you to Fishpole; to the left you soon come to a bridge over the outlet of the pond, which you cross, and then follow another old lumber road along the crest of the ridge to a big swamp. From here on there are so many branch lumber roads it is impossible to describe the way. But with a map one can find it easily enough.

Near Grass Pond, by a group of double-header rollways, the trail up Grass Pond Mountain branches off.[2] We were delighted to find it had gotten much use since we cut it out. When we got above timberline (caused by fire) we opened a large can of red paint we had brought along and blazed the trail with it. The view from the summit was magnificent, the weather being perfect. We stayed on top forty minutes and gazed with delight on this unrivaled view of the Bog River watershed.

It was just noon when we started down through the bad slash, heading for the big slough on the Third Pond of Bog River. We ate lunch at a little brook at the foot of the mountain. After crossing a low bridge we came out on the characteristic open flat of the Bog River country, covered only by grass and ferns.

Here we picked up the Long Lake West trail and were soon thereafter informed by frequent signs that we were on the A.A. Low Preserve.[3] We got a very good view of Graves Mountain. We crossed the head of the slough on a beaver dam and after a little difficulty picked up the trail on the other side. It soon branched in three, the left-hand fork going to Graves Pond, the right to Bog River, while we kept the center trail, which passed by Spring and Three Pound Pond on its way to Long Lake West. We took a couple of side trips to the right to catch another glimpse of Third Pond and one of Second and First. We also walked off trail to the left to see Spring Pond. They were all far from inspiring. At Second Pond we were surprised to hear the chug-chug of a motorboat and see a party of young men and girls land. But the slash held more attraction for us, so we hastened on. Soon we left the trail for good and cut across a burned flat, now densely overgrown. Here we found in the two Hornet Ponds and Three Pound Pond probably as ugly a trio of bodies of water as were ever grouped within half a mile of each other. Nothing but slash, backed by hills, burned to the bare rock, surrounded them. Yet, I have been told by a guide who has fished and hunted much in this section that they furnish the best trout angling he ever knew.

It was about three o'clock when we left these ponds and cut through the notch in the hills for Otter Pond. Here the going was particularly rough. Roy, who had done little walking during the summer, stood the hard traveling remarkably well.

There were many deer tracks here, and we saw a couple of those animals. Just before Otter Pond we struck a good trail which evidently came from Graves Pond and led to Iron Pond. To the left, at the center of the pass, was a big cliff which, as I recall it, must have been two or three hundred feet high. Otter and Iron ponds were better than the others we had been seeing, but there wasn't anything very good about frogging the slash along the shores of the latter. When this ended at Lake Marian we anxiously looked for a trail, and after a little difficulty found one leading directly up the hill to the left. This brought us, after fifteen minutes, to the houses of Lake Marian Association. Evidently the members were making good use of the great weather, for we counted no less than ten boats on the lake.

At the main building we received faulty instructions in regard to the trail to Cranberry and proceeded. We soon found we were wrong, so we cut again by compass, as Bill and I had done eight weeks before. The woods did not furnish particularly delightful traveling. They had been entirely lumbered and partly burned, so that slash was bad. Old lumber roads helped us a little bit, but most of the time it was a case of bucking the brush. Finally, after an hour and a half, we reached the Sucker Brook tote road. Here, at 7:30, we hastily ate supper and then rushed over the rough way as fast as we could, coming out on the main Horseshoe-Cranberry Road at Proulx's First Camp just before dark. From here it was an easy half-hour's walk home.

NOTES

1 Pigs Ear Flow gets its name from Pigs Ear Island, named for its shape (Fowler 1959, 90).

2 This is the trail that Marshall and other students cut a few weeks earlier. See p. 115. A rollway is where logs were piled to roll into a waterway.

3 Abbot Augustus Low owned about 36,000 acres in the Bog River region. He dammed the river in 1907 to create the Bog River Flow (McMartin 2004, 100-1). See historical map on p. 105.

Five Ponds
August 12-13

The Five Ponds trip was the only one I had definitely planned before coming to camp, for along with everyone else, I had been told of the virgin timber and the white pines of that region.[1] In fact, practically everyone in the class had planned that trip, but no one except Os Brown and Hank Clark had carried their plans through. Finally, on the third-last weekend Bill Osborn and I determined to make the trip we had almost taken the third week.

It was 9:30 one bright Saturday morning when we paddled away from camp. It was very pleasant on the calm lake, so we took our time and did not reach Cat Mountain Landing until two hours later. After putting up our canoe we set out on the High Falls trail. Nothing of interest occurred on the way, except that a bag of rice at the bottom of one of the packs burst open and its contents trickled all over the landscape. The Plains[2] was a decidedly hot place at noon, and when we finally came to the Boiling Spring, which Bill rightly remarked looked like a pot of boiling wheatina, we welcomed the refreshing drink. Shortly later we came to the old railroad grade and turned to the right.[3] After following it about a mile we saw a dim trail leading off through a hollow to the left. Just beyond was a low hill. This trail soon brought us out to a ford on the Oswegatchie, which we were able to cross without getting wet above the shins.

Across the river were a few old lumber cabins by which the trail led. We followed it through the slashed land, checking upon the topographical features as we went. After twenty-five minutes we entered virgin timber and realized that we must be in Herkimer County. It is no use trying to describe the beauty of an unmarred spruce-flat forest. Suffice it

Photo by Phil Brown

Big Shallow Pond in 2005.

to say that we thoroughly enjoyed every one of the 14.7 minutes it took us to traverse this stretch of timber to Big Shallow. After depositing our packs at the campsite on the foot of this tarn, we set out to explore the Five Ponds.

Big Shallow, as its name implies, hasn't very much water. It is oval in shape and about three hundred yards along its greater axis. To the right a very steep hill rises, covered with large spruce and pine. The latter average about two feet in diameter. All along the shores of the pond is a magnificent coniferous growth.

Little Shallow lies about an eighth of a mile south of Big Shallow, just across a low ridge. It is as long as the latter but narrower. A bend makes it impossible to see the full length. Beaver are doing a great deal of damage here.

The Washbowl is the smallest pond of the five. It is almost round and is a good illustration of a pond filling in. The soil near the edge of the water is extremely toxic, and as a result the vegetation is greatly dwarfed. Gradually, as one goes back from the margin, the trees become larger, giving what is known as an amphitheatre effect. This pond is located between the two Shallows but is a trifle east of them.

A long, narrow knife-edge ridge, about 150 feet high, separates the Fives from the Shallows. It is covered with a great growth of spruce and

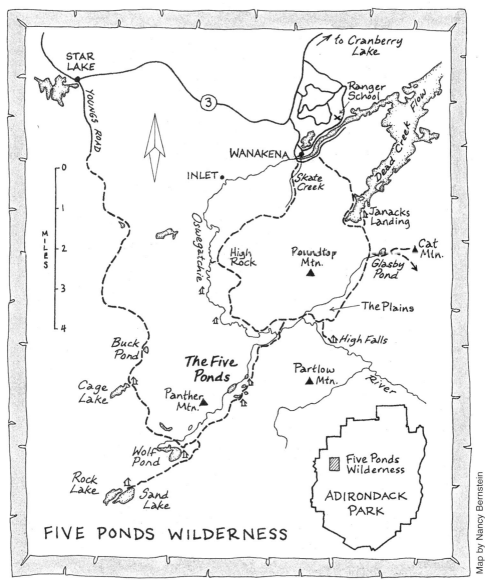

The map shows today's trail system in the vicinity of the Five Ponds.

white pine. So dense is the shade under the canopy of this forest that bushes, ground cover and even reproduction are entirely wanting. At one place, however, a windfall had cleared about a quarter of an acre, and here conditions were reversed. We crossed this ridge and descended to the lower end of Big Five.

We both agreed that Big Five was the finest pond of all. It was surrounded by virgin timber, as the others were, but in addition was tucked away in a little ravine with steep hills rising from the very shore on either side. At the far end, to complete the vista, rose Panther Mountain. The pond is narrow, but the longest of this group.

Little Five is more or less triangular. The most impressive thing about it is the white pines. They are finer around this tarn than any of the others. The hills rise steeply on all three sides. The beaver had done much damage here, and this alone prevents the pond from being perfect. There is now a fringe of dead timber all along the shoreline. These rodents had cut softwoods as well as hardwoods. They gnawed down one paper birch fourteen inches in diameter. Deer signs were also very plentiful, one of the tracks being so big we suspected it might have been made by an elk.[4]

We took our time on these explorations, and so it was 6:30 before we reached camp again. While I was cooking supper Bill pushed out in a leaky scow to try to snare some members of the order pisces. He failed, however, to take in anything but the scenery, so we had a troutless supper. But I defy anyone to beat that meal of macaroni, eggs, bread and jam.

It was so pleasant, as we lay down to reflect, that we were in the heart of a tract of virgin timber about forty miles square, absolutely unmarred by man. And yet we could not help regretting that there should be so very few of such tracts left, due to the almost criminal lack of foresight of our legislatures of the nineteenth century.

During the night we were awakened once or twice by the splashing of deer in the pond and frequent loud snorts close at hand. But these were very welcome disturbances.

Next morning we left camp at seven o'clock, heading southward, with the motto of "Wolf Pond or bust." We climbed the sharp ridge which divided the Five Ponds and followed it. Soon we came to a place where almost all the old trees were gone but where a young crop of white pine had taken their place. This we judged was the site of an old windfall. The ridge extended for about a mile beyond Big Five and then gradually flattened out. Here we crossed the stream which is the outlet of Wolf Pond, and the inlet of Big Five, and climbed the hill on the other bank. Somewhere on this hillside we knew was Lone Duck Pond, for which we were looking. So we proceeded carefully through a forest which was now of the hardwood-slope type. The yellow birches were of particularly large size, many being three feet in diameter. In one of these old fellows was a black animal which looked big enough to be a young bear. It was almost four feet long. Actually, it was by a large margin the biggest porcupine I ever saw.

Lone Duck Pond looked as if it hadn't been visited by anything since the glacier left, except the one bird after which it was named. It has a remarkable variety of trees along its small shoreline, including beech, yellow and paper birch, hard and soft maple, ash, cedar, hemlock, spruce, tamarack and white pine, not to mention many different shrubs. We soon left it with reluctance and followed the top of the hillside, keeping the main brook in sight or sound. On top of the hill the land was very flat. There was a great deal of raspberry and witch-hobble which we at first supposed was caused by lumbering but which absence of stumps indicated must have arisen from an ancient fire or windfall. We hoped to be able to see Muir Pond[5] across this flat but could not. However, we soon struck its outlet. We would have liked to have followed it to the pond but decided we would not have time. So we followed the stream down and soon reached the naturally broad swamp, made even bigger by beaver, at the foot of Wolf Pond.

If there is any wilder body of water in the Adirondacks of a size equal or greater than that of Wolf, I should like to hear about it. This pond lies in the very heart of that tract of virgin timber referred to above. No trail penetrates to it, the old one shown on the map being now almost entirely overgrown. The only sign of civilization along its two miles of shoreline is the mouldering remains of a trapper's lean-to.[6] The land all around is flat, so there is not even a prominent feature by which you can tie yourself to well-known territory. The nearest habitation is seven miles north on the air line at Inlet.[7] Nehasane and the railroad are eleven miles east as a bird would fly, while the Beaver River settlements are fifteen miles to the south. To the west is a lumbering country in which the nearest permanent dwelling is sixteen miles distant, Jerden Falls. But as one would actually have to travel, these distances would be greatly increased.

We followed along the north shore of the pond to the main inlet. The tree formation was different from any I had ever seen in the Adirondacks. Instead of the characteristic close, compact forest, the trees, entirely white pine and tamarack, grew as if in a park, standing about twenty-five or thirty feet apart, with very large crowns and relatively short boles. In the open spaces between them, on the very sandy soil, grew grasses, sedges, ferns, raspberries and heaths. A careful examination of the ground indicated an ancient fire which must have occurred before the white race ever entered the Adirondacks, for the trees were at least 150 years old.

Finally we decided we would have to return, after more than an hour spent at this remote pond. We headed for the south end of the knife ridge and stuck it just about right. As we cut across country we found the park type of forest even more accentuated than around the pond. The line of demarcation between it and the spruce-flat type was very sharp. After returning to camp I was much interested in finding the following quotation from Colvin, written forty-five years before, in regard to the same region: "The ridge was almost singular. Open and picturesque with superb white pine trees here and there upon it, with numerous deer paths deeply stamped, leading through its carpeting of moss and whortleberry bushes, the beautiful lake on the one side, and the shallow winding river on the other, made it far more entrancing than the choicest ramble of guarded park."[8]

We followed up the ridge till we saw Big Five below us. We could not resist the temptation of visiting it again, for perhaps the last time in years, or forever. Then we crossed the ridge and descended to our camp on Big Shallow, after a great morning.

After a good lunch, we set out on our return journey to camp fifteen miles away. The trip back was thoroughly enjoyable as well as thoroughly uneventful. It took us four and a half hours. Darkness was almost at hand when we landed on the beach after the best trip of the summer.

NOTES

1 The fifty thousand acres of virgin timber is the largest tract of primeval forest in the Northeast. Since Marshall's day, many of the ancient trees have been toppled in windstorms

2 In 1922 the High Falls trail cut through the Oswegatchie Plains, a largely treeless area north of High Falls. Early settlers hiked to the Plains to cut hay and graze sheep. Today's trail skirts the Plains.

3 Rich Lumber Co. built a railroad from Wanakena to High Falls in 1902 to gain access to its sixteen thousand acres of timberlands. The state bought most of the Rich land in 1919, three years before Marshall's hike, and later converted the rail bed into a truck trail. Today it is a hiking trail.

4 Elk were not native to most of the Adirondacks, but at least three hundred were released in the region between 1895 and 1916 (Kogut, 509).

5 Named for George Muir, a hunter and trapper who was still alive in Marshall's day.

6 Marshall might be disappointed to learn that two marked trails lead to Wolf Pond today and that a lean-to sits on its northern shore.

7 Located a few miles west of Wanakena, Inlet is the starting point for canoe trips up the Oswegatchie and was once the site of a hotel.

8 Verplanck Colvin, who surveyed the Adirondacks for the state, explored the region twice in the 1870s. Colvin is describing the section of the esker that divides Sand Lake and Rock Lake, a few miles south of Wolf Pond. Colvin had also visited the Five Ponds. In his *Report on the Topological Survey of the Adirondacks for the Years 1873 and 1879* he described them as "another collection of lakelets unknown to maps." They do appear on a map he created for the report. The arrangement of the ponds, however, is inaccurate: it shows three ponds on the west side of the esker instead of two. All but one of the Five Ponds are nameless. The pond that appears to be Big Shallow is called "White Pond." He gives the elevation of White Pond as 1,687 feet, which is only about 10 feet higher than the measurements of modern surveyors.

East Mountain
August 20

The track meet, circus and the late retirement consequent to the dance of the night before left me not particularly peppy this morning. But there were a couple of mountains close at hand which I had wanted to climb all summer, which could easily be made in a day. So I set out rather late on the Horseshoe trail, at a very dignified gait. At Proulx's Second Camp I turned off the main highway and followed the haul roads to Dog Pond. Then I cut by compass for Long Tom Mountain.

At first the traveling was pleasant enough, but soon I came to the old fire slash. As there was no hurry, however, I went through it at a speed that would disgust an earthworm, and so it did not seem as unpleasant as would otherwise have been the case. I crossed a low ridge and the headwaters of Sucker Brook and then commenced the real climb, which did not amount to very much. About when I began to warm up to the work I came out on bare rock and soon stood on the summit of Long Tom.

The weather was cold and the air clear, but a storm was brewing in the northeast, so I could not see the big mountains. But Tupper, part of the Bog River chain, Graves Mountain, Cranberry and the East Mountain range stood out very clearly. Directly below me lay Lake Marian, and I could distinctly see several rowboats on it. But, though much territory could be seen, there was far too much slash to permit this view to rank very high.

Quite a wind was blowing, and as it was decidedly cold, I soon left the mountain. I now headed in the direction of East Mountain, crossing the headwaters of the Grasse River. Accidently I stumbled across Little Dog Pond, an unimpressive and very small body of water. Just beyond I struck the Horseshoe trail again and soon came to the famous forks, where forty-seven young foresters had gone astray two months before.[1] I followed the same branch they took, soon leaving it to cut up the side of East Mountain. There were many large boulders encountered on the way. The woods had been lumbered for the biggest conifers a good many years before and so made pleasant walking.

East Mountain is long and flat on top. For more than a mile it varies but little in elevation. The highest peak is the one nearest Dog Pond, but there is another high point to the west, just before the ridge breaks away. From here, by much twisting of neck, you can get a view of much of Cranberry. But there is too much brush in the way. From the main summit one can see almost nothing, but by following along the ridge below the summit, I got occasional views from rocks or across openings made by the lumberman. Tupper could be seen to the northeast, and I got a fleeting glimpse of some of the High Peaks. Shurtleff's Hotel[2] was plainly visible to the north, while directly below lay the big valley connecting the headwaters of the Grasse River with East Creek. Burntbridge Pond stood out conspicuously. To the south one could look across the flat at the head of Sucker Brook toward the chain of hills and low mountains separating the Oswegatchie and Racquette watersheds. There was a great deal of slash both along the summit of this mountain and in the surrounding landscape.

As I slowly descended toward East Inlet I pondered with regret upon the fact that for the first Sunday since camp opened I would eat two regular meals in camp. But salvation was close at hand. Upon approaching the lake I heard chopping and soon found six of the fellows cutting trees for the cabin. They were practically finished with their cutting, but I stayed and helped for three hours to skid the logs down to the lake. It was almost dark when we finished, and long before we had covered the two-and-a-half miles to camp, night had blotted out the last streaks of daylight.

NOTES

1 Marshall recounts this incident in an unpublished manuscript titled "Summer Camp." His fellow students had set out to walk to Horseshoe Lake en route to the village of Tupper Lake. When they reached what they assumed was Horseshoe they learned they had circled back to Cranberry Lake (Marshall 1922, 3).

2 Shurtleff House was located in the hamlet of Conifer.

Nehasane
August 26-27

The last weekend trip of the summer was one of the first I had planned. I was going to follow the Old Military Road from High Falls to Nehasane[1] and return by train and the Horseshoe trail.

It was about nine o'clock on an autumnlike Saturday morning that I set out on the squally lake in a canoe left by the rangers.[2] No need to go into details about the seven-mile journey to Wanakena. As a paddler, I'd grade about number six common anyway, but with a hurricane from the southwest dead against me, progress, like a face in a Turkish harem, was invisible. Every stroke of the paddle seemed to put me in exactly the same spot as before, perhaps a bit behind. Yet, somehow, I finally found myself standing at the Ranger School, with the borrowed canoe safely beached.

There is a good dirt road from the Ranger School to Wanakena, beaten hard by the feet of generations of rangers seeking the delights of the city. This Paris of the Upper Oswegatchie failed to hold me for very long, and crossing the river I started out on the trail to High Falls. This first followed an old railroad grade[3] by a dreary-looking pond. Ed Hamill's wonderful array of ball-tossers were soon encountered,[4] preparing for the final battle of the season by loading bricks on a wagon for the cabin. My watch having paid the penalty of a twenty-foot drop, they gave me the

A logging train in the Oswegatchie Plains.

time, which was high noon. The grade led up the valley of Skate Creek through as ugly country as can be imagined. After a mile, the direct trail to the falls branched off to the left.[5] In three miles it crossed two young mountains, heavily lumbered, and joined the trail across the Plains near the Boiling Spring. And gosh, didn't that water taste great! A pack, a hot day, a steep slope and a lumbered country form a great combination to promote thirst. Not long after the spring the trail ran into the grade again, having cut off about eight or ten miles.[6]

Turning to the left, I soon reached the falls. Here was a sight to soothe sore eyes, but mine weren't sore. However, I was sorry that the I.M.C. and Sunset Inn[7] fiends were not here, for a dozen maidens were sporting on the rocks. I made my way straight to the one man there, who was of a safe age. We had a very interesting conversation in regard to the ecology of the Plains, and he described the Moose River Plains, the only other similar formation in the Adirondacks.[8]

After this pleasant conversation I crossed the Oswegatchie on a newly constructed bridge. I found a little difficulty at first picking up the trail shown plainly enough on the map. It was not until reaching the virgin timber of Herkimer [County] that I was sure of being right. Here the trail forked. The most plain branch to the right said: "Beaver River 18 miles." The one to the left seemed to have no designation, but finally I made out dimly on a young spruce, "Old Albany Trail."[9]

Courtesy of Susan Smeby

An old postcard of High Falls on the Oswegatchie.

There now ensued a delightful walk through the virgin forest. Only a subdued light filtered through the dense crowns of the dark spruce and hemlock. There was little undergrowth. The old trail underfoot was the last connecting link with the pioneers of a century ago. Its ancient moss-covered logs had borne the hunters and trappers of that distant day when the North Woods were one unbroken stretch of luxuriant forest, where the wolf, the panther, the moose and the deer lived and died without once being frightened by that most bloodthirsty of all creatures, termed man.

The trail had been roughly blazed and had been cut out here and there. Sometimes both blazes and trail were plain. At other places either one or the other distinctly showed the way. But there were many spots where it appeared as if the right of way had not been brushed out since the original constructors had come through in 1815. I was glad at such places that I had my map, for I could travel as indicated by it, feeling confident of picking up the trail in a short time. Soon the Robinson River, a wild, tumbling stream, seeming to come from an unknown region, was crossed. It was certainly a temptation to follow it up and let Stem Analysis[10] and camp and civilization take their course without my presence.

Just beyond the river the trail seemed to end, and upon confidently reaching for my map, I discovered that it was gone. This was a rather

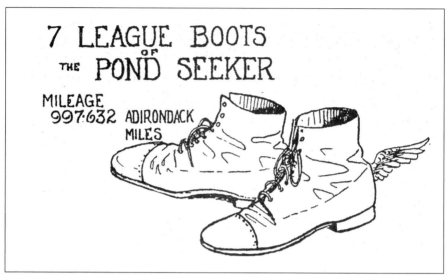

Drawing of Marshall's boots in the Forestry College Summer Camp's yearbook.

disappointing discovery, for I knew that with the limited time and the dim trail the chances of ever reaching Gull Lake were poor. Then a vision flashed in my mind of a hunter of the century before, who had lost the trail, groping aimlessly through the unknown forest fifty miles from the edge of civilization through a dismal, impenetrable wilderness. What a change a hundred years made even in this unmarred forest, for all I had to do anytime I wanted to get out of the woods was to cut due east by compass to the railroad but ten miles away.

After much difficulty I picked up the trail again at the top of the hill above the river. Soon I saw Gull Pond[11] through the trees, an almost perfect little pond. I followed along its shore to the southwest end, and then cut through the woods for about three hundred yards to the West Pond, which was almost as fine as its neighbor. There was a campsite along the trail right next to Gull Pond, which would have made a wonderful place to stop for the night, but I wanted to make Gull Lake so that I might spend the evening chatting with George Muir, the last of the great hunters—George Muir, who had killed 67 of the 108 panthers and 39 of the 98 wolves slain since 1870.[12]

After one or two more difficult places, I again caught the gleam of water through the trees, and knew I must be seeing Crocker Pond.[13] It was some distance from the trail, but I cut over to it. While also surrounded by fine timber, the pond itself was not as fine as the other two.

It seemed to have little water and much mud.

Just across the brow of the hill half a mile beyond I met my Appomatox. Here the trail ran into the cut-over land of the Webb preserve and effectually lost itself. Try though I did for half an hour, I could not pick it out from among the old logging roads. But there was a big valley below where I figured Gull Lake must lie. I descended to it and found only a shallow brook. "This is too small for the outlet of so big a lake," I reasoned, "so I will follow it down." This was beautiful theory, and I expected momentarily to come out on the shore of my dreams. The only trouble was that I missed my guess. Gull Lake and the old hunter were across the next broad bridge. I realized this after half an hour. But by this time the sun had long set behind the rugged hill to the west, and it was too dark to travel further.

As my stomach was out of order, as a result of the strain placed on it by some of the concoctions of my fellow timber cruisers, I did not bother about cooking supper but just ate a few pieces of bread and butter. When the short meal was over twilight was also gone.

I spread my blankets on the wood-sorrel leaves, which had never before been disturbed by man. As I dropped off to sleep it was a sad sound that came to my ears from the treetops above and the brook below, and the wind and the water seemed to unite to blow taps for the millions of acres of primeval forest that had gone, while about at attention stood some of the few surviving veteran acres of the Grand Forest of the Adirondacks.

I awakened next morning before sunrise. While leisurely eating a light breakfast I decided on my plans for the day. If Gull Lake was really in the next valley, as I now supposed, it was out of the question to visit it and return that day. There was just a possibility it might still be below me. So I determined to follow down the brook another mile and if nothing showed up then to cut for the railroad, which I knew I was sure to reach eventually by traveling east.

Gull Lake did not show up, so I left the brook and headed a little south of east. Suddenly I was startled by the whistle of a locomotive ahead. It didn't sound to be more than a mile away, though I knew it must be six or seven by air line. Three more times during that long morning as I approached the tracks I heard that whistle, and each time it sounded further away.

For quite a while my trailless course led through pleasant virgin timber. I crossed several brooks, flowing in a northerly direction to the

Oswegatchie. Then I suddenly came across some white signs telling the world that the private property of W. Seward Webb and the Ne-ha-sa-ne Park Association lay just beyond and that trespassing was forbidden. These signs continued for miles in an east and west line. I followed them over several rolling hills, soon entering a section which had been logged for softwood. Then, upon crossing a hill, I found myself out of the forest looking over a great, open waste area of ferns, grass, blackberries, raspberries, fallen trees and here and there dense thickets of fire cherry, aspen and birch. This was all the result of some little spark escaping from a locomotive on the tracks several miles away.[14]

The open character of the land gave me a fine opportunity to take in the topography. I could pick out the valley where I figured the railroad must lie. When I reached it after a long time, there was no sign of tracks. So I figured it must be beyond the next hill, but it wasn't, nor behind the next, or the next, or the next. While the traveling wasn't bad, it was tantalizing to have the objective keep continually moving further away. It was not as easy walking as it would have been without a pack, either. The streams were all dried up, so a drink was out of the question, and the sun was very hot in the open. What an awfully monotonous country it was! Every hill just like the last one. The only relief was in the occasional sight of Grass Pond Mountain to the north and some distant mountains toward Long Lake ahead. But there's no use to go into details about this endless journey. I had long ago made up my mind that I would never reach anywhere when I came to signs of fairly recent lumbering in a marsh which the fire had not reached. This was encouraging, but the sluggish stream in the center was not. It was too wide to jump, especially with a pack, and too muddy to ford. Tested with a four-foot stick, the mud was bottomless. I didn't care to chance slipping up to my neck in the slime, with no one apt to come that way till doomsday, so I trudged upstream for some distance and finally crossed on a beaver dam. Just beyond, to my great joy, was a good tote road. It led in a direction which was parallel to the tracks, but I knew it must lead somewhere, so I followed it north. Twice it seemed destined to go right back to the slash from whence I came, but it changed its mind. I shall never forget the pleasure I felt when, after hours of seemingly aimless travel, I at last saw the gleam of steel through the trees which told me that somewhere had been reached.

I knew I was a short distance north of Nehasane and Lake Lila, so

Burned landscape near Long Lake West after the 1908 fire.

leaving my pack, I walked down the tracks a mile, almost to the station, and then descended to the shore. Lila is the sixteenth-largest lake in the Adirondacks[15] and quite nice looking. It was distinctly worth seeing. However, perhaps the most interesting part about it is that the four topographical sheets join right in its center. A railroad is not an ideal pathway for a pedestrian, but it seemed like the finest boulevard compared with the scene of my morning's travels. My first stop was Robinwood, three miles from Nehasane. Here I met one of the employees of the Robinwood estate, who invited me to visit the two lakes on the property, Bog and Anne.[16] They were certainly nothing to rave about. I liked Bog the better of the two. I left him at 2:30 and was soon pounding the ties again, pack on back. I stopped once on the four miles to Long Lake West to eat a lunch of bread, butter and cheese.

The country around Long Lake West was certainly barren. The fire of 1908 had burned over acres right down to bedrock. There didn't seem to be many people in town, and all those I did see were sleeping. However, I managed to get a mighty welcome drink of water. The five miles in Horseshoe were dull, without mistake. After six miles of tie walking, I began to tire of the highway for which I had so yearned a few hours before. Seventeen miles of packbasket travel was also beginning to scratch my back. About the only joys on these five miles were five mileposts. Even a side trip through the swamp to Hitchings Pond did not bring much pleasure, for the pond was so terribly ugly. There was so much bare rock it looked like a good place for a penitentiary.

It was 5:15 as I walked by Horseshoe Station and left the tracks at last. As the sky was now overcast, I figured that it would be dark in two hours, so I knew I would have to do some real hustling if I wanted to make camp. I hit upon a pace of almost five miles an hour and maintained it. If I could reach Curtis Pond by dark I knew there would be little trouble getting out. But I didn't relish the idea of traveling the treacherous road east of that point at night. I checked in at Pine Pond, High Grass Meadow and Center Pond with plenty of light, ahead of schedule. But at the Second Camp[17] it was growing dusky, while at Irish Pond there was just a streak of scarlet on the western clouds and the daylight was almost gone. Night had completely settled in shortly after passing Curtis, but I didn't care. The remaining two-and-a-half miles were easy, though I made them at a slower pace. It was 7:51 when I pulled up at Tent 10 after a thirty-nine-mile day, thirty-four of which had been made with a pack.

I saw a lot of beautiful scenery, but there wasn't a better part of the trip than the great macaroni supper I cooked myself to break my diet of fifty hours. It was a fitting climax to the last trip of the summer.

NOTES

1   Nehasane was the name William Seward Webb gave his preserve near Lake Lila. Its meaning is uncertain, but one proposed translation is "crossing on a stick of timber" (Donaldson 1921, vol. I, 41). Throughout, I have corrected Marshall's spelling, "Nehasne."

2   That is, students at the New York State Ranger School in Wanakena.

3   The railroad was built by the Rich Lumber Co. in 1902. It is now a hiking trail.

4   Ed Hamill, a forestry student from Massachusetts, was captain of the Summer Camp's baseball team.

5   Now closed, this trail was created by guide Bert Dobson, who ran a rustic resort at High Falls in the early 1900s.

6   Actually, the Dobson trail saved the hiker about four miles.

7   The Sunset Inn was a small hotel near Bear Mountain on Cranberry Lake (Tupper Lake Historian William Frenette, personal communication, November 2004).

8   The Moose River Plains are located several miles east of Old Forge in the western Adirondacks.

9   This is the Old Military Road referred to earlier. The rough road ran from the Sacandaga River in the southern Adirondacks to Russell in St. Lawrence County. The state legislature authorized its construction in 1812 (Donaldson 1921, vol. II, 129).

10 A course in which students learned to analyze tree rings to reconstruct a tree's growth.

11 Apparent reference to Gal Pond.

12 Over twenty-one years, Muir made $705 in state bounties for killing wolves and mountain lions—more than any other Adirondack hunter (Terrie 1993, 93). He died one spring while hiking twelve miles through snow from Wanakena to his cabin on Gull Lake. He was eighty years old. (Keith 1976, 118-121.)

13 Cracker Pond. See Marshall's own etymology, p. 152.

14 A fire that destroyed much of the forest in the Bog River and Cranberry Lake region in 1908 was blamed on a spark from a train near Long Lake West (Fowler 1959, 58-62).

15 Marshall had made a list of the Adirondacks' hundred largest lakes in 1922. The Adirondack Park has been expanded since then. Lake Lila is now the twenty-third-largest lake.

16 Anne Pond is called Clear Pond on the maps.

17 A reference to one of Oliva Proulx's lumber camps.

Ratings

At the end of the summer I made a rating of the beauty of all the lakes and ponds I visited. Of course, any such rating is very uncertain and subject to much criticism. No two people would regard any one pond alike. Even the same person seeing a pond under varying weather conditions or from different angles might rank it quite differently. But on the whole, a fairly good idea may be gotten of the desirability of visiting the various ponds by this rating.

As certain names are very common appellations for ponds, I have indicated in each case by letter the region in which the body of water lies. The key to the meaning of these letters follows:

A—Bog River drainage (Cranberry quadrangle)
B—Bog River drainage (Tupper Lake quadrangle)
C—Chair Rock Creek drainage
D—Along New York Central Railroad
E—Between Cranberry and New York Central Railroad
H—Herkimer County
M—Massawepie section
S—South of Cranberry (unless otherwise included)
T—Tupper Lake section
W—West of Cranberry

1. Nicks	H	19. Fishpole	C	37. Marian	B
2. Big Five	H	20. Town Line	M	38. Graves	A
3. Wolf	H	21. Cranberry		39. Horseshoe	D
4. Moosehead	W	22. Nehasane	D	40. Olmstead	S
5. Gull Pond[1]	H	23. Little Shallow	H	41. Dillon	W
6. Big Tupper	T	24. Big Simons	T	42. Darning Needle	C
7. Big Shallow	H	25. Little Moosehead	W	43. Indian Mountain	S
8. Massawepie	M	26. Curtis	E	44. Third Pond	A
9. West	H	27. Dog	E	45. Otter	B
10. Big Deer	S	28. Washbowl	H	46. Clear (Anne)	A
11. Grass	A	29. Horseshoe	M	47. Little Center	E
12. Center	E	30. Cowhorn	S	48. Crane	W
13. Little Five	H	31. Mud	A	49. Toad	S
14. Hedgehog	E	32. Boot Tree	M	50. Upper Twin	W
15. Long	M	33. Bog	A	51. Silver	E
16. Crocker[2]	H	34. Irish	E	52. Slender	S
17. Lone Duck	H	35. Tooley	W	53. Catamount	M
18. Deer	M	36. Star	W	54. Lower Twin	W

55. Scott	C	69. Spring		83. Cook	
56. Second Pond	B	70. Upper Spectacle		84. Heath	
57. Iron	B	71. Lower Spectacle		85. Three Pound	
58. Spruce Grouse	A	72. Chaumont		86. Piercefield Flow	
59. Little Dog	E	73. Muskrat		87. Pine	
60. First Pond	B	74. Silver Leaf		88. Big Hornet	
61. Little Wolf	T	75. John		89. Harrington	
62. Glasby	S	76. Panther		90. Newton Falls	
63. Simmons	S	77. Esker		91. Robinwood	
64. Raquette	T	78. Tamarack		92. Little Hornet	
65. Clear (Crystal)		79. Hitchings[3]		93. Wanakena	
66. Cat Mountain		80. Nicks		94. Little Fish Pond	
67. Bassout		81. Sunny			
68. Triangle		82. Grassy			

There are really no eminences in this region worthy of being designated as mountains. The maximum elevation is found on what is called Long Tom Mountain, and this is only 2,620 feet above sea, or less than 1,200 feet higher than Cranberry. I managed to climb every prominent hill visible from Cranberry, and my rating of the beauty of their views follows:

NAME	HEIGHT	NAME	HEIGHT
1. Grass Pond	2,400	6. Indian	2,260
2. Graves	2,300	7. East	2,460
3. Cat	2,261	8. Wolf	2,420
4. Bear	2,240	9. State Ridge	1,940
5. Long Tom	2,620	10. Hedgehog	2,060

The rating of my ten trips in the region, as far as enjoyment was concerned, follows:

1. Five Ponds	6. Star Lake
2. Bog River	7. Horseshoe Circle
3. Nehasane	8. Hornet Pond
4. Massawepie	9. Heath Pond
5. Nicks Pond	10. East Mountain

NOTES

1 Now known as Gal Pond.

2 Cracker Pond.

3 Spelled "Hitchins" on modern maps.

The Oswegatchie from High Rock.

Origin of Names
in the Region

Marshall appended this historical account of toponyms to the end of "Week-End Hikes in the Cranberry Lake Region."

Adirondacks. "The mountainous district known as the Adirondacks takes its name from a well-known Mohawk word, ratirontaks, 'they eat trees.' This term is in regular use at the present day among the Mohawks to denote the so-called Algonquin tribe who formerly had their head-quarters not far from Montreal. … These Algonquins … were wont in former days to hunt extensively in the Adirondack region." Professor J. Dyneley Prince.

These Indians were called "Ratirontaks" or "Tree-eaters" because in winter when game grew scarce in their inhospitable climate, they were often driven by hunger to live for weeks upon the buds, roots, bark and even the wood of the forest trees. The name Adirondacks was first applied to the group of highest mountains in 1838 by Ebenezer Emmons, the first scientific explorer of the region.[1] From this local application it spread to the whole wilderness of northern New York.

Bassout Pond. John Bassout was a well-known hunter and trapper of the mid-nineteenth century. He had a camp on the trail from Cat Mountain to Cowhorn Pond.

Benson Mines. Founded by the Magnetic Iron Ore Company, of which Benson was a director, 1887. This concern had about ten mines in New York and Pennsylvania.

Bog River and Lake. Named from the low, boggy character of the surrounding country.

Brandy Brook. The water after rains is a brandy color.

Burnt Bridge Pond. The old Lake George road crossed the outlet of this pond on a high bridge, which was burnt, supposedly by some Indians, early in the last century.

Cat Mountain. The father of George and John Muir, while following a trap line around the mountain, saw a wildcat standing on a ledge just above him.

Chair Rock Creek. Named from a peculiarly formed rock on an island near the mouth of the creek.

Chaumont Swamp and Pond. In the early part of the nineteenth century James Donatianus Le Ray de Chaumont, a distinguished French courtier, acquired several hundred thousand acres of land in the northern and western part of the Adirondacks. He later sold 100,000 acres to Joseph Bonaparte, brother of the great Napolean, who built a hunting lodge on Lake Bonaparte.

Colvin Pond. Named after Verplanck Colvin by some of his guides in 1873. It was at this time that Colvin discovered and mapped more than half the ponds in the region. Colvin, in my opinion, did more for the Adirondacks than any man who ever lived.

Conifer. Named after the type of lumber manufactured at the mill.

Cook Pond and Cook's Corners. Named after an early settler at the Windfall. The place now termed Cook's Corners on the map was formerly called the Windfall, as it was located in the clearing made by the worst cyclone New York ever experienced. For an interesting description see 112 in *The Forest Arcadia*.[2]

Cowhorn Pond. The shape of the pond is supposed to resemble a cow's horn.

Cracker Pond. Called on the topographic map Crocker Pond. Some early traveler left some crumbs from his lunch here just before Colvin passed it, so he named it.[3]

Cranberry Lake. Before the dam was built there was a great cranberry marsh where Dead Creek Flow now is.

Cranberry Lake in the 1920s.

Curtis Pond. Lanson (Lant) Curtis was a trapper who had a camp on East Inlet, less than a mile from Summer Camp.

Dillon Pond. George Dillon was another hunter and trapper of the latter part of last century.

Dog Pond. Jesse Irish killed an animal here which seemed to be a cross between dog and wolf. This pond was formerly called Ami Pond after Ami Brumley, a noted wolf hunter and a noted wit.

Dunning Pond. Alvah Dunning was one of the very greatest of the Adirondack hunters and guides.

Esker Pond. Named from the glacial formation which caused it.[4] Formerly Bean Pond, so called from its shape.

Gale. Emery Gale was the first settler in this little community. He came there in 1864 and founded a home among the unbroken wilderness. His son, who came with him, still lives there, being postmaster and running the only store.

Glasby Pond. Nick Glasby was one of the greatest of the early hunters and trappers.

Grass Pond. The Indian name for this body of water was O-sa-ken-ta-ke, meaning "Grass Lake." "Kentucky" is derived from a similar word.[5]

Grasse River. Named after Admiral de Grasse, a noted French naval officer.[6] The Indian name was Ni-kent-si-a-ke, meaning "full of large fish."

Graves Pond and Mountain. Bill Graves was a Tupper Lake hotel-keeper who used to come into this region every fall to hunt. He was accidentally shot and killed by his son near Horseshoe.

Hitchings Pond. Named after an old guide.[7]

Horseshoe Lake. Named from its shape.

Irish Pond. Jesse Irish was the first permanent settler in the Cranberry Lake region.

Iron Mountain and Pond. The early visitors to the Adirondacks were particularly interested in the possibilities of exploiting the iron known to occur in the region. Many of the early maps indicated the location of supposedly rich deposits and so-called Iron Mountains were not infrequent. One of the most famous of these was in Township 2, Great Tract 2 of Macombs Purchase. This township lies east of Cranberry and was called Oakham. Iron Mountain included what are today known as Long Tom, Rampart, Silver Lake and Iron mountains.

I quote a sentence from *The Forest Arcadia*, published in 1864: "Standing upon the shore of the lake (Cranberry) where the river commences its descent, and looking east, we have the iron mountain in Oakham, four miles distant, looming up over the surrounding hills." Note here the typical Adirondack mile, for Iron Mountain is really nine miles distant by air line.[8]

Joe Indian Island. Before the dam was constructed in 1865 this was a point. Here Joe Naughton, a prominent Ogdensburg barrister, frequently camped and left his name.

Lake Lila. Named after the wife of W. Seward Webb, in whose property it is included. It was formerly known as Smith's Lake, after David Smith, a hermit who lived on its shores for fifteen years prior to 1845. See Donaldson, Volume I, Page 135.

Long Lake West. The railroad station of Long Lake, about twenty miles west of that place. Also called Sabattis Post Office, after the greatest guide of the lake region of the Adirondacks.[9]

Lake Marian. Named after the wife of A.A. Low, the owner of the lake. Formerly called Silver Lake, from which the nearby mountain derived its name.

Massawepie Lake. So called by the Indians, from "massa," meaning large, and "sepia," water.

Moody. "Uncle Mart" Moody, who was perhaps the greatest of the Saranac guides, built the Mount Morris House here in 1879. The place, however, was always called Moody's, and this became the official designation of the settlement, which forms one of the three parts of Tupper Lake.

Moosehead Pond. When Jesse Irish first discovered this pond he found the decaying remains of a moose skull on the shore.

Mud Lake. This was mentioned by all the early writers as the wildest spot in the east, and each had to take a trip there to see the lake and kill a moose. They were all impressed upon the appropriateness of the name, which well described its low shoreline.

In 1858 Headley wrote: "But alas! when our boats a length floated on its dead, stirless bosom, they sank lower than before, and we looked at each other in mute inquiry or blank astonishment. … 'So this is Mud Lake,' I said, with a tone that was meant to be cheerful. There was no response except from John who, with an expression of intense disgust on his face, slowly muttered, 'Mud Hole.'"

"… Round the whole circle of the marshy lake there seemed not a dry spot big enough to pitch our tent upon."

Muir Pond. George Muir killed 67 of the 108 panthers slain in New York since 1871 and 39 of the 98 wolves. His brother, John Muir, and his father were also famous hunters.

Ne-ha-sa-ne Lake and Park. An Indian word meaning "crossing on a stick of timber," applied by Webb to his estate and a lake on it. It was formerly called Albany Lake because the old Albany Road crossed over the foot of it.

Newton Falls. James Newton of Watertown was one of the owners of the paper mill started here in 1890. He was made general manager of the mill but was not successful, losing his company's money and his own mind.

Nicks Pond. "The second little lake was called Nick's Lake after one who had trapped there."–Colvin.[10] The one was Nick Glasby, after whom three ponds in the region were named.

Olmstead Pond, Mountain and Landing. Olmstead was one of the post-Civil War hunters and trappers. He had a camp at Olmstead Pond, which he reached by trail from Olmstead Landing on Dead Creek Flow. Roundtop Mountain was formerly called Olmstead.

Oswegatchie River. Oswegatchie was the Indian for "black water" and was applied by them to the river.[11] Francis Piquet, a French missionary, called it River la Presentation, when he founded a mission for the Indians at its mouth in 1749. The savages who came to live there were called Oswegatchie.

Oven Lake. Some very early visitors to the region built a large Italian sod oven on the shores of this lake.

Partlow Pond and Mountain. Webster Partlow was a great hunter and trapper. Several of his relatives were also famous hunters. Webster is still living at Wanakena.

Piercefield. Township 6 in Macombs Great Tract No. 2 was called Piercefield after the first settler. The falls were a famous scenic spot until the construction of the mill and the founding of the town about 1890.

Raquette River, Pond and Lake.[12] Donaldson mentions two plausible reasons for this name. When Sir John Johnson fled across the wilderness from Johnstown to Canada early in 1776, he and his party took the old Indian trail from Fish House to Raquette Lake. There was snow in the woods when the party started, so they used snowshoes. But on reaching the lake they were overtaken by the spring thaw and had to abandon their raquettes. They piled them together near South Inlet, where traces of them could be seen for years.

The theory which Donaldson favors is the one brought forward by Hough in his *History of St. Lawrence and Franklin Counties*. He says that the name was applied by a Frenchman because of the shape of a morass at the mouth of the river.[13]

Scott Pond. Fide Scott was one of the best woodsmen and one of the most eccentric characters the region ever produced. He worked for Colvin when the section was first explored. For years he had a cabin near Big Deer Pond.

Simmons Pond. Simmons was another of the early hunters.

Tupper Lake. Tupper was a surveyor who worked around the lake which bears his name, at the end of the eighteenth century. He was probably the first white man to penetrate that region.

Union Point. Early in the summer of 1862 a number of young fellows camped on this point. Here they made up their minds to enlist in the army and joined the Union forces in time to get into the bloodiest single day's battle of the war at Antietam.

Usher Farm. Luke Usher was a prominent citizen of Potsdam, born in 1830. He was a civil engineer and a bank president. About 1890 he became interested in the lumber game and was the head of the Potsdam Lumber Company. This concern maintained a farm for the benefit of its woods workers, which bore the name of the president of the company.

Wanakena. This is a recently applied name. It means good or pleasant place. The Indians never were sarcastic enough to give it to the town which now bears that title.

Wolf Mountain. Some of the early visitors to the region fancied a resemblance in the shape of this mountain to a wolf. Wolf Mountain was called the Old She-Wolf, while Grass Pond Mountain was known as the Little Wolf.

NOTES

1 A New York state geologist, Ebenezer Emmons led an expedition to the summit of Mount Marcy in 1837. It was the first ascent of the state's highest mountain (Carson 1927, 53).

2 *The Forest Arcadia of Northern New York*, published in 1864, described the wilderness of the northwestern Adirondacks.

3 Today's topographical maps call it "Cracker."

4 An esker is a narrow ridge formed by the deposits of a glacial river when the ice melts.

5 One dictionary says "Kentucky" is likely related to "kenta," the Iroquois word for prairie.

6 Others argue that the correct spelling is "Grass" and that the name was inspired by the meadows along the river (Jamieson 1994, 44-5). In any case, "Grass" is the spelling on modern maps.

7 The accepted spelling today is "Hitchins."

8 Marshall thought Adirondackers typically underestimated distances.

9 Mitchell Sabattis was an Abenaki Indian who lived in Long Lake (Donaldson 1921, vol. 2, 81-87).

10 Colvin 1874, 55.

11 Several other etymologies of "Oswegatchie" have been proposed, none of them definitive (Jamieson 1994, 4).

12 Elsewhere, Marshall uses the older spelling "Racquette."

13 See Donaldson, vol. 1, 43.

Dawn in the Woods

Marshall wrote this poem for the 1923 issue of Empire Forester, *the yearbook of the New York State College of Forestry. He was then a junior. It may have been inspired by his backpacking trips in the Cranberry Lake region the previous summer.*

In the early morning when the first faint light
Cuts the murky blackness of the cool calm night,
While the gloomy forest, dismal, dark, and wild,
Seems to slowly soften and become more mild,

When the mists hang heavy, where the streams flow by
And reflects the rose-tints in the eastern sky,
When the brook trout leaps and the deer drinks slow,
While the distant mountains blend in one soft glow,

'Tis the precious moment, given once a day,
When the present fades to the far-away,
When the busy this-time for a moment's gone,
And the Earth turns backward into Nature's dawn.

Hauling white-pine logs in the early 1900s.

History of Cranberry Lake

Marshall wrote this historical sketch for the 1922 Camp Log, *an annual publication produced by students to record their experiences at the Forestry College Summer Camp.*

The history of the Cranberry Lake region does not date back very far. The region was never much inhabited by the Indians, although at times they entered it to hunt. There was one important Indian trail which traversed it, running from Albany to the St. Lawrence. Over this in 1776, Sir John Johnson and some of his Tory followers fled from the Mohawk Valley to Canada. This is the first definite knowledge we have of any white men entering the region, although it seems probable that a few old hunters or trappers may have been there previously.[1]

During the next three-quarters of a century the region was almost unvisited. The few who came there might almost be enumerated. Some unknown surveyor ran the boundary line between the Macomb and the Totten and Crossfield purchases[2] at the very end of the eighteenth century. Early in the next century the old Albany Road and the Chester and Canton Road were put through this region. The former ran west and south of Cranberry, the latter north and east. For years they were the main entrances to this section of the woods. Hunters and trappers from the settlements to the north and west would come into the region in the summer along these rude highways. Among the earliest to come in this way were Nat Foster and Nick Stoner, famous in pioneer history and fiction of the state.[3] Old Bill Ward, whose son still lives, was known to have seen the lake around 1820.

The number of visitors increased slowly but surely. Soon occasional people from the city appeared, the forerunners of the present great army

Fide Scott's camp on Big Deer Pond.

of vacationists. It is from the latter class that we get our earliest descriptions of the region in books of travel. These writings created great interest and brought to the wilderness hundreds who would not otherwise have come. Headley's *Adirondack* (1853), Street's *Woods and Waters* (1860) and Northrup's *Camps and Tramps in the Adirondacks* (1880) contain the earliest published accounts of the region. One quotation from Headley's book well describes the wildness of the country in those days. Talking of the view from Mud Lake he said:

"To the left far inland rises a lofty, stern-looking mountain.[4] Standing way back in the solitude by itself, nameless, it awakens strange feelings. A wilderness probably never trodden by human foot stretches away from its base, while from its lonely summit spreads a view never seen by the eye of man. To the right frowns a savage precipice[5] scowling across at its solitary neighbor. Between these two silent monuments stretches a vast extent of natural meadows, interspersed with fir trees, standing sometimes singly and sometimes in groups. But no details can give you any conception of the undescribable loneliness of the scene."[6]

A new era for the region started in 1865, with the building of a dam at the foot of Cranberry, which raised the height of the lake fifteen feet, and doubled its area.[7] Not only did this bring the works of man into the heart of the wilderness, but it also brought the beginning of the first permanent settlement, as Hugh McConnell, the dam tender, became the first resident of Cranberry Lake. It is true that an old mine had been opened just below the dam a few years before, but it was soon deserted. About the same time Jesse Irish settled on the windfall three miles northwest of the lake.

The windfall mentioned above was the result of the most terrific cyclone New York has ever known. It occurred in 1845 and cut a path about half a mile wide from west of Cranberry to Lake Champlain. As far as Upper Saranac there was one continuous lane in which not a tree was left standing. From there to Champlain there were some breaks. Until it rotted down, the windfall was passable only on the occasional trail the woodsman cut through it.

During the rest of the century the hamlet of Cranberry Lake grew very slowly. Twelve years later, in 1877, it contained only three houses. Gilbert Dodds, who succeeded McConnell, had a dwelling and barn near the dam.[8] A short distance east was a school, while near where the Birches now stands was a boarding house kept by Dick Thomas. The fourth house was built by Chancy Westcott on the west side of the lake, and the fifth by Bill Rossbach near the present church. The first store was opened in 1895, by Bishop. As late as 1900, there were only eight or nine buildings.

During these thirty-five years the surrounding wilderness was penetrated by an ever-increasing number of hunters, trappers, guides and tourists. As the works of these pioneers has left a profound effect on the region, and their names in many cases have been given to geographical features, it might be well to briefly mention some of the more prominent men.

Nick Glasby, John Bassutte,[9] Lant Curtis, Webb Partlow, Olmstead and Dillon were well-known hunters and trappers in their day. Glasby was probably the best known of this group, for not only is his last name given to a pond, like the others, but his first has been conferred on two. Smith Bruner, Ami Brumley, John and George Muir were particularly famous wolf hunters. Muir is still living at Gull Lake.[10] Bruner was a half-breed. Brumley was a well-known wit. He used to get drunk quite often and say, "Am I Ami or am I not Ami. If am not Ami, who am I?" Dog Pond was called Ami Pond for years.

Seth Howland, father of the present well-known Cranberry guides, killed the last panther near Tooley Pond in 1864.[11]

Steve Ward was one of the earliest to visit this region, coming with his father in 1846, as a boy of nine. Since that time he has come every year except 1864, when he was fighting with the old Fifth Corps in Virginia. During the seventy-six years he has been coming to Cranberry he has seen it change from a wilderness as dark and unknown as any in Africa to a highly civilized recreational rendezvous. Today he is a hale and hearty veteran of eighty-five.

The region also had its eccentric hermit in old Ezra Wheeler, who cultivated a few acres near Pleasant Lake. He was considered crazy but pleasant.

Jack Ormston, or "Adirondack Jack" as some called him, was famous alike for his strength and his misfortunes. He was continually having some accident or other.

Fide Scott, John Sullivan and Albert Mackenzie guided for Verplanck Colvin. Scott had for years a log cabin in the clearing above Big Deer Pond. He was among the most daring of the stalwart hunters and trappers and one of the most eccentric characters the Adirondacks has ever produced.[12]

Other famous guides of the early days were Ed Young, George Sawyer, Jack and Charlie Thomas, the Howland brothers, Chancy Westcott, and Sam and George Bancroft.

Only a few of the prominent visitors from the city can be mentioned. Perhaps the best liked of all was Reuben Wood of Syracuse, famous angler and sportsman.[13] Judge Vann of Syracuse was another well-known figure around the lake. He first came up in 1878 and revisited the region for forty-two consecutive years, until his death. Judge Kennedy and A. Judd Northrup were also well-known visitors from central New York.

Joe Naughton of Ogdensburg, a prominent barrister, used to be a regular visitor even before the Civil War. Joe Indian Island, then a point, was named after him.

Bill Graves was a hotel keeper from Tupper Lake who used to come to hunt every fall. He was accidentally shot and killed by his son near Horseshoe.

But most important of all the visitors was Verplanck Colvin. When he entered the region in the autumn of 1873 as chief of the state survey not half the ponds were known. Those that were on the maps were gen-

Emporium Forestry Company's mill at Cranberry Lake.

erally miles out of position. Rivers and mountains were placed on the maps by mere guess. Due to lack of funds with which to carry on the work Colvin was forced to face all sorts of perils, including starvation and freezing, but he persevered, and it is to him that we are principally indebted for our present knowledge of the region.

The development around the lake has mostly occurred since 1900. The first summer cottage was built by Albert Ames Howlett on Dead Creek Flow in 1885.[14] He called it Tramps Retreat. It was full of curiosities, including the skin of a snake forty-two feet long.

Indian Mountain Club started in 1898 and acquired quite extensive holdings of land. It broke up in 1908, but in 1911, it reopened as a hotel and has thus prospered. Bear Mountain House, Sunset Inn and Lone Pine Camp are recent developments. Numerous cottages, both summer and permanent, have sprung up around the lake, taking away much of its former wildness.

In 1919, the Emporium Forestry Company opened a mill at Cranberry, which resulted in a very rapid growth in the town, so that today it has more than three hundred people. Other towns have also sprung up in the vicinity of Cranberry Lake. Benson Mines started in 1887 and has experienced the regular ups and downs of a mining town.

Today it is down. Newton Falls started in 1890, with the opening of a pulp mill. It has experienced the regular ups and towns of a lumbering town. Today it is up. Conifer is another lumbering town where the Emporium Forestry Company has one of its mills. Wanakena commenced with the Rich Lumber Company's mill in 1900. Massawepie was the summer home of a number of very wealthy people. Though located in the woods, no expense was spared to make the interior like the most costly city houses, but despite the vast amount of money sunk in the project, the owners of the place soon tired of it, and it has been deserted since 1908.

As late as 1880, the whole northwestern Adirondacks was a continuous stretch of virgin timber except for the occasional clearing of a settler. But soon the lumbermen came in, including Abbott, Barber, Webb, Low, Usher, Rice, the Canton Lumber Company, the Rich Lumber Company, the Emporium Forestry Company and the International Paper Company. Following the lumbermen came fires, of which the most disastrous was the one of 1908, which burned over tens of thousands of acres, particularly east of Cranberry. As a result there is very little virgin timber left in what was comparatively recently the wildest part of this state.

Frequent houses now dot the formerly unbroken shoreline of Cranberry. The shouts of people and the noise of motorboats now resound over the lake which a generation ago echoed to the shrill cry of the panther and the wolf. The great pines once disturbed only by wind and lightning have given place to gardens and lawns. The present seems all important, the past very distant. Yet it is well to pause occasionally and think of the men and events of yesterday that have caused the conditions of today.

NOTES

1 Paul Jamieson writes that Joseph Poncet, a French Jesuit priest, went down the Oswegatchie in 1653 after traveling overland from the central Adirondacks (Jamieson 1994, 6.)

2 These two purchases were the largest land grants in northern New York. The Totten and Crossfield purchase of 1771 involved 1,150,000 acres. The Macomb purchase of the 1790s encompassed 3,693,755 acres. (Donaldson 1921, vol. 1, 51-77.)

3 The hunter-trappers Nat Foster and Nick Stoner both arrived in the Adirondacks in the late 1700s (Brumley 1994, 3).

4 Grass Pd Mt. [Marshall's note.]

5 Graves Mt. [Marshall's note.]

6 Marshall's quotation contains minor inaccuracies. See Letter XLIV in Headley 1875, p. 375.

7 The state legislature authorized the dam in 1865, but it was not built until 1867 (Fowler 1959, 11-12).

8 Jesse Irish succeeded McConnell. Michael G. Dodds then succeeded Irish (Fowler 1959, 16).

9 Bassout Pond is named for him. Early variant spellings include "Barsout" (Colvin 1873, see foldout map) and "Bossout" (Wallace 1894, 149).

10 He is referring to George Muir. Muir died while hiking twelve miles through the snow from Wanakena to his cabin on the remote Gull Lake. He was eighty years old. (Keith 1976, 118-121.)

11 The last panther killed in the Adirondacks was shot in 1894 in Herkimer County (Kogut 1990, 506).

12 Philo "Fide" Scott was the model for the main character in Irving Bacheller's 1906 novel *Silas Strong: Emperor of the Woods* (Brumley 1994, 54).

13 Reuben Wood, a champion fisherman, designed the fly that bears his name. A boulder at the mouth of Sucker Brook, near the site of the Forestry College Summer Camp, is inscribed: "In memory of Reuben Wood, a genial gentleman and great fisherman who was fond of these solitudes" (Smeby 2002, 55).

14 Some of Marshall's dates in the next three paragraphs are slightly off: Tramps Retreat was built in 1886; Emporium opened its Cranberry Lake mill in 1917; Rich Lumber Company built Wanakena in 1902 (Fowler 1959, 9-10).

Courtesy of Susan Smeby

Reuben Wood Rock at the mouth of Sucker Brook.

Why I Want to Become a Forester in the Future

Marshall wrote this short essay in 1918 while a student at the Ethical Culture School in New York City. In the final paragraph, he demonstrates a remarkable self-knowledge for a 17-year-old and a prescient vision of his future.

Most people have only a very hazy conception of what forestry is, and so, in case you may happen to be one of the majority, I will explain this profession in a brief way. There are three big branches of forestry. Firstly, there is the landscape forestry. This is conducted in cities, towns and estates. The job of the landscape forester is to see that trees are planted ornamentally, so that they may present the greatest possible amount of beauty to the person who comes in contact with them. An example of the landscape forester's work is the city parks. He also must plan out large country estates or plant trees on city streets. A second branch of forestry is scientific lumbering. Aside from having to know all that any needs to know, a scientific lumberman must be able to cut for the future. He must be able to cut with the least possible waste. And finally, he must be able to cut with the least possible expense. The third branch of forestry is state or government forestry. The state or government forester must have the widest knowledge. Besides knowing the principles of landscape forestry and lumbering, he must know how to be a ranger, a firefighter and a great many other things. But all foresters who want to be successful must have a knowledge of the woods, they must be conscientious, hard-working men, and they must be morally strong men.

The future forester peeking out of a tepee.

Foresters are needed. The American Forestry Association recently issued a statement saying that at least forty thousand more foresters are wanted. Surely, there are few fields with so many openings. You may ask what such a horde of trained men is needed for. A complete answer to such a question would fill pages. But some of the most important needs for new foresters are in rebuilding and replanting the devastated lands of Europe, hundreds of square miles in area. This alone could occupy thousands of men's lifetimes. But there are other tasks. Scientific lumbering is still in its infancy. At the present only forty percent of a lumbered tree is usefully used. The government forestry service has a very inadequate force of trained foresters. Hundreds of other, smaller branches also cry out for men. There is indeed a great need for foresters.

Probably the most important point a person must consider in looking for his life's work is how well he likes the job and how well he is fitted for it. As far as liking forestry is concerned, I entertain not the slightest doubt. I love the woods and solitude. I love the various forms of scientific work a forester must do. I would hate to spend the greater part of my lifetime in a stuffy office or crowded assembly or even in a populous city. If I can combine my greatest pleasure with a useful work, then surely I will have a great advantage over most business and professional men. In regard to fitness, I do not think I would fail. Certain I am that if my mind is fit for anything, that thing is forestry. And physically speaking I do not think I am below normal in fitness. My love of the woods, the necessity of more foresters and my fitness for the task, all these are reasons why I want to be a forester.

An old-growth forest in the Adirondacks.

Part Three

PRESERVATIONIST

"There is nothing in the world to equal the forest as nature made it. The finest formal forest, the most magnificent artificially grown woods, cannot compare with the grandeur of primeval woodland."

– Bob Marshall
RECREATIONAL LIMITATIONS
TO SILVICULTURE IN THE ADIRONDACKS

Adirondack lumberjacks, circa 1888.

Recreational Limitations to Silviculture in the Adirondacks

In his first foray into the politics of preservation, Marshall argues against open-ing up the public Forest Preserve to logging. He compares a virgin forest to a museum: Just as society spends money to safeguard art or artifacts in a museum, it ought to be willing to pay a little—in the form of lost timber profits—to preserve the Adirondack wilderness. It's a theme he would expand on in later years. Marshall wrote this article for one of his courses at the New York State College of Forestry. It was published in the February 1925 issue Journal of Forestry.

There are probably few parts of the New York state constitution which have withstood so much criticism as Article 7, Section 7.[1] This provides that no timber on the Forest Preserve shall be sold, removed or destroyed. During the thirty years since its adoption a steady barrage of disapproval, ridicule or pseudo-logic has been hurled against it, which, however, has failed to impress the great majority of fair-minded citizens because some fundamental points are generally overlooked. However, in dealing with the problem of the New York state Forest Preserve, the following facts must be considered:

■ The aesthetic advantages of the virgin forest are of even greater moment than the economic drawbacks.

■ Lumbering and recreation are not practical on the same area in the Adirondacks.[2]

■ The recreational problems cannot be met by laying aside a few hundred thousand acres of scenic reserves.

■ There is no adequate assurance that cutting in the Forest Preserve would be done in such a way as to leave the requisite area of scenic reserves unmarred.

Virgin Forests

From a forestry standpoint virgin forests are undesirable. They are usually overstocked with older trees, which results in slow growth and an inadequate representation in the younger age classes. A great deal of wood which could be utilized goes utterly to waste. Growth merely balances loss through decay. But though economically wasteful, there are thousands of people who sincerely believe that there is nothing in the world to equal the forest as nature made it. The finest formal forest, the most magnificent artificially grown woods, cannot compare with the grandeur of primeval woodland. In these days of overcivilization it is not mere sentimentalism which makes the virgin forest such a genuine delight.

A couple of centuries ago there was scarcely a break in the untrammeled forest which covered New York. Today 99 1/2 percent of those forests have been cleared, lumbered or burned. There are probably less than a hundred thousand acres of virgin timber now owned by the state,[3] nor one percent of the fifteen million acres of potential forest land. We can certainly afford to set aside this relatively small area even though it involves an annual financial loss of sixty-five cents per acre.[4] Many times that amount of money is tied up in museums and parks. But there never was a museum that had a more interesting exhibit than this last remnant of the woods that were, nor a park that could compare with them in beauty.

Recreation and Lumbering

One of the favorite points brought up by those who desire to open the Adirondacks for logging is the example of the National Forests where there is both exploitation and recreation. The weakness of this analogy is readily apparent. The National Forests have about eighty-five times the area of the New York state Forest Preserve. The demand for recreational opportunities, due to a less dense population, is not nearly as great. As a result there is ample room for exploitation and camping on separate areas. But, despite this, we have about 7,200,000 acres set aside in National Parks where regulations against cutting are just as stringent as in the Adirondacks or Catskills. The example of the National Forests and Parks would really seem to be an argument in favor of Article 7, Section 7.

Under certain silvicultural systems, as a conservative selection, logging may not seriously injure the aesthetic value of the forests. But let us note what silvicultural methods the exponents of opening the Adirondacks advocate for each of the four types found in the region.

Swamp. Clear-cutting is the method unanimously agreed upon for this type. Reproduction is abundant, and the roots of the trees are so shallow that any other system would result in serious windfall.

Spruce Flat. There is more diversity of opinion here. Recknagel recommends a heavy selection, cutting spruce roughly to ten inches diameter breast high and balsam to five inches.[5]

Mixed Hardwood. Various systems have been suggested for this type, of which clear-cutting and planting is the one earnestly advocated by the Cornell Forestry Department, one of the organizations most in favor of opening the Forest Preserve for exploitation.

Spruce Slope. The method recommended here is clear-cutting, although it is admitted that steep upper slopes should be reserved for protection and recreation forests.[6]

Unfortunately, no accurate estimate has been made as to what percent of the Adirondack forest the spruce-flat type occupies. Graves estimated it at ten percent of Nehasane Park and thirty percent of the Whitney Preserve.[7] Let us assume twenty percent for the sake of argument. Then eighty percent, or all the rest of the merchantable area, should be clear-cut according to those who propose opening the Forest Preserve for lumbering.

Now it cannot be denied that clear-cutting is aesthetically the least desirable of any high forest method of reproduction. A young plantation may be beautiful to look at from the road, but no person who goes to the woods for recreation gets the real benefit of the forest if it consists mostly of small poles. Some people assume that as long as you have any trees, the woods have full recreational value. This is not so. The vital factor is the type of woods. As an example, in climbing Mount Marcy from Keene Valley the average party gets little pleasure out of the heavily culled forest at the base of the mountain, but many claim that the beautiful woods higher up the trail are worth almost as much as the view itself. Any number of similar instances can be cited.

Obviously, there is no specific diameter which the trees as a whole must attain to be considered of recreational value. But if none of the trees are even twelve inches in diameter, you certainly won't have a very desirable forest from an aesthetic standpoint.

According to Colonel Henry S. Graves,[8] under favorable conditions it is possible for red spruce to grow twelve inches in diameter in ninety years. Norway spruce grows faster, but this fact is balanced by the less favorable growing conditions over most of the Adirondack region. Recknagel recommended an eighty-year rotation for spruce on private land.[9] Of course, in state forests this rotation could be lengthened, so let us assume on an average a rotation of one hundred years. For ninety percent of that time there would not be a spruce over twelve inches. The hardwoods would be even smaller. Remembering that clear-cutting is to be applied to eighty percent of the territory logged it will be seen that seventy-two percent of the area will be constantly almost worthless from a recreational standpoint and the remainder seriously impaired.

Aside from the internal appearance of the woods themselves the wild views from the mountains will be irreparably ruined. And the lakes, even with the proposed belt of timber to be left along the shores, will have rising from them, instead of magnificently wooded mountainsides, a checkerboard of all-aged cutting areas. It is obvious that if you clear-cut the Adirondacks you practically ruin their recreational potentialities.

Area of Scenic Reserves

Since the economic conditions and silvicultural requirements in the Adirondacks seem to require clear-cutting over most of the region and since this system is highly injurious to recreational usage, it is certain that whatever areas are needed for this latter purpose must be set aside as scenic reserves. But here there is room for a great deal of honest difference of opinion. To decide on any definite area will require much further research in both forestry and sociology. However, it will be well to observe certain facts.

1. The recreational demands which will be made on the Forest Preserve cannot be judged by the present number of tourists and campers. People cannot live generation after generation in the city without serious retrogression, physical, moral and mental, and the time will come when the most destitute of the vast city population will be able to get a vacation in the forest. The Palisades Interstate Park and the Allegheny Park will be totally inadequate to meet the extensive demand which is certain to come, so the Forest Preserve will have to provide for the great majority. Therefore, it is imperative that we do not make this future impossible.

2. West of the Mississippi River there are about 7,200,000 acres in National Parks. The vast area is devoted almost exclusively to recreation. But the population of the trans-Mississippian states is only 31,689,445, giving 0.23 acres of National Park for every person, without considering the vast National Forests areas devoted to the same purpose. On the other hand, the 1,847,193 acres of the New York forests leaves only 0.18 acres for each New Yorker.

3. It has frequently been stated that New York is the biggest consumer of wood and hence should be a large producer. This is perfectly true, but it must also be borne in mind that the Empire State also has by far the greatest population of any state in the Union.[10] So, while lumber is a bulky commodity, people are even more difficult to transport and though freight rates are high, passenger rates are much higher. Therefore, where production and recreation conflict, the latter must be given precedence in order to avoid the expensive necessity of moving people great distances for their recreation.

4. The Forest Preserve embraces only twelve percent of the fifteen million acres of potential forest land in New York. Adding to this all other lands devoted primarily to recreation it would not exceed fifteen percent of the area. This would not seem to be too much land to dedicate to the upbuilding of the health, minds and morals of our vast population. Therefore, until far more definite studies are made, the New York Forest Preserve should remain intact.

Control of Cutting

No matter how much a person may be opposed to lumbering on a large scale on state land, it cannot be denied that the right to do limited cutting in the Forest Preserve would be beneficial. Release, improvement and salvage cuttings would frequently be of great advantage to the forest. In addition, it might be desirable to exploit commercially certain limited areas. But before any change in the constitution can be made there must be positive assurance that all logging can be kept under perfect control. So far no plan has been brought forward which gives this assurance. There would have to be absolute provision made for the following points:

1. Administration of all cutting must be entirely out of political control.

2. The administrative organization must be assured a sufficient sustained financial support, or otherwise the legislation might in the future curtail the forestry appropriations to such an extent that adequate regulation would be impossible.

3. The scenic reserves must be absolutely safeguarded against logging that would ruin their aesthetic value.

4. Assurance must be given by leading lawyers that any amendment that may be proposed cannot be construed to mean anything which is not apparent on the surface.

Perhaps when the exponents of opening the Forest Preserve have satisfied the justifiable apprehension in regard to these four points, the so-called "absurd conservationists" will be more amenable toward changing the constitution.[11] For those conservationists have seen in the past the most outrageous exploitation of the public domain; they have seen during the past year the almost successful attempt of private interests to push through an amendment at the polls after favorable action by the legislature granting special privileges in the Forest Preserve, which the people defeated by an overwhelming majority.[12] They are not the selfish, sentimental type of conservationist. But they know that the only thing which has prevented the utter devastation of the Adirondacks has been Article 7, Section 7, and so they are naturally quite wary about giving it up.

NOTES

1 The article, drafted at the state's 1894 constitutional convention, mandates that the public Forest Preserve "shall be forever kept as wild forest lands." Marshall's father, a delegate to the convention, helped draft the article (Glover 1985). It was renumbered Article 14 at the 1938 constitutional convention.

2 In recent years, the state has purchased recreational easements on vast tracts of commercial timberlands in the Adirondacks. The lands are open for hiking, biking, snowmobiling and other outdoor pursuits. This would seem to contradict Marshall's claim, but the recreation he has in mind is the experience of natural wilderness.

3 Barbara McMartin estimates that there are as many as 500,000 acres of old-growth forest in the Adirondacks (McMartin 1994, 190).

4 A.B. Recknagel, Forests of New York, p. 74 [Marshall's note].

5 "Suggested Forest Management Requirements in Forests of New York State." New York Lumber Trade Journal, November 15, 1922 [Marshall's note].

6 A.B. Recknagel, "Sample Working Plan for Adirondack Softwoods," Empire State Forest Products Association, Bulletin 15 [Marshall's note].

7 Henry S. Graves, Practical Forestry in the Adirondacks [Marshall's note. Nehasane Park and Whitney Preserve were private lands within the Adirondack Park.].

8 Henry S. Graves, Principles of Handling Woodlots [Marshall's note].

9 A.B. Recknagel, "Sample Working Plan for Adirondack Softwoods," Empire State Forest Products Association, Bulletin 15 [Marshall's note].

10 In 2003, New York had the third-largest population in the nation.

11 Marshall may be referring to a 1923 article by Frank A. Waugh titled "Conservation Ad Absurdum" that attacked the constitution's forever-wild clause. Even if Marshall's conditions were met, conservationists today would not support logging in the Forest Preserve.

12 In 1923, voters rejected a constitutional amendment that would have allowed the construction of power dams in the Forest Preserve (Brown 1985, 83).

The Perilous Plight
of the Adirondack Wilderness

In 1932, New Yorkers were asked to vote on an amendment to the state constitution that would have permitted the state to construct cabins and ancillary facilities in the Forest Preserve. It was backed by Robert Moses, the influential director of the New York State Council of Parks. Marshall wrote this article in opposition. It was published in the October issue of High Spots. *In November, voters rejected the proposal by a 2-1 ratio.*[1]

Hundreds of thousands of people, with a great variety of pleasures, visit the Adirondacks annually. Some want to ride on paved highways and spend the night in luxurious hotels. Others prefer their sustenance from hotdog stands by the side of the road and their sleep in comfortably prepared tourists' campsites. Still others desire to tramp the forest trails in an effort to escape from the constant presence of the mechanical and to feel the exhilaration of depending entirely on their own competence and power. Finally, there is a small group which desires the joy of getting back where even trails cease and where man may live intimately with the purely primitive. It is idle to attempt an absolute evaluation of the merits of these different types of forest recreation, for each type ranks highest to many individuals. The important consideration is that all of these forms of recreation may be enjoyed simultaneously in the Adirondacks if a well-directed and tolerant administration of the Forest Preserve is maintained.

All of these forms of forest recreation, in addition to golfing, tennis, baseball, skiing, bobsledding, ice skating, swimming, rowing, canoeing, motorboating, aqua-planing and dancing are enjoyed in the Adirondacks as they are administered today. One may now circle the entire Forest Preserve, traveling almost entirely on first-rate highways, stopping exclusively at first-rate hotels (if one has the money) and leading a life which differs in scenic setting but not in the immediate details of life from what one might lead in the heart of any large city. At the other extreme, one may also do as Herb Clark and I did the other day when we turned our backs on both roads and trails and followed the torrent of Roaring Brook to its source on the high slopes of Lost Pond Mountain.[2] The stream as we ascended was a constant succession of waterfalls tumbling over the hard, granite outcrops,[3] with clear, deep opalescent pools of water below them. There were flumes and chasms and one narrow gorge which extended for almost a mile, with sheer rock walls sometimes as much as thirty feet high. On either bank were the shady depths of the primeval forest in which, though the individual trees were all different, the general appearance was unchanged from those days before white men had ever penetrated to the wilderness of northern New York. Indeed, for all we could observe, as we followed up the unmarred valley of Roaring Brook, northern New York still was an aboriginal wilderness and the mechanical twentieth century was much more remote than the primitive eighteenth.

I do not contend that the exultation which Herb and I derived from our day on Roaring Brook was superior to what the tourist on the porch of Paul Smith's Hotel, the speedboat driver on Lake Placid, the golfer on the Saranac links or the couple gliding over Durgan's dance floor experienced. I do contend, however, that Herb and I and the tens of thousands like us are entitled to our form of exultation. Under the present laws which govern the management of the state Forest Preserve we may continue to enjoy it.

But the continuance of present conditions is threatened, and if these conditions are changed the Adirondack wilderness is in the utmost danger of extermination. For the so-called Recreation Amendment to the constitution would subject the few remaining primitive areas in the Adirondacks to almost certain invasion by the improvements of civilization which if once made would ruin forever the unmarred nature of the wilderness. There is only a very small fraction of the Adirondacks which remains unaltered by the activities of man. On the other hand, for those who desire their forest recreation in ways which the wild forest cannot provide, more than two-thirds of the entire Adirondack Park is at present privately owned and may be developed in any manner desired.[4] In addition there are hundreds of miles of roads across state lands and thousands of miles of trails. Every conceivable type of outdoor recreation may be pursued in the Adirondacks under the existing laws. The undeveloped state lands are not vital for any type of outdoor recreation except the enjoyment of the primeval and of the wilderness. But the passage of the proposed Recreation Amendment would not only imperil but actually doom this one form of recreation most unique to the forest, this one form which cannot be experienced in any other part of the entire state.

NOTES

1   Brown 1985, 154.

2   Also called Lost Pond Peak, it's located south of Street Mountain.

3   There is no granite to speak of in the Adirondacks. The outcrops probably were anorthosite, gneiss or another hard rock.

4   Today, a little more than half the land inside the Park is private. Since 1973, development on this land has been regulated by the Adirondack Park Agency.

Photo by Carl Heilman II

A telemark skier on Tongue Mountain.

Zoning the Forest Preserve

In 1933, Russell M.L. Carson invited a number of preservationists, foresters and others to write down their opinions as to how to balance public use of the Adirondacks with its protection. High Spots published the submissions in January 1934. It also ran the following excerpt from a letter by Marshall, written nearly a year earlier, in which he calls for keeping parts of the Forest Preserve trailless.

For the Adirondacks to afford their greatest benefit to the greatest number of people I would not talk so much in terms of changes as in terms of creating a carefully thought-out program. This program would not radically alter the status quo of the present Adirondacks, but it would stress the necessity of planning so that they might afford the maximum recreational values to the people. Consequently I believe that such a program should consider the desirability of zoning the Adirondack Park for different types of use. Thus there would be areas set aside in which no trails, camps or any improvements would be made. These would be genuine wilderness areas of the highest type. It is unfortunately true that there are relatively few such areas of more than fifty square miles that can still be set aside in the Adirondacks. These seem so precious from the standpoint of primitive forest recreation that they should be safeguarded in the near future by all means.[1]

Other areas would have occasional trails through them but would not be intensively developed. They would be semi-wild areas but not as wild as entirely trailless sections.

Finally there would be areas such as the region around Johns Brook Lodge where trails would be developed very intensively so that visitors might have a great variety of possible trips over well-traveled paths.[2]

If the development of these types of areas is left entirely to chance it is inevitable that the first type would soon disappear while the last type would be developed in inferior fashion. It takes a great deal of skill to really lay out a good trail to take advantage of all the aesthetic possibilities of the region in which it runs. A poor trail may eliminate the possibility of constructing a good one.

Less important than the zoning matter but still of much value for the adequate use of the region is the desirability of encouraging as wide a variety of uses of the Forest Preserve as is reasonably possible without seriously affecting the most important uses. At present automobiling, ordinary hiking, canoeing, rowboating and motorboating are much encouraged, and splendid facilities for them have been developed in the Adirondacks. On the other hand horseback riding and skiing have been very little encouraged. I think that a change in policy in regard to these two sports is desirable so that more trails may be fixed up for horseback riding and more ski trails opened. In each case this would generally involve simply a little extra work in clearing and in the case of horseback riding in fixing a decent tread underfoot. This, of course, does not imply that I think that all or even most trails should be made available for riding and skiing, but I do think that a sufficient number should be developed so that those who are fond of these very splendid sports may get more opportunities of enjoying them. Of course considerable skiing can be done on ordinary hiking trails. I do not believe that it is necessary to clear as wide trails as have already been cleared in the vicinity of Lake Placid and Adirondack Lodge. However, some additional work must be done, and I think this should be considered in changing the recreational policy in the Adirondacks.

NOTES

1   Marshall's point of view is reflected in the state Department of Environmental Conservation's management plans for Wilderness Areas in the Adirondacks. Such plans often recommend keeping certain tracts trailless. Most of the Pepperbox Wilderness Area, for example, lacks formal trails.

2   Johns Brook Lodge, owned by the Adirondack Mountain Club, sits at the base of the Great Range in the eastern High Peaks Wilderness, where there is an extensive network of popular trails.

Comments on Commission's Truck Trail Policy

In 1935, the New York State Conservation Department started building truck trails to enable firefighters to reach remote areas of the Forest Preserve. When John Apperson and other preservationists objected, Conservation Commissioner Lithgow Osborne suspended work while a committee appointed by the governor studied the matter. Osborne argued in favor of the truck trails in the January 1936 issue of American Forests. *Marshall's rebuttal below appeared in the same issue. Eventually, the committee voted 4-1 to allow the truck trails, with Apperson dissenting.[1] In the years to come, preservationists would complain that both state officials and the public improperly used the truck trails to drive into the Preserve.*

In my disagreement with practically all of Commissioner Osborne's defense of Adirondack truck trails, I want to make it clear that I genuinely respect the sincerity of Mr. Osborne's argument. The issue is not that of one personality against another. It involves the fundamental soundness or unsoundness of the whole wilderness viewpoint.

Mr. Osborne quotes a portion of Judge Crane's decision in the famous bobsled run case to justify his interpretation of the constitution.[2] He omits another equally significant portion: "Trees could not be cut or the timber destroyed, even for the building of a road."

Mr. Osborne says: "In 1934, for all the improvement of our equipment and for the increase in our personnel, we only missed by the narrowest of margins an even worse fire year [than in 1908]." This "narrowest margin" would seem to be pretty broad. In 1908 there were 346,953 acres burnt in the Adirondacks; in 1934, 10,853 acres, or approximately one thirty-second of the area burnt in that earlier fire year. Similarly, the estimated fire loss in 1908 amounted to $802,139 and in 1934 to $26,199.

This was in spite of the extraordinarily severe climatic conditions to which Mr. Osborne properly pointed in his annual report. Clearly, the fire organization which the state has developed is immensely more capable to cope with fires than it was in 1908, and the danger from fires because of this splendid organization is immensely less. The general public is right in believing that no radical departure from past policies needs to be taken to safeguard the Adirondacks from fire. It is right in holding that the necessity of truck trails for the purpose of decreasing one-tenth of one percent of the Adirondacks burned on the average annually is too uncertain to justify giving the Conservation Department a blanket discretion to invade the wilderness with routes for mechanized transportation.

Mr. Osborne feels that the Bay Pond fire "might easily have been the worst on record if it had not been for the good system of roads in that section."[3] He also states that when the truck trails he contemplates are completed they will only be "needles in the North Woods haystack." My interpretation of the significance of the Bay Pond fire is that, in spite of the fact that there were better road facilities in that section than Mr. Osborne hopes to provide for the North Woods generally, this fire developed into the worst one in the Adirondacks "since 1913." Many other fires which started in far less accessible areas under equally dry climatic conditions were readily controlled in 1934. The Bay Pond fire seems to indicate clearly that there is no close correlation between the degree of road or truck trail development and the effectiveness of fire control in the Adirondacks.

Mr. Osborne states that "these so-called fire truck trails are in reality simple one-way woods-roads . . . ." Because the building of truck trails in the Adirondacks has fortunately not yet progressed very far, Mr. Osborne is probably unaware that from a purely technical standpoint "simple one-way woods-roads" have not proven a success for fire transportation where they have been built by the Forest Service and the Indian Service in timber types similar to those which are found in the Adirondacks. In the mixed hardwood forests there are two bad fire seasons—one in the spring before the green leaves come out and one in the autumn after the leaves have fallen. At a time when there is already high inflammability on the more exposed cut-over areas and old burns, the narrow truck trails, where they lead through less exposed places, still have unmelted piles of snow and impassable mud holes because there has not been time for sunlight to dry out the ground. It has therefore generally been necessary for both the Fire Service and the Indian Service to widen the clearing for their truck trails to a minimum of twenty-four feet in order to facilitate the melting of snow and drying of the ground which makes possible the use of these truck trails in reaching spring fires. I can see no reason why Mr. Osborne in the Adirondacks will have any different experience than have the Indian Service and Forest Service in similar timber types in the Lake States.

Mr. Osborne assumes that truck trails are certain to decrease the area burned. Truck trails, however, do not only work to decrease the fire danger. In some cases they increase it. Passable trails have the genuine advantage that they do get firefighters and equipment more quickly and easily to the fires. Especially they hasten the speed of getting to lightning fires which have the habit of starting away from the normal routes of transportation. However, in the Adirondacks lightning fires are of almost no significance. There were only seventy-eight acres burned over by lightning fires, even in the exceedingly dry year of 1934. On the other hand, truck trails tend to bring more fires into the woods if they are not kept closed to vehicular traffic. Even if they are kept closed, they greatly increase the forest inflammability along the right-of-way. Through the opening made in the forest when usable truck trails are built, the sunlight is given a better chance to dry the natural fuels of the forest. There is plenty of excellent research by forest experiment stations which clearly shows that the more sunlight which reaches the floor of the forest, the drier the dead leaves, needles, twigs and logs alongside become. Consequently, at the edge of any cutting of the forest, regardless of whether it is a logging operation, or a fire lane, or a road, or a truck trail, fires burn more fiercely and spread more rapidly because the materials which burn are drier. In addition, when the mineral soil of the wild forest is exposed in road building, weeds which dry up in the autumn and make a much greater fire hazard than the normal forest vegetation, tend to become prolific.

Mr. Osborne thinks that one of the causes of increased fire danger attributed to truck trails can be eliminated by keeping the new truck trails closed to unofficial use. Personally, I do not believe this can be done. Already several of the recently built truck trails have been invaded by automobiles, in spite of the gates which protect them. Furthermore, once a road passable for automobiles is actually built, there will immediately be a strong argument that the Conservation Department is like a dog in the manger in not permitting the general public to use it.[4] It will be much easier to open by constitutional amendment a road which already exists than it would be to authorize the cutting of an entirely new road.

Even if truck trails could be kept closed to general travel, no attempt will be made to keep hunters, fishermen and hikers from walking along them. Because of the much greater drying of forest fuel which occurs at the edge of the opening made by truck trails than occurs along a narrow foot trail, the spread of man-caused fires will generally be more rapid along these truck trails, even if those who use them walk. This is especially important when one considers that sixty-seven percent of the Adirondack fires in 1934 were caused by smokers, hunters, campers and fishermen.

Mr. Osborne states that "the trails are dead-end roads running nowhere, from a communication point of view, and hence would fit into no conceivable state or county highway system." The whole history of wilderness invasion in the United States is replete with examples of "dead-end roads, running nowhere from a communication point of view," which nevertheless have later been expanded and connected into communication systems. As an example, the Ely-Buyck road, which cuts the wilderness of northern Minnesota in two, was started as a couple of far-removed stub truck trails, to be used purely for fire protection. Gradually these stub truck trails were lengthened, and then all at once, before anybody seemed to realize it, there was a highway right through the heart of this wild country.

The wilderness, uninvaded by any signs of mechanization, has a value unique to outdoor recreation. It has a value which to countless individuals exceeds any other value there is. Except for northern Maine, the Adirondacks contain the last wilderness areas of any large size which remain in the East.[5] Enjoyment of the wilderness depends not only on whether one actually is traveling at a given moment by primitive methods, but also on whether the whole environment is in rhythm with the primitive. An automobile road, even though it is disguised by the name of truck trail and traveled only Conservation Department cars, wrecks the sense of wilderness completely. Therefore, Mr. Osborne's truck trails, regardless of whether or not he keeps them locked up, will destroy the character of the Adirondacks as "wild forest lands," a priceless character which the New York state Constitution for forty-one years has tried to preserve.[6]

NOTES

1   For more details, see Graham, 190-95.

2   In 1930, Judge Frederick C. Crane wrote a decision for the Court of Appeals, the state's highest tribunal, that a legislative act authorizing construction of an Olympic bobsled run in Forest Preserve violated the state constitution, which mandates that the Preserve "shall be forever kept as wild forest lands."

3   Bay Pond is a private estate in the northern Adirondacks.

4   In fable, the dog in the manger would not allow the horse or ox to eat the hay even though the dog did not want the hay for itself.

5   See "Largest Roadless Areas in United States," p. 199. Marshall's list does not include the Florida Everglades.

6   See note 2.

Calkins Brook Truck Trail in 2006, seventy years after Bob Marshall saw it.

Calkins Creek

Marshall wrote this article about 1936, during the controversy over building truck trails in the Forest Preserve.[1] It was not published until 1953, in Ad-i-ron-dac. *The Conservation Department was then proposing to build more truck trails to enable forest rangers to reach remote places where dead timber from the Great Blowdown of 1950 posed a fire hazard.*

As a child I used to look out across the waters of Saranac Lake toward the rugged skyline of Ampersand Mountain and the Sawtooth Range. They were wild-looking summits, showing no sign of civilization anywhere upon their timbered slopes. I remember, once, asking one of the old guides what lay beyond them, and he answered: "Ampersand Valley, and it's a lonesome country." Then I asked what lay beyond Ampersand Valley, and he pointed out the distant peaks of Seymour and Seward. Then I asked what lay beyond Seymour and Seward—beyond the furthermost beyond which one could see—and he replied: "That's the Cold River country, but I've never been there. Few people go there. It has no settlements and no roads."

In 1919 I took my first trip in this country of no settlements and no roads and found the statement not quite literally true. There were old logging roads, but most of them were overgrown, and all of them were part of an unmotorized wilderness. In 1920 we followed up Cold River from its mouth to Duck Hole and then cut through Ouluska Pass, the old Indian "place of shadows," to Ampersand Pond. We did not see a single human being in four days of travel. We carried all the requirements for livelihood upon our backs and were elated by the realization that we were traveling where only competent people could go. Here in truth there remained the wild country of my childhood's imagination, where automobiles which had wrecked all semblance of the wilderness over most of New York state seemed to be barred forever.

I recollect camping one night by a beaver pond on a remote stream called Calkins Creek.[2] I remember a deep-red sunset in a strange world, cut off gorgeously from everything but the moss-grown forest and the evening mist.

Later, when the full moon of August rose above the ancient tree-tops, we watched the unconcerned beaver splashing in its calm candescence, listened to the undisciplined hooting of the owls and felt the fresh north wind blowing on our cheeks without a single dissonant impression to spoil the perfect primitive harmony.

After 1924 I was away from the Cold River country for twelve years. However, I thought of it very often, even when I was traveling among the larger wildernesses of the West and arctic Alaska. It always seemed glorious that in the most populous state of the Union there should yet exist an entire drainage, embracing several hundred square miles, which was free from a single route for mechanized transportation.

Once, I remember, while camping in northern Idaho I had a nightmare. I dreamed that a road had been built down the Cold River. It was just one road, but it wrecked the whole world of wilderness. Fortunately, it wasn't really a road but only a nightmare.

Last May I returned to Cold River and found my nightmare had come true. The Cold River drainage is no longer a whole world where one can live the splendid life of the primeval. It is no longer possible for those who still want above all else to enjoy the unique emotions of the primitive environment to do so without an accompanying discord of mechanical modernity.

Calkins Creek now has a modern road down most of its length. It is called a truck trail, which means that it is actually a dirt-and-gravel road built on higher standards than many which the farmers of New York are using today. There are great scars along its edge where material for the roadbed has been gouged out of the hillside. The tire tracks which blot out the footprints of the deer seem to symbolize the twentieth century which has come to steal from the primeval one of its rare remaining interests.

The constitution of the state of New York says that "the lands of the state, now owned or hereafter acquired, constituting the forest preserve as now fixed by law, shall be forever kept as wild forest lands." In spite of the constitution, the "wild forest lands" have been irrevocably shattered.

NOTES

1 See "Comments on Commission's Truck Trail Policy," p. 189.

2 Called Calkins Brook on modern maps.

Largest Roadless Areas
in the United States

Marshall and a colleague, Althea Dobbins, wrote the following article for the November 1936 issue of The Living Wilderness, *the magazine of the Wilderness Society. Although most of the roadless areas they identified were in the West, Adirondack aficionados will note that three lie within the Blue Line: Moose River (430,000 acres), Mount Marcy (380,000 acres) and Cranberry Lake-Beaver River (380,000 acres). These three areas remain largely roadless.*

The fight to save the wilderness has grown during the past ten years from the personal hobby of a few fanatics to an important, nation-wide movement. All over the country, people are beginning to protest in a concerted manner against the invasion of roadless tracts by routes of modern transportation. Encouragingly enough, a number of these protests have been heeded, and several splendid roadless areas have thus been saved. Others have been preserved by federal and state officials before any protest had to be launched. Yet others, unfortunately, have been invaded either because nobody happened to realize that invasion was imminent or because no one was aware that there was a significant area to be saved.

The battle to protect the wilderness is a critical one. Definitely there have not been enough large roadless tracts safely reserved from invasions. There is important need to make a study at an early date concerning which officially designated roadless areas should be enlarged and which areas on which official action has not been taken should be established.

As a step preliminary to such a study, it is necessary to know what are the potential roadless areas which still can be saved. With this objective in mind, we have made a rough analysis of all the forest areas in the United States, embracing 300,000 acres or more, which have not yet been invaded by routes of mechanized transportation. We have made a similar study of desert areas embracing 500,000 acres or more, under the assumption that a considerably larger area is needed in open country than in forest country to give one the feeling of wilderness. The study of such areas was made from accurate road maps for all National Forests, National Parks and Indian reservations, as kept by the federal bureaus administering these lands; from the excellent maps of the New York State Conservation Department; from the most accurate available automobile maps, and from the knowledge of a number of people familiar with specific locations which are not well mapped. We wish to express our appreciation to the following for their kind assistance: Lee Kneipp and Helen Smith of the U.S. Forest Service; H.S. Teller of the National Park Service; E.H. Coulson and J.P. Kinney of the Indian Service; Depue Falck of the Grazing Division of the Interior Department, and William G. Howard of the New York State Conservation Department. As this is only a preliminary study, we realize there will be a number of mistakes. This is especially true of the desert areas where existing road maps are unusually poor. We would greatly appreciate any corrections which the readers of this article can make.

In drawing the boundaries of our roadless areas, we placed the edge one-half mile back from all roads, under the assumption that this distance was necessary to isolate the more annoying influences of mechanization. Where a stub road penetrated into a wilderness area, we drew our boundaries half a mile back from the road on each side, thus in effect eliminating a finger reaching into such a wilderness area for a width of approximately one mile.

In view of the fact that most people do not visualize areas in terms of acres, we would like to point out that the 300,000 acres is not a roadless area in any pioneering sense. Actually, a 300,000-acre tract is only about 21½ by 21½ miles, something which a reasonably good walker could traverse readily in a day if there were a trail. A desert area of 500,000 acres is only 27½ by 27½ miles, across which even a poor horseman could ride in a day. Of course, most of these areas are not square but are much attenuated, so that a 300,000-acre area might have the dimensions of approximately 47 miles by 10 miles, instead of 21½ by 21½ miles.

The following table and map indicate those forest areas in the United States of 300,000 acres or more and those desert areas of 500,000 acres or more which are not yet accessible to mechanized transportation.

FOREST AREAS

NAME	STATE	ACREAGE
1. Aroostock-Allagash	Maine	2,800,000
2. Northern Cascade	Washington	2,800,000
3. Salmon River	Idaho	2,800,000
4. High Sierra	California	2,300,000
5. South Fork of Flathead	Montana	2,000,000
6. Selway	Idaho-Montana	2,000,000
7. Upper Yellowstone	Wyoming	2,000,000
8. Upper St. John	Maine	1,300,000
9. Olympic	Washington	1,200,000
10. Superior	Minnesota	1,200,000
11. Wind River Mountains	Wyoming	1,200,000
12. Beartooth	Montana-Wyoming	960,000
13. Absaroka Range	Wyoming	930,000
14. Siskiyou	Oregon	830,000
15. Sawtooth	Idaho	820,000
16. Syaladopsis	Maine	780,000
17. San Juan	Colorado	690,000
18. Umpqua	Oregon	640,000
19. North Yosemite	California	630,000
20. Dead River	Maine	600,000
21. High Uinita	Utah	580,000
22. East Grey River	Wyoming	560,000
23. Foss River	Washington	550,000
24. Gila	New Mexico	530,000
25. North Glacier	Montana	480,000
26. Marble Mountains	California	440,000
27. Moose River	New York	430,000[1]
28. Bechlor River	Wyoming	420,000[2]
29. Madison Range	Montana-Wyoming	430,000
30. South Fork of Salmon	Idaho	410,000
31. White River	Colorado	410,000

32. Salmon-Trinity Alps	California	410,000
33. Okefenokee	Georgia	400,000
34. South Yosemite	California	400,000
35. Mount Marcy	New York	380,000[3]
36. Cranberry-Beaver River	New York	380,000[4]
37. Gros Ventre	Wyoming	370,000
38. Goat Rocks	Washington	370,000
39. South Glacier	Montana	340,000
40. Tonto Basin	Arizona	340,000
41. Wallowa	Oregon	330,000
42. Eagle Cap	Oregon	320,000
43. Electric Peak	Wyoming-Montana	320,000
44. Pintlar	Montana	320,000
45. Blue River	Arizona	310,000
46. Big Horn	Wyoming	310,000
47. Mission Range	Montana	310,000
48. Teton Range	Wyoming	300,000

DESERT AREAS

NAME	STATE	ACREAGE
101. Colorado River	Utah-Arizona	8,890,000
102. Owyhee	Idaho-Oregon-Nevada	4,130,000
103. Grand Canyon	Arizona	4,000,000
104. Nevada Desert	Nevada	2,670,000
105. Book Cliffs	Utah-Colorado	2,420,000
106. North Mohave Desert	California	1,970,000
107. San Rafael Swells	Utah	1,930,000
108. Red Desert	Wyoming	1,900,000
109. Sevier Lake	Utah	1,900,000
110. Little Snake River	Wyoming-Colorado	1,800,000
111. Carrizozo Plains	New Mexico	1,800,000
112. North Salt Lake Desert	Utah	1,700,000
113. South Salt Lake Desert	Utah	1,600,000
114. South Mohave Desert	California	1,500,000
115. White Sands	New Mexico	1,200,000
116. Black Mesa	Arizona	1,200,000
117. West Mojave Desert	California	1,100,000

118. Painted Desert	Arizona	1,000,000
119. Guano Lake	Oregon-Nevada	980,000
120. East Mojave Desert	California	950,000
121. Harqua Hala Desert	Arizona	740,000
122. Bill Williams River	Arizona	700,000
123. Kingston Range	California-Nevada	650,000
124. Bruneau River	Idaho-Nevada	650,000
125. Cignus Peak	Arizona	620,000
126. South Pass	Wyoming	610,000
127. Salton Sea	California	610,000
128. Summer Lake	Oregon	540,000
129. Monument Butte	Wyoming	540,000

NOTES

1   The Moose River area would include, among other lands, the 157,000-acre West Canada Lake Wilderness.

2   This figure seems to be out of order.

3   The High Peaks Wilderness would account for 193,000 acres of the Mount Marcy area.

4   This would include the 118,000-acre Five Ponds Wilderness. The Adirondack Council, an advocate for wilderness preservation, has proposed establishing a 409,000-acre Bob Marshall Great Wilderness in this region of the western Adirondacks. See p. 307 for details.

The South Fork of the Teton River on the edge of the Bob Marshall Wilderness.

Photo by Carl Heilman II

The Problem of the Wilderness

In this article, published in Scientific Monthly *in 1930, Marshall lays out his strongest case for preserving wilderness. Because of its influence, we reprint it here even though Marshall did not write it with the Adirondacks in mind—or at least not only the Adirondacks.*

I

It is appalling to reflect how much useless energy has been expended in arguments which would have been inconceivable had the terminology been defined. In order to avoid such futile controversy I shall undertake at the start to delimit the meaning of the principal term with which this paper is concerned. According to Dr. Johnson a wilderness is "a tract of solitude and savageness," [1] a definition more poetic than explicit. Modern lexicographers do better with a "tract of land, whether a forest or a wide barren plain, uncultivated and uninhabited by human beings." [2] This definition gives a rather good foundation, but it still leaves a penumbra of partially shaded connotation.

For the ensuing discussion I shall use the word *wilderness* to denote a region which contains no permanent inhabitants, possesses no possibility of conveyance by any mechanical means and is sufficiently spacious that a person in crossing it must have the experience of sleeping out. The dominant attributes of such an area are: first, that it requires anyone who exists in it to depend exclusively on his own effort for survival, and second, that it preserves as nearly as possible the primitive environment. This means that all roads, power transportation and set-tlements are barred. But trails and temporary shelters, which were common long before the advent of the white race, are entirely permissible.

When Columbus effected his immortal debarkation, he touched upon a wilderness which embraced virtually a hemisphere. The philosophy that progress is proportional to the amount of alteration imposed upon nature never seemed to have occurred to the Indians. Even such tribes as the Incas, Aztecs and Pueblos made few changes in the environment in which they were born. "The land and all that it bore they treated with consideration; not attempting to improve it, they never desecrated it."[3] Consequently, over billions of acres the aboriginal wanderers still spun out their peripatetic careers, the wild animals still browsed in unmolested meadows and the forests still grew and moldered and grew again precisely as they had done for undeterminable centuries.

It was not until the settlement of Jamestown in 1607 that there appeared the germ for that unabated disruption of natural conditions which has characterized all subsequent American history. At first expansion was very slow. The most intrepid seldom advanced further from their neighbors than the next drainage. At the time of the Revolution the zone of civilization was still practically confined to a narrow belt lying between the Atlantic Ocean and the Appalachian valleys. But a quarter of a century later, when the Louisiana Purchase was consummated, the outposts of civilization had reached the Mississippi, and there were foci of colonization in half a dozen localities west of the Appalachians, though the unbroken line of the frontier was east of the mountains.[4]

It was yet possible as recently as 1804 and 1805 for the Lewis and Clark Expedition to cross two-thirds of a continent without seeing any culture more advanced than that of the Middle Stone Age. The only routes of travel were the uncharted rivers and the almost impassable Indian trails. And continually the expedition was breaking upon some "truly magnificent and sublimely grand object, which has from the commencement of time been concealed from the view of civilized man." [5]

The exploration inaugurated a century of constantly accelerating emigration such as the world had never known. Throughout this frenzied period the only serious thought ever devoted to the wilderness was how it might be demolished. To the pioneers pushing westward it was an enemy of diabolical cruelty and danger, standing as the great obstacle to industry and development. Since these seemed to constitute the essentials for felicity, the obvious step was to excoriate the devil which interfered. And so the path of empire proceeded to substitute for the undisturbed seclusion of nature the conquering accomplishments of man. Highways wound up valleys which had known only the footsteps of the wild animals; neatly planted orchards and gardens replaced the tangled confusion of the primeval forest; factories belched up great clouds of smoke where for centuries trees had transpired toward the sky, and the ground cover of fresh sorrel and twin-flower was transformed to asphalt spotted with chewing gum, coal dust and gasoline.

Today there remain less than twenty wilderness areas of a million acres,[6] and annually even these shrunken remnants of an undefiled continent are being despoiled. Aldo Leopold has truly said:

> The day is almost upon us when canoe travel will consist in paddling up the noisy wake of a motor launch and portaging through the back yard of a summer cottage. When that day comes canoe travel will be dead, and dead too will be a part of our Americanism. . . . The day is almost upon us when a pack train must wind its way up a graveled highway and turn out its bell mare in the pasture of a summer hotel. When that day comes the pack train will be dead, the diamond hitch will be merely a rope and Kit Carson and Jim Bridger will be names in a history lesson.[7]

Within the next few years the fate of the wilderness must be decided. This is a problem to be settled by deliberate rationality and not by personal prejudice. Fundamentally, the question is one of balancing the total happiness which will be obtainable if the few undesecrated areas are perpetuated against that which will prevail if they are destroyed. For this purpose it will be necessary: first, to consider the extraordinary benefits of the wilderness; second, to enumerate the drawbacks to undeveloped areas; third, to evaluate the relative importance of these conflicting factors, and finally, to formulate a plan of action.

II

The benefits which accrue from the wilderness may be separated into three broad divisions: the physical, the mental and the esthetic.

Most obvious in the first category is the contribution which the wilderness makes to health. This involves something more than pure air and quiet, which are also attainable in almost any rural situation. But toting a fifty-pound pack over an abominable trail, snowshoeing across a blizzard-swept plateau or scaling some jagged pinnacle which juts far above timber all develop a body distinguished by a soundness, stamina and élan unknown amid normal surroundings.

More than mere heartiness is the character of physical independence which can be nurtured only away from the coddling of civilization. In a true wilderness if a person is not qualified to satisfy all the requirements of existence, then he is bound to perish. As long as we prize individuality and competence it is imperative to provide the opportunity for complete self-sufficiency. This is inconceivable under the effete superstructure of urbanity; it demands the harsh environment of untrammeled expanses.

Closely allied is the longing for physical exploration which bursts through all the chains with which society fetters it. Thus we find Lindbergh, Amundsen, Byrd gaily daring the unknown, partly to increase knowledge but largely to satisfy the craving for adventure. Adventure, whether physical or mental, implies breaking into unpenetrated ground, venturing beyond the boundary of normal aptitude, extending oneself to the limit of capacity, courageously facing peril. Life without the chance for such exertions would be for many persons a dreary game, scarcely bearable in its horrible banality.

It is true that certain people of great erudition "come inevitably to feel that if life has any value at all, then that value comes in thought,"[8] and so they regard mere physical pleasures as puerile inconsequences. But there are others, perfectly capable of comprehending relativity and the quantum theory, who find equal ecstasy in non-intellectual adventure. It is entirely irrelevant which viewpoint is correct; each is applicable to whoever entertains it. The important consideration is that both groups are entitled to indulge their penchant, and in the second instance this is scarcely possible without the freedom of wilderness.

III

One of the greatest advantages of the wilderness is its incentive to independent cogitation. This is partly a reflection of physical stimulation, but more inherently due to the fact that original ideas require an objectivity and perspective seldom possible in the distracting propinquity of one's fellow men. It is necessary to "have gone behind the world of humanity, seen its institutions like toadstools by the wayside."[9] This theorizing is justified empirically by the number of America's most virile minds, including Thomas Jefferson, Henry Thoreau, Louis Agassiz, Herman Melville, Mark Twain, John Muir and William James, who have felt the compulsion of periodical retirements into the solitudes. Withdrawn from the contaminating notions of their neighbors, these thinkers have been able to meditate, unprejudiced by the immuring civilization.

Another mental value of an opposite sort is concerned not with incitement but with repose. In a civilization which requires most lives to be passed amid inordinate dissonance, pressure and intrusion, the chance of retiring now and then to the quietude and privacy of sylvan haunts becomes for some people a psychic necessity. It is only the possibility of convalescing in the wilderness which saves them from being destroyed by the terrible neutral tension of modern existence.

There is also a psychological bearing of the wilderness which affects, in contrast to the minority who find it indispensable for relaxation, the whole of human kind. One of the most profound discoveries of psychology has been the demonstration of the terrific harm caused by suppressed desires. To most of mankind a very powerful desire is the appetite for adventure. But in an age of machinery only the extremely fortunate have any occasion to satiate this hankering, except vicariously. As a result people become so choked by monotony of their lives that they are readily amenable to the suggestion of any lurid diversion. Especially in battle, they imagine, will be found the glorious romance of futile dreams. And so they endorse war with enthusiasm and march away to stirring music, only to find their adventure a chimera and the whole world miserable. It is all tragically ridiculous, and yet there is a passion there which cannot be dismissed with a contemptuous reference to childish quixotism. William James has said that "militarism is the great preserver of ideals of hardihood, and human life with no use for hardihood would be contemptible."[10] The problem, as he points out, is to find a "moral equivalent of war," a peaceful stimulation for the hardihood and competence instigated in bloodshed. This equivalent may be realized if we make available to everyone the harmless excitement of the wilderness. Bertrand Russell has skillfully amplified this idea in his essay on "Machines and the Emotions." He expresses the significant conclusion that "many men would cease to desire war if they had opportunities to risk their lives in Alpine climbing."[11]

IV

In examining the esthetic importance of the wilderness I will not engage in the unprofitable task of evaluating the preciousness of different sorts of beauty, as, for instance, whether an acronical view over the Grand Canyon is worth more than the Apollo of Praxiteles.[12] For such a rating would always have to be based on a subjective standard, whereas the essential for any measure is impersonality. Instead of such useless metaphysics I shall call attention to several respects in which the undisputed beauty of the primeval, whatever its relative merit, is distinctly unique.

Of the myriad manifestations of beauty, only natural phenomena like the wilderness are detached from all temporal relationship. All the beauties in the creation or alteration of which man has played even the slightest role are firmly anchored in the historic stream. They are temples of Egypt, oratory of Rome, painting of the Renaissance or music of the Classicists. But in the wild places nothing is moored more closely than to geologic ages. The silent wanderer crawling up the rocky shore of the turbulent river could be a savage from some prehistoric epoch or a fugitive from twentieth-century mechanization.

The sheer stupendousness of the wilderness gives it a quality of intangibility which is unknown in ordinary manifestations of ocular beauty. These are always very definite two- or three-dimensional objects which can be physically grasped and circumscribed in a few moments. But "the beauty that shimmers in the yellow afternoons of October, who ever could clutch it."[13] Anyone who has looked across a ghostly valley at midnight, when moonlight makes a formless silver unity out of the drifting fog, knows how impossible it often is in nature to distinguish mass from hallucination. Anyone who has stood upon a lofty summit and gazed over an inchoate tangle of deep canyons and cragged mountains, of sunlit lakelets and black expanses of forest, has become aware of a certain giddy sensation that there are no distances, no measures, simply unrelated matter rising and falling without any analogy to the banal geometry of breadth, thickness and height. A fourth dimension of immensity is added which makes the location of some dim elevation outlined against the sunset as incommensurable to the figures of the topographer as life itself is to the quantitative table of elements which the analytic chemist proclaims to constitute vitality.

Because of its size the wilderness also has a physical ambiency about it which most forms of beauty lack. One looks from outside at works of art and architecture, listens from outside to music or poetry. But when one looks at and listens to wilderness he is encompassed by his experience of beauty, lives in the midst of his esthetic universe.

A fourth peculiarity about the wilderness is that it exhibits a dynamic beauty. A Beethoven symphony or a Shakespearean drama, landscape by Corot [14] or a Gothic cathedral, once they are finished become virtually static. But the wilderness is in constant flux. A seed germinates, and a stunted seedling battles for decades against the dense shade of the virgin forest. Then some ancient tree blows down and the long-suppressed plant suddenly enters into the full vigor of delayed youth, grows rapidly from sapling to maturity, declines into the conky senility of many centuries, dropping millions of seeds to start a new forest upon the rotting debris of its own ancestors, and eventually topples over to admit the sunlight which ripens another woodland generation.

Another singular aspect of the wilderness is that it gratifies every one of the senses. There is unanimity in venerating the sights and sounds of the forest. But what are generally esteemed to be the minor senses should not be slighted. No one who has ever strolled in springtime through seas of blooming violets, or lain at night on boughs of fresh balsam, or walked across dank holms in early morning can omit odor from the joys of the primordial environment. No one who has felt the stiff wind of mountaintops or the softness of untrodden sphagnum will forget the exhilaration experienced through touch. "Nothing ever tastes as good as when it's cooked in the woods" is a tribute to another sense. Even equilibrium causes a blithe exultation during many a river crossing on tenuous foot log and many a perilous conquest of precipice.

Finally, it is well to reflect that the wilderness furnishes perhaps the best opportunity for pure esthetic enjoyment. This requires that beauty be observed as a unity and that for the brief duration of any pure esthetic experience the cognition of the observed object must completely fill the observer's cosmos. There can be no extraneous thoughts—no question about the creator of the phenomenon, its structure, what it resembles or what vanity in the beholder it gratifies. "The purely esthetic observer has for the moment forgotten his own soul";[15] he has only one sensation left, and that is exquisiteness. In the wilderness, with its entire freedom from the manifestations of human will, that perfect objectivity which is essential for pure esthetic rapture can probably be achieved more readily than among any other forms of beauty.

V

But the problem is not all one-sided. Having discussed the tremendous benefits of the wilderness, it is now proper to ponder upon the disadvantages which uninhabited territory entails.

In the first place, there is the immoderate danger that a wilderness without developments for fire protection will sooner or later go up in smoke and down in ashes.

A second drawback is concerned with the direct economic loss. By locking up wilderness areas we as much as remove from the earth all the lumber, minerals, range land, water-power and agricultural possibilities which they contain. In the face of the tremendous demand for these resources it seems unpardonable to many to render nugatory this potential mineral wealth.

A third difficulty inherent in undeveloped districts is that they automatically preclude the bulk of the population from enjoying them. For it is admitted that at present only a minority of the genus *Homo* cares for wilderness recreation, and only a fraction of this minority possesses the requisite virility for the indulgence of this desire. Far more people can enjoy the woods by automobile. Far more would prefer to spend their vacations in luxurious summer hotels set on well-groomed lawns than in leaky, fly-infested shelters bundled away in the brush. Why then should this majority have to give up its rights?

VI

As a result of these last considerations the irreplaceable values of the wilderness are generally ignored and a fatalistic attitude is adopted in regard to the ultimate disappearance of all unmolested localities. It is my contention that this outlook is entirely unjustified and that almost all the disadvantages of the wilderness can be minimized by forethought and some compromise.

The problem of protection dictates the elimination of undeveloped areas of great fire hazard. Furthermore, certain infringements on the concept of an unsullied wilderness will be unavoidable in almost all instances. Trails, telephone lines and lookout cabins will have to be constructed, for without such precaution most forests in the west would be gutted. But even with these improvements the basic primitive quality still exists: dependence on personal effort for survival.

Economic loss could be greatly reduced by reserving inaccessible and unproductive terrain. Inasmuch as most of the highly valuable lands have already been exploited, it should be easy to confine a great share of the wilderness tracts to those lofty mountain regions where the possibility of material profit is unimportant. Under these circumstances it seems like the grossest illogicality for anyone to object to the withdrawal of a few million acres of low-grade timber for recreational purposes when one hundred million acres of potential forest lie devastated.[16] If one-tenth portion of this denuded land were put to its maximum productivity, it could grow more wood than all the proposed areas put together. Or if our forests, instead of attaining only twenty-two percent of their possible production,[17] were made to yield up to capacity, we could refrain from using three-quarters of the timber in the country and still be better off than we are today. The way to meet our commercial demands is not to thwart legitimate divertissement but to eliminate the unmitigated evils of fire and destructive logging. It is time we appreciated that the real economic problem is to see how little land need be employed for timber production, so that the remainder of the forest may be devoted to those other vital uses incompatible with industrial exploitation.

Even if there should be an underproduction of timber, it is well to recall that it is much cheaper to import lumber for industry than to export people for pastime. The freight rate from Siberia is not nearly as high as the passenger rate to Switzerland.

What small financial loss ultimately results from the establishment of wilderness areas must be accepted as a fair price to pay for their unassessable preciousness. We spend about twenty-one billion dollars a year for entertainment of all sorts.[18] Compared with this there is no significance to the forfeiture of a couple of million dollars of annual income, which is all that our maximum wilderness requirements would involve. Think what an enormously greater sum New York City alone sacrifices in the maintenance of Central Park.

But the automobilists argue that a wilderness domain precludes the huge majority of recreation-seekers from deriving any amusement what-ever from it. This is almost as irrational as contending that because more people enjoy bathing than art exhibits therefore we should change our picture galleries into swimming pools. It is undeniable that the automo-bilist has more roads than he can cover in a lifetime. There are upward of 3,000,000[19] miles of public highways in the United States, traversing many of the finest scenic features in the nation. Nor would the votaries of wilderness object to the construction of as many more miles in the vicinity of the old roads, where they would not be molesting the few remaining vestiges of the primeval. But when the motorists also demand for their particular diversion the insignificant wilderness residue, it makes even a Midas appear philanthropic.

> Such are the differences among human beings in their sources of pleasure, that unless there is a corresponding diversity in their modes of life, they neither obtain their fair share of happiness, nor grow up to the mental, moral and esthetic stature of which their nature is capable. Why then should tolerance extend only to tastes and modes of life which extort acquiescence by the multitude of their adher-ents?[20]

It is of the utmost importance to concede the right of happiness also to people who find their delight in unaccustomed ways. This prerogative is valid even though its exercise may encroach slightly on the fun of the majority, for there is a point where an increase in the joy of the many causes a decrease in the joy of the few out of all proportion to the gain of the former. This has been fully recognized not only by such philoso-phers of democracy as Paine, Jefferson and Mill, but also in the practical administration of governments which spend prodigious sums of money to satisfy the expensive wants of only a fragment of the community. Public funds which could bring small additional happiness to the mobil-ity are diverted to support museums, art galleries, concerts, botanical gar-dens, menageries and golf links. While these, like wilderness areas, are open to the use of everyone, they are vital to only a fraction of the entire population. Nevertheless, they are almost universally approved, and the appropriations to maintain them are growing phenomenally.

VII

These steps of reasoning lead up to the conclusion that the preservation of a few samples of undeveloped territory is one of the most clamant issues before us today. Just a few years more of hesitation and the only trace of that wilderness which has exerted such a fundamental influence in molding American character will lie in the musty pages of pioneer books and the mumbled memories of tottering antiquarians. To avoid this catastrophe demands immediate action.

A step in the right direction has already been initiated by the National Conference on Outdoor Recreation,[21] which has proposed twenty-one possible wilderness areas. Several of these have already been set aside in a tentative way by the Forest Service; others are undergoing more careful scrutiny. But this only represents the incipiency of what ought to be done.

A thorough study should forthwith be undertaken to determine the probable wilderness needs of the country. Of course, no precise reckoning could be attempted, but a radical calculation would be feasible. It ought to be radical for three reasons: because it is easy to convert a natural area to industrial or motor usage, impossible to do the reverse; because the population which covets wilderness recreation is rapidly enlarging, and because the higher standard of living which may be anticipated should give millions the economic power to gratify what today is merely a pathetic yearning. Once the estimate is formulated, immediate steps should be taken to establish enough tracts to insure everyone who hungers for it a generous opportunity of enjoying wilderness isolation.

To carry out this program it is exigent that all friends of the wilderness ideal should unite. If they do not present the urgency of their viewpoint the other side will certainly capture popular support. Then it will only be a few years until the last escape from society will be barricaded. If that day arrives there will be countless souls born to live in strangulation, countless human beings who will be crushed under the artificial edifice raised by man. There is just one hope of repulsing the tyrannical ambition of civilization to conquer every niche on the whole earth. That hope is the organization of spirited people who will fight for the freedom of the wilderness.

NOTES

Unless otherwise noted, the following footnotes were included with the original article.

1   **Editor's note:** Samuel Johnson published his *Dictionary of the English Language* in 1755.

2   *Webster's New International Dictionary*.

3   Willa Cather, "Death Comes for the Archbishop."

4   Frederic L. Paxson, "History of the American Frontier."

5   Reuben G. Thwaites, "Original Journals of the Lewis and Clark Expedition, 1804-1806," June 13, 1805.

6   **Editor's note:** In "Largest Roadless Areas of United States," published six years later, Marshall cataloged eleven forested wilderness areas and eighteen deserts greater than a million acres. See p. 199.

7   Aldo Leopold, "The Last Stand of the Wilderness," *American Forests and Forest Life*, October 1925.

8   Joseph Wood Krutch, "The Modern Temper."

9   Henry David Thoreau, "Journals," April 2, 1852.

10   William James, "The Moral Equivalent of War."

11   Bertrand Russell, "Essays in Scepticism."

12   **Editor's note:** Sculptor in classical Athens (Oxford Classical Dictionary, 3d edition, 1996).

13   Ralph Waldo Emerson, "Nature."

14   **Editor's note:** Camille Corot (1796-1875) was a French painter (Enyclopaedia Britannica, 15th ed.).

15   Irwin Edman, "The World, the Arts and the Artist."

16   George P. Ahern, "Deforested America," Washington, D.C.

17   U.S. Department of Agriculture, "Timber, Mine or Crop?"

18   Stuart Chase, "Whither Mankind?"

19   "The World Almanac," 1929.

20   John Stuart Mill, "On Liberty."

21   National Conference on Outdoor Recreation, "Recreation Resources of Federal Lands," Washington, D.C.

Untrammeled

In describing his visit to Nicks Pond in 1922, Bob Marshall imagines himself transported back to the "untrammeled country" of the early trappers. He uses the same curious adjective—"untrammeled"—in later writings, most notably in his essay "The Problem of Wilderness," to describe pristine lands. In 1964, long after Marshall's death, the word cropped up again in the oft-quoted line of the Wilderness Act that defines wilderness as "an area where the earth and its community of life are untrammeled by man." Howard Zahniser, who labored over the act for years, often revising drafts at his cabin in the Adirondacks, chose "untrammeled" after much deliberation and stuck with it over the objections of colleagues who considered the term vague or obscure. It often is misunderstood as a synonym for "untrampled," but its true meaning is "unimpeded" or "unrestrained." (A trammel is a net used to catch birds or fish.) As Zahniser explained, the idea he had in mind is that wilderness

Courtesy of Association for the Protection of the Adirondacks

Howard Zahniser at Hanging Spear Falls in the High Peaks Wilderness.

areas should not be "subjected to human controls and manipulations that hamper the free play of natural forces." Zahniser was familiar with Marshall's writings, but he got the inspiration for "untrammeled" from another source. The Wilderness Society, which Marshall helped found, notes on its Web site: "While drafting the Wilderness Act, Zahniser felt compelled to go beyond the constraints of formal bureaucratic language. He particularly struggled to find the best word to accurately describe wilderness lands. Not just any word would do for a connoisseur of both literature and nature. One day when a friend remarked to him that she enjoyed the 'untrammeled' Olympic National Park seashore, he knew his search was over. Although the Wilderness Act went through numerous revisions, the word 'untrammeled' was retained in all 66 versions, including the last."

For more on Zahniser's choice of words, see Douglas W. Scott's article "'Untrammeled,' 'Wilderness Character,' and the Challenges of Wilderness Preservation," *Wild Earth Journal*, Fall/Winter 2001-2002, pp. 72-78.

Part Four

PORTRAIT
ARTIST

*"Herb has been not only the greatest teacher
that I have ever had but also the most kindly and
considerate friend a person could even dream about, "*

– **Bob Marshall,** on HERB CLARK

Bob and Herb on a backpacking trip.

Herbert Clark

Bob and George Marshall were robust teenagers when they started climbing the High Peaks in 1918, yet they had trouble keeping up with their 48-year-old guide, Herb Clark. In this good-humored profile–written for High Spots *in 1933– Marshall describes Clark as "the fastest man I have ever known in the pathless woods." This assessment came after Marshall had hiked with numerous companions all over the West and in Alaska. When the Marshalls and Clark climbed Iroquois Peak for the first time, the boys dubbed it Herbert Peak. Only later did they discover that the mountain already had a name (see Philip G. Terrie's article, p. 285). Although today there is no peak named for Clark, there is a Herbert Brook on Mount Marshall. Appropriately, it leads hikers to the summit.*

Herbert Clark was born near Keeseville, New York, on July 10, 1870, in the days when life was mysterious, wild and harsh.

Herb's grandmother, while driving the produce of her farm to market one night, suddenly found her horses stopping in horrible fright, while close at hand she heard chains rattling. Being a very pious woman, she said her prayers and got out to look at what had happened. She found the horses in a lather and all the tugs in the harness loose and concluded that the devil must have been after her. A few weeks later she got news that her mother had died. Similarly, Herb's father was walking home from the forge at Clintonville one night when he saw an empty ore car whiz past him down the center of the road at a terrific speed as if the devil were in it. A few days later he too got news of his mother's death. When Herb was two years old his parents bought a farm along the road from Clintonville to Augur Pond. The people from whom they bought it had been very poor for many years but suddenly became exceedingly rich. At the same time the peddler who customarily visited the neighborhood disappeared. Whatever the relationship between these events, the fact remains that throughout Herb's childhood the kettle on the stove would commence to rattle all at once, people would be heard talking upstairs when the whole family was in the kitchen, and one night Herb woke up to find a woman dressed in white standing by his bed.

Of wilderness there was also plenty in those days. Augur Pond lay just outside the true Adirondack wilderness, but it was in sight of the high mountains and still had in its vicinity many large blocks of unmarred timber. Such roads as existed were full of holes, and a journey by buggy of forty miles was considered a big day. Wild animals were common. From their house the Clarks often heard panthers screaming. One night when Herb was about twelve, while he was walking home from Clintonville, he had to pass through a dark piece of woods. Suddenly he heard an animal following him. As soon as Herb emerged into the fields beyond the forest he broke into a run. As he approached the house his mother heard him coming and opened the door. The light flooded into the darkness outside, and simultaneously a panther emitted a most terrible screech. "My scalp was sore for three days after that," says Herb after half a century. "I guess that's when my hair started to turn gray."

Herb was born just before the great depression of 1873. His father, who had served three years with the army of the Potomac, commenced to get an $8.00-a-month pension in 1880, but from 1873 until 1880 the family was very much pinched for finances. There were eleven children, nine of whom survived infancy, and their support put a terrific strain on the diminutive income which the family got from the sale of its produce and from the odd jobs which the father and the older boys could pick up. Once the whole family went two or three days without anything to eat until someone gave them some potatoes. They had salt in the house, and that with the potatoes tasted to Herb the best of any meal he has ever eaten.

In spite of the austerity which this background may suggest, Herb from his childhood was a jocular and dashing young blade. His fondness for poking the keenest sort of satire at hypocrisy and sham, for twisting up blusterers in their own boastful stories, was something which friends who knew Herb in his youth tell me he possessed while he was in the early teens. He apparently was a very handsome young man in those days and a great favorite with the girls, whom he rushed by the wholesale.

In spite of his lightheartedness and his fondness for gay times, Herb was also a terribly hard worker, and he had a tremendous sense of loyalty to his family. He contributed materially to its income from the time he was twelve. For about five years he worked on the farm and in such odd jobs as he could pick up around Clintonville. In those days they paid fifty cents for a twelve-hour day at loading pulpwood. "They gave you a drink of water and that was all in the line of food."

Herb's first job away from home came in the summer of 1887 when he went up to Hank Allen's farm at North Elba to cut hay. After his father died in 1889 Herb went away to work every summer but returned to his mother in the winters. Most of his jobs required twelve hours' work in the day, but he was always fresh enough to spend a good half of the night in jollity. His wanderings took him to Miller's old hotel on Lower Saranac, to Vermont, to New Hampshire and to Saranac Village. In 1896 he commenced ten years of work at the old Club House at Bartlett's Carry between Upper Saranac and Round Lake.[1] After his first winter there his mother died, and thereafter he made his home around the Saranacs.

He acted as night watchman at Bartlett's for two years, then for five summers rowed the freight boat twenty-four miles [round trip] between Bartlett's and Ampersand[2] in the morning and guided in the afternoon and finally for three years devoted himself exclusively to guiding. The freight boat was a huge Adirondack guideboat, nearly twice the length of the normal crafts of that design, and Herb sometimes rowed as high as 2,200 pounds in one load. While at Bartlett's he made the record of having rowed about sixty-five miles in one day, twenty-four of them with this freight boat.

Perhaps it was such training which enabled Herb in those days to become undisputed champion among the rowers on the Saranac waters. In 1908 they held an all-Adirondack rowing race on Lower Saranac. This was won by a Blanchard of Long Lake, but Herb, although then thirty-eight years old, came in a close second, only a half a boat length behind in a field of eight or ten of the best rowers in the entire Adirondacks. The next year, with Blanchard out, everybody expected Herb to be champion, but the race was canceled. Herb continued as leading oarsman of the Saranacs through 1919, after which he retired from competition, as he always said he would do when he became fifty.

In the spring of 1906 Ed Cagle, who had guided for our family at Lower Saranac for six years, decided to open a livery stable, and by an almost impossible combination of circumstances it just chanced that Herb came to work for my father. At this time my brothers, sister and I were all under ten years of age. I cannot speak authoritatively of what Herb meant to the others, although I have strong suspicions. I do know positively that to me Herb has been not only the greatest teacher that I have ever had but also the most kindly and considerate friend a person could even dream about, a constantly refreshing and stimulating companion with whom to discuss both passing events and the more permanent philosophical relationships and, to top it all, the happy possessor of the keenest of humor I have known.

I remember one night as children we were camping on an island in Round Lake. A couple of greenhorns from Schenectady were also on the island, and discerning in Herb an old-time guide, they asked him if there were any dangerous wild animals left in the Adirondacks. With a perfect seriousness, Herb regaled them for two hours on panthers, on wild boars, on rugarues[3] and on horrible snakes of many species. They became so frightened that they were going to leave right away, until Herb kindly assured them that none of these animals could swim, and so they retired in their tent on this oasis in a wilderness of bristling fury.

For my brothers and myself Herb would make up the most amazing fables. A rock on Lower Saranac with a peculiar dent was where Captain Kidd had bumped his head. The Ausable River below the present Olympic ski jump was where the *Monitor* and the *Merrimac* had fought their famous battle, and an old lady who came limping along as he told this tale was used as circumstantial evidence, for her shinbone had been taken off by a stray shell at the time of this great conflict. There were those great heroes of a reverse Paul Bunyan, who did everything inconceivably poorer than you would imagine it could be done: Jacob Whistletricker, a man with many marvelous drugs; Joe McGinnis, who got the fantod, a disease in which one shrinks to the size of a baseball; Susie Soothingsyrup, a gay young lass of many virtues, and of course the grandfather pickerel, which we would someday catch, with gold teeth and spectacles.

Herb is full of songs. Almost every year he adds to his repertoire, which consists either of garbled versions of ancient popular ditties, fitted to suit his needs, or of jingles which he makes up expressly for the occasion. I recall once, while we were battling our way through the clumps of mountain balsam on Colden, hearing Herb's cheerful voice from above us booming out:

> "Say, old man, will you give me a chew?"
> "No, sir," says he, "I'll be damned if I do."
> "If you'd saved up your money, been as
>   cunning as fox
> You'd always have tobacco in your old
>   tobacco box."

In 1903 Herb married Mary Dowdell, a waitress at the Club House, and they are still happily wedded. They have had six children who have gone through high school; they have a splendid house, a large and excellent garden, and a garage for the cars of two of Herb's sons. But it has required very hard work to get these things. I remember that Herb would often row the two miles to his home when the day's work at our place was over, labor in his garden until dark and then get up before daylight to work until about six in the morning. When there was no work to be done in his garden he would be out early, catching small frogs for which bass fishermen used to pay sixty cents a dozen. Even at sixty-three he is unable to loaf and always finds something for his spare moments, if it is only rubbing an extra coat of oil into a pair of shoes or putting an especially fine edge on an axe.

One of Herb's greatest joys is fishing. "I was born fishing, I guess," he says. "At least as early as I can remember I used to like to go off to Augur Pond and fish." It seems to make no difference to him what the fish is, for he sets out with equal enthusiasm after pickerel, bass, brook trout, whitefish or lake trout, and with all his success is abnormal. For a number of years his eighteen-and-a-half-pound pickerel held the record for the Saranac waters. As a hunter Herb was even more enthusiastic, though less successful.

Although Herb's greatest fame has come as a mountain climber, strangely enough he had never scaled a peak in the four-thousand-foot class until he, George Marshall, Carl Poser and I ascended Whiteface in 1918. Thereafter, for the next six years, Herb, George and I found

Herb Clark was the inspiration for this poem, written by Lenore Marshall, Bob's sister-in-law. It appeared in No Boundary *(1943, Henry Holt), a collection of her verse.*

The Old Guide Spoke

The old guide spoke; our voices had been mute,
Awed by the vast futility of words.
The mountains rose above us resolute,
Streaked swiftly by the dip and lift of birds;
And subtly, irretrievably, the night
Poured darkness on the water at our feet,
Until we lost the final link of light,
Heard nothing but the lap and the retreat.

We drank the hush, we kept our silence well,
Dreading some tortuous sentence that might fall,
Yet longed to be articulate and tell;
Until in answer to our inarticulate call
The old guide spoke; he did not break the spell:
"To think that we must die and leave it all."

Adirondack mountain climbing our greatest joy in life. We spent from twenty to thirty days during each of these summers on the woodland trails and in the later years even more delightfully where there was no sign of pathway.

When we first commenced our climbing there were few signboards and no trail markers at all. Neither was there the present heavy travel which really makes markers superfluous. It took some skill in those days to find your way about, particularly with the numerous fresh lumber roads which forked off from the similar lumber roads which constituted many of the trails. It was often quite a problem to decide which fork would bring you to your destination and which might end at some loading deck in a jungle of second growth. In solving these problems we all took a part, but Herb's interpretations showed the greatest frequency of correctness.

In our later adventures on trailless peaks, and back in 1921 only twelve of the forty-six high peaks had trails to their summits, Herb was really a marvel. At the age of fifty-one he was the fastest man I have ever known in the pathless woods. Furthermore, he could take one glance at a mountain from some distant point, then not be able to see anything two hundred feet from where he was walking for several hours and emerge on the summit by what would almost always be the fastest and easiest route. Just as examples, I recall how perfectly he hit the dike which leads to the top of Calamity, traveling from Adams; how he found just the right slide which cut off a long battle with aspen and cherry thickets on Cascade; how he led the way straight to the top of Panther Peak, which we didn't see for nearly five hours after we left the dam on Cold River.

I spent the early part of this summer at our home on Lower Saranac, living alone with Herb. Every morning he would wake me up with some different song or quotation. On July 10th he came in shouting: "Sixty-three years ago this morning there was wild rejoicing in the Clark household. Let's celebrate by taking that trip into the Wallface Ponds." So it was arranged that to celebrate Herb's sixty-third birthday we would take the jaunt which he had been urging on me for several weeks.

We started from Adirondack Lodge and followed the Indian Pass trail for eight miles, past the stupendous grandeur of the rock mass of Wallface. We left the trail to follow up the Wallface Pond outlet, a turbulent brook which tumbles over great boulders and smooth granite slides to meet the stream from Indian Pass. About halfway up to the pond there were bad beaver slashings and beyond a steep climb over the slippery rocks of the creek bed. Soon, however, we stood at the outlet of Lower Wallface, which we had not seen for eight years, and though it had been seriously marred by beavers, its remoteness from the paths of men was a cause of genuine exultation.[4] Around the Wallface Ponds we delighted in the shady freshness of one of the most beautiful virgin spruce forests on the continent. Leaving the Upper Pond we dropped steeply through another splendid stand of virgin spruce to that glorious series of cascades which is known as Roaring Brook. This seldom-visited stream cut its way through canyons, tumbled over waterfalls, brushed by thickets of lush, green herbage and reflected the primeval forest of spruce and birch and hemlock. We followed along in silence and elation until we came to where the creek took a sharp bend to the left. Then we realized that we must cut across a narrow range of hills which separated us from the Moose Pond trail.[5] Once this was reached, when the spell of the primeval was lost, Herb suddenly became his most jocular self. He invented gay songs to tease me and reminisced pleasantly on the days before the trails were so heavily marked, traveled and covered with orange peels. On the last lap into Averyville, Herb set a jaunty four-mile-an-hour pace, and when we emerged on the meadows after twenty-five miles, ten of them without a trail, he was virtually as fresh as when he had started.

This makes as appropriate an ending as I can conceive for the autobiography of this clear-headed, strenuous, exultant climber of mountains, this kindly, humorous, sensitive lover of the wilderness, Herb Clark.

NOTES

1   Round Lake was another name for Middle Saranac Lake.

2   Ampersand Bay is at the eastern end of Lower Saranac Lake, on the edge of Saranac Lake village.

3   An imaginary monster (*Dictionary of American Regional English*, Vol. 4, 2002).

4   Today there is a state-maintained trail to Wallface Ponds.

5   Moose Pond lies along the Northville-Placid Trail.

Mills Blake,
Adirondack Explorer

As a boy, Marshall developed a passion for wilderness adventure by reading about the exploits of Verplanck Colvin, the nineteenth-century Adirondack surveyor. Colvin died in 1920, but his right-hand man, Mills Blake, was still alive when Marshall wrote this encomium about nine years later. The article, which quotes liberally from Colvin's official reports, was not published until 1951 (in Ad-i-ron-dac*), long after both its author and subject had passed away.*

In the autumn of 1873 four explorers were encamped in the remote and seldom visited wilderness of the western Adirondacks. Its best-known portion was Bog River, up the uncharted channel of which only a handful of hardy adventurers had ever forced their boats. These wanderers described the mysterious stream and especially bleak Mud Lake at the head of navigation as one would have written of the jungles of central Africa. Off this waterway, scarcely anyone had penetrated, and the multitude of ponds hidden in the surrounding forest were mostly nameless and unknown to man. Even the Indians had never roamed to their shores. The deer came down from the hills in the evening to drink, the loons dove and cried shrilly at dusk, and the hawks soared against the western afterglow just as they had done for uncounted centuries.

Today that wilderness is gone. The Adirondack Division of the New York Central crosses the waters of Bog River. The shores of Mud Lake, which half a century ago had echoed to nothing more civilized than the gun of the intrepid moose hunter, now echo six times daily to the whis-

Courtesy of Association for the Protection of the Adirondacks

Mills Blake, at far right, on Roaring Brook in the western High Peaks.

tle of the rumbling passenger trains. The obscure ponds of the seventies are all mapped and designated, trails lead down to their shores, and the shadowy primeval forest in which they were hidden has vanished in smoke and ashes.

The explorers have disappeared with the forests which they first penetrated–all except one man, Mills Blake. He remains as a living reminder of the time when the Adirondacks were a far darker retreat than any place in present-day United States.

Mills Blake was born in Albany, New York, in 1848. When he was twelve years old both of his parents died, and he went to live with a guardian in Nassau, New York.[1] Here he met young Verplanck Colvin in 1863, and a friendship which lasted fifty-seven years had its inception. The two boys spent much time tramping over the Rensselaer hills, and probably this had an important effect in establishing that extreme love for the woods which became the motivating influence in both of their lives.

Blake studied for three terms at Nassau Academy. In 1864 he moved back to Albany, where he worked in the law office of Verplanck's father for eight sempiternal years. The indoor occupation proved exceedingly distasteful, and furthermore his health commenced to break under the confinement. With a thoroughly miserable life in store, fate suddenly entered and, just as in the most dramatic of Mrs. Southworth's contemporary novels,[2] with one dexterous snap reversed everything.

Fate in this case took the form of the peripatetic Verplanck Colvin. His family's fortune was sufficiently large that he did not have to worry about work, and so from the close of the Civil War he had been making sporadic trips of exploration into the unfrequented Adirondacks. He had gone into the woods purely for pleasure, but finding them poorly mapped he determined to locate accurately the major geographical features. For several years he received no official support, but in 1872 the New York Legislature appropriated a small sum of money to commence a state survey. This had for its primary objectives a map of the Adirondacks conforming to actual topography and the relocation of the early survey lines which fifty to one hundred years had almost obliterated. Colvin immediately offered a position to his unhappy friend, and together for twenty-eight years they blazed, measured and mapped the Adirondacks. No Aeneas ever had a more faithful Achates, no Lee a more dependable Stonewall Jackson, than this quiet Mills Blake, assistant and chief of the Division of Levels.

In the latter part of July 1872 the survey got under way in the vicinity of Lake Pleasant. After a few preliminary sketch maps and barometric measurements, Colvin, Blake and two guides, Ed Sturgis and Banage LaPage, moved north through the wilderness to Lake Lewey. From here they ascended 2,300 feet, which the best existing maps showed to be level ground, and made the first altitudinal measurement of Snowy Mountain.[3]

West of Snowy was a region entirely unmapped. Only a few illiterate trappers had encroached upon it. It was reputed to contain the semi-mythical Cedar Lakes, but no one could tell within eight hundred miles where their waters flowed into the ocean. The St. Lawrence advocates were in the majority, but a few contended that these lakes were sources of the Hudson. Colvin, Blake, Sturgis and LaPage shouldered back-break-

Verplanck Colvin

Courtesy of the Association for the Protection of the Adirondacks

ing packs and set out upon a journey of unknown duration into this country of unknown topography and dimensions. When they returned to civilization four days later the country was no longer unknown, and the Hudson River minority was vindicated.[4]

The greatest year of the survey from a standpoint of genuine adventure was 1873. August and September found the party engaged in the first systematic reconnaissance of the mountain region. This period was filled with first ascents[5] of virgin peaks, startling discoveries of cloud-capped summits where the maps showed valleys, perilous traverses along the edge of thousand-foot precipices, and the breathtaking night descents. The following random excerpt from the official report retains something of the original flavor of those romantic explorations.

> Asborbed in our work [on Mount Dix] we were startled by sunset to the consciousness that night had already settled in the chasm valleys below. It would be impossible to descend in the dark, amid the cliffs and ledges, where only the footprints of the catamount had guided us by daylight to places which could be scaled; and our camp and camp guard and provisions were miles away. There was no time for discussion and I ordered a descent in the Hunter's Pass, so far down as it would be necessary to find water and a resting place. Water, unfortunately, was not be to readily found, and soon we became entangled amid ledges, slides and cavernous rocks that rendered the previous night descent of the Giant inferior in danger. In the darkness, clinging by roots, aiding each other from ledge to ledge, and guiding with special care the footsteps of those carrying the theodolite,[6] etc., we finally found ourselves slipping on the edge of rocks draped in cold, wet, sphagnous moss, and a little lower we found water! A moment's rest and we descended further only to find that we were in a cul-de-sac ... with walls of air ... turn which way we would, save toward the mountain top; and we reached the verge of an overhanging cliff, so high that even the tree-tops below were not distinguishable. The slender stream lept the edge and was lost in the depths. Here were we compelled to halt, and reclining at the edge of the precipice, passed the night; the feeble fire, by its suggestion of supper only giving edge to our hunger.[7]

On October 15, when reasonable men in that boreal clime were thinking about holing up for the winter, Colvin, Blake, John Solomon and Albert Mackenzie, the two last Saranac Lake guides, had the audacity to set out on a first exploration of the vast and gloomy western plateau. The wilderness of that thousand-square-mile tract, as described above, was almost undefiled as when the last ice sheet receded.

The remainder of October was devoted to reconnoitering the Bog River drainage. With a shifting base along the river, expeditions were projected in every direction. New ponds were mapped at the rate of one a day, and two prominent mountains were climbed from which many angular measurements were taken. The vague and legendary Bog River country became familiar terrain, and perhaps the explorers would soon have considered themselves in civilization had they not unexpectedly run out of food. This forcibly recalled the fact that it was ninety to one hundred miles round trip with difficult portages to the nearest source of supplies. A guide was dispatched to the settlements, and the remaining three buckled down to double hours on half rations. Two days later Colvin wrote: "We had food for reflection, but little else."[8] However, that night the guide returned, and sustenance was once more available.

> November first found Mud Lake still open, though the upper portion was partially frozen over. Embarking we passed up the lake and now reached the end of navigation. Drawing the boats out on the ice margin we turned our backs upon even the remote and desert shores of Mud Lake–lonely, doleful water–and with winter closing in around us, loaded with baggage and drawing our boats with ropes over the yielding snow, we started directly westward into an unknown region of dismal wilderness, with whose dangers or obstacles we were unacquainted; a small sack of flour forming our principal reliance. The desolate snows of the barren marshes–the drear, wintry aspect of everything–gave the scene the appearance of an arctic exploration.[9]

Their objective was Lost Lake, which after a century's oblivion they had rediscovered a few days before. Here they added to their party George Muir, the Adirondacks' most illustrious wolf trapper and panther hunter, whom they encountered at this mystic tarn. In four days they mapped and determined the elevation of eighteen more ponds, sketched the unknown headwaters of the Oswegatchie, and located two or three small mountains.

On November 6th the party started on the most difficult phase of the entire exploration, the forced march from the Oswegatchie headwaters to the Beaver River. After a week of unremitting hardships, struggling through pathless jungles, bridging unfordable streams, breaking through ice-covered lakelets and nearly freezing in the performance of their onerous duties, they had battled their way through the last large, unexplored wilderness of the Adirondacks. It took six more days, plodding through two or three feet of snow, to arrive at the nearest settlement, Long Lake.

To Mills Blake, in the early years of the survey, came dozens of other experiences nearly as thrilling. They are dramatically described in Colvin's *Reports* from 1872 to 1878 and in Russell M.L. Carson's *Peaks and People of the Adirondacks*. Such adventuresome days, however, were of necessity self-destructive, because after a few years the wildest places had all been explored. Thereafter came the less spectacular but probably more important routine of finding and remarking century-old survey lines; moving step by step with level and rod from known to unmeasured elevations; locating for all time by an intricate system of triangulation countless peaks, ponds and streams; traversing shorelines, sketching contours, meandering the devious courses of rivers. It involved wearisome backpacking and breaking through half-frozen lakes and grueling marches in the heat of summer; detouring over precipitous, icy mountains in late autumn; searching on snowshoes for decaying township lines at forty below in midwinter; fighting slush, sleet and blustering winds in early spring for hours which stretched far on both sides of daylight.

Carson tells how Blake spent thirty-nine consecutive days on the summit of Marcy in the autumn of 1883, engaged in measuring angles. This adventure is typical of Blake's indefatigable loyalty, for storms which soaked his entire equipment, freezing weather which made the adjustment of the delicate transit screws an agony, drifts of snow five feet deep, glare ice which rendered even the short descent from the summit to the timberline camp perilous, and the deadly monotony of patiently sighting on distant objects day after day could not cause him to forsake his alpine duty or read one angle hastily and without scientific exactness.

In 1900 the survey was abolished, and after more than a quarter of a century Colvin and Blake ended their Adirondack labors. Their subsequent work was connected with railroad promotion and real estate. Neither ever married. In 1872 they commenced living together in the old Colvin homestead in Albany, which also served as headquarters for the survey, and here they dwelt until Colvin's death in 1920.

The most important result of Colvin and Blake's work was its contribution to the preservation of the Adirondacks from total scenic destruction. The attention which the survey attracted to the entire region showed even the indifferent public the tremendous economic values and irreplaceable beauty which the state was sacrificing to timber thieves and incendiaries. Of lesser significance were the conveniences which the new maps afforded, the opening of the woods to a far wider use than had previously been possible and the elimination of endless litigation which would have been inevitable had the early survey lines disappeared.

NOTES

1   A rural town in Rensselaer County east of Albany.

2   Emma Dorothy Eliza Nevitte Southworth was a popular author in the nineteenth century. She wrote sixty-six novels. (*Encyclopaedia Britannica* CD-ROM, 1999.)

3   This is also the first recorded ascent of Snowy [Marshall's note].

4   The Cedar Lakes drain into the Cedar River, a tributary of the Hudson.

5   Although Colvin made first ascents of seven of the forty-six High Peaks, Blake only made one. Curiously, Blake's first ascent was of Mount Colvin, August 20, 1873. [Marshall's note.]

6   A surveying instrument for measuring horizontal and vertical angles (*Encyclopaedia Britannica* CD-ROM, 1999).

7   New York State, Report of the Topographical Survey of New York for the Year 1873 by Verplanck Colvin, pp. 29-30 [Marshall's note].

8   Colvin Report, 1873, p. 58 [Marshall's note].

9   Colvin Report, 1873, p. 60 [Marshall's note].

Mills Blake, 1881.

Mills Blake

Marshall wrote this short obituary for High Spots *soon after Mills Blake's death in 1930.*

The days of exploration in a geographical sense are so long a thing of the past in the eastern United States that any survivor from that adventuresome period seems almost like an anachronism. Such an anachronism, and a most charming one, was Mills Blake, who died in Albany on March 4th at the age of eighty-two.

The Adirondack career of Mills Blake started nearly sixty years ago. In the summer of 1872 Verplanck Colvin got the Adirondack Survey under way and chose for his right-hand man his boyhood friend, Mills Blake. Together for a quarter of a century the two of them explored, surveyed and mapped the Adirondacks. Mills Blake's task through all these years was never the brilliant or conspicuous one, nor did his shy, retiring nature ever give to him fame which came to the better-known Adirondack heroes such as Colvin himself, Cheney, Sabattis, Dunning and Murray.[1] But for sheer faithful service, for variety of thrilling adventures with the uncertainties of the wilderness, for amount of unmapped territory first explored by him and for thorough knowledge of the entire Adirondacks, few of the more famous Adirondack characters could equal his record.

It is interesting to recall in these days of high-class trails, copious signposts and markers, complete maps and frequent cabins that when Blake first entered the Adirondacks none even knew, for example, which way the country west of Indian Lake drained. There was no record of anyone having ever crossed the wilderness from Bog to Beaver River, and the region of high mountains contained but a single major trail while over half of the high peaks were unscaled.

Yet Mills Blake was so quiet, so untheatrical, so thoroughly abhorrent of sensationalism that to speak with him you would never guess how stirring some of the adventures in such a wild country really were. He would make the account of the winter march from remote Mud Lake to the half-frozen Beaver River seem less perilous than the average present-day camper's account of a summer night in the cabin at Colden. But if you looked at his eyes you would see a very happy twinkle at the recollection of those glorious days which made you feel that here was a man who truly appreciated the unassessable privilege of communion with the unexplored.

NOTES

1   John Cheney, Alvah Dunning and Mitchell Sabattis were nineteenth-century guides. William H.H. Murray's book *Adventures in the Wilderness* (1869) helped popularize the Adirondacks.

An Evening with Professor Einstein

Albert Einstein renounced his German citizenship in 1933, after Adolf Hitler became chancellor, and took a position at the Institute for Advanced Study in Princeton. In the summer of 1936, he brought his wife to Saranac Lake for the sake of her health. (Einstein often went sailing on Lake Flower.) On the evening of August 7, Marshall had dinner with Einstein at Knollwood, the family camp on Lower Saranac Lake, and later jotted down the following notes. Previously unpublished, the typescript is in the Bancroft Library of the University of California at Berkeley.

Billy[1] and I called for Albert Einstein at the house where he was living in Saranac Lake village at five o'clock in the evening. We drove him up to Knollwood. Then we all went out in a rowboat, Professor Einstein doing the paddling and I the rowing, while Billy sat in the center. I took them around among many channels between the islands and up into Pope Bay,[2] and I have seldom seen a person more delighted with the natural scenery than was Professor Einstein. Repeatedly he exclaimed about how different it was in America, where you could still see places which did not indicate the evidences of man.

We came back from the lake about seven o'clock and had an enjoyable supper with Florence and David[3] and then went down to the boathouse to watch the long northern twilight slowly disappear. Thereafter, we drove Einstein back to his cottage, where his wife is critically ill and where he has come especially for her health.

Einstein spends his mornings sailing on Lake Flower.[4] Sailing is his

Albert Einstein with state Senator John J. Dunnigan on Lake Flower.

favorite diversion. He says that he has never gone in for any sort of athletics except sailing. He never dances. He always needs at least eight hours' sleep.

Of course, he has been very much overrun by those who wanted to get a glimpse or a souvenir from the most noted scientist in the world. He has taken it extremely good-naturedly and patiently and tolerantly and with a really fine sense of humor.

Even when sensation lovers have quoted him as telling them certain things which he has never said at all, he does not seem to get irritated but only a little bewildered. The day before an old fiddler from Saranac had quoted Einstein as saying that he had a Stradivarius violin, which as a matter of fact Einstein had not said at all, and this statement had been quoted in all the Eastern papers. Instead of getting furious about this, Einstein merely asked us whether we thought he ought to get out a formal denial, and he seemed perplexed at what could have caused the man to make such a statement. But he talked in a very friendly way about the old fiddler.

Some of his views were especially interesting. He thinks that the subconscious thoughts of the experimenter influence many queer experimental results, such as the Miller variation of the Michelson-

Morley experiment[5] and Carrell's pendulum.

Einstein believes that some day inheritances of acquired characteristics will be demonstrated, but he does not think that any experimenters so far have done so.

He does not consider the Japs original investigators but admires very much the scientists of India.

It seems to him that the United States is more different from all European countries than the difference between most extremely divergent European nations.

He fears that fascism will come to the United States.

Here are a few verbatim statements which he made:

"It's wonderful how many foolish things you must try in order to find one good idea."

"Only when a man is attacked you can tell how modest he is."

"After all, we [scientists] get our bread and butter from society, so we owe it to society to let it know a little of what we are doing." (This was expressed while we were discussing whether scientists should try to popularize their work.)

"If there is anything in which Roosevelt is an expert, it is getting elected."[6]

NOTES

1 Nickname of Jacob Billikopf, who was married to Marshall's sister, Ruth.

2 Bay on the southwest shore of Lower Saranac Lake.

3 Marshall's niece and nephew, the children of Jacob and Ruth Billikopf.

4 In village of Saranac Lake. Named for Roswell Flower, New York's governor 1892-94.

5 In the nineteenth century, scientists believed that space was filled with an invisible ether and that light traveled through the ether in waves. In 1887, the American researchers Albert Abraham Michelson and Edward Williams Morley tried to measure the Earth's velocity relative to the ether. They hypothesized that light beams transmitted in opposite directions would travel at different speeds, depending on whether the light was traveling with or against the ether. Their experiment, however, detected no difference in the velocities of light. Eventually, this led scientists to reject the ether hypothesis and Einstein to propose, in his theory of relativity, that the speed of light is a constant. Dayton Miller was an American scientist who continued to argue for the existence of the ether.

6 At the time, Franklin Delano Roosevelt was nearing the end of his first term as president. He would be elected three more times.

Drawing by Verplanck Colvin from his *Topographical Survey of the Adirondack Wilderness for the Years 1873-74.*

Part Five

NOVELIST

"A man was crazy to go into the Bog River country at that time of year. He'd freeze to death, like as not. But if Mr. Colvin insisted on being a damn fool he'd better take somebody with no sense and young blood. Why not take Jim Allen's kid?"

– *AN ISLAND IN OBLIVION*

An Island in Oblivion

Among Marshall's papers in the Bancroft Library at the University of California at Berkeley is the manuscript of a novel titled An Island in Oblivion. *The narrator, Bart Allen, grew up near Lake Placid in the 1800s. He seems to be an alter ego, for Marshall wished he had been born a generation or two earlier, when the Adirondacks were largely pristine and unexplored. Like Marshall, Bart Allen eventually moved west and then to Alaska. Two excerpts from the Adirondack portion of the novel are reprinted below. In the first, Bart describes climbing Mount Marcy with his sister, Betty; John Ferris Thornton, a summer boarder, and Bill Nye, a guide. In the second, he describes working for Verplanck Colvin's survey crew—which would have been Marshall's dream job.*

On his 1871 visit Mr. Thornton invited Betty and myself to accompany him and Bill[1] on their expedition to Marcy that year. They were going out by way of Indian Pass and the abandoned Adirondack Iron Works. Of course we were thrilled. It was the adventure of a lifetime. During the two days before starting we thought nothing but the trip, and mundane matters like milking and cutting the hay were done while our minds roved the clouds.

We set out on a Monday morning carrying packs which ranged from Bill Nye's sixty pounds to Betty's twenty-five, she of course wanting to carry more. I thought there could never have been such verdure anywhere as we passed through after the trail left the cuttings which the North Elba folk had made. With many twists and turns our path brought us steadily closer to where the precipice of Wallface jutted straight up out of Indian Pass. The Ausable, which I had so long

Verplanck Colvin captioned this drawing: "Oven Lake. Accident to the second boat–The guides' baggage and instruments in danger."

dreamed of following to its source, kept getting smaller hour by hour and finally when the dusk of evening commenced to settle, it was nothing but a trickle of water. Here we camped in a crude shelter made of spruce boughs, with the cliffs of Wallface almost overhanging us.

That night around the campfire Bill and Mr. Thornton told stories appropriate to our primitive home. They were of infuriated animals, of untraversed desolations, of beauty beyond the power of man to conceive. Bill Nye had roamed the forests for years and years, summer and winter, day and night. A camp like ours, a dozen miles from the closest human being, was as commonplace to him as our barnyard was to us. John Ferris Thornton had traveled widely among the scenic marvels of the world. He spoke of the thundering falls of Niagara, the fjords of Norway, the barely scalable chimneys of the Alps, the floodplains of the Nile as casually as we would have talked about Lake Placid. All at once I got a glimmer of an immense earth, big enough that all the people who had been born since Adam had only found time to know a little bit of it, a world with places where even the perilous adventures of Bill Nye would be tame.

The following day we picked our route between huge boulders across the famous Indian Pass. We dropped down through heavy spruce forests to the mountain-locked waters of Henderson Lake. Here we were at last on the far side of the circling range which had always girded our existence. When we reached the deserted village which had been, quarter of a century before, the metropolis of the Adirondacks, and saw the ancient forest encroaching on its forlorn-looking streets, it seemed as if we must have discovered some strange, fantastic land where permanence and decay merged together and ultimately were the same.

Next morning we followed up Calamity Brook through bright mountain meadows, studded with a profusion of delicate bluets, and through deep virgin woods, carpeted with yielding moss. That afternoon we camped on the undesecrated shore of Lake Colden. It was still daylight when we went to bed in preparation for the acme of adventures on the morrow. For a long time I could not go to sleep but lay with a great contentment, looking cozily over the top of my blankets. Through the trees I saw the mist rising from the unruffled surface of Lake Colden and MacIntyre looming beyond in impressive grandeur. I heard the trout jumping in the water, heard the airy notes of the thrush and robin. I felt as if the world was all perfection and life nothing but a glorious lark.

Before six o'clock of the great day we were on the trail, climbing steadily along the rugged bank of the Opalescent River. Betty and I wanted to rush ahead, but Bill and Mr. Thornton curbed us with pleasantly sarcastic comments. The trail climbed out of the forests of spruce and cedar into paper birch and balsam and spruce. The trees grew ever smaller, the moss wetter, the flora different than anything I had ever seen. Then the cheerful white of the paper birch became scarce, and finally there was nothing left but black forests of strangely shrunken evergreens. Up, up we clambered, pulling ourselves now by roots, now taking precarious foothold on slimy rocks. The world seemed to be dropping off all around us, and we were mounting to a solitary pinnacle in space. Mounting, mounting, till even the last, prostrate outposts of the forest were no more, and there were only rocks and sphagnum and seas of white sandwort. Then the moss and sandwort were gone, a few jagged rocks alone jutted into the sky, and in a few moments we stood upon the crest of the state.

When we looked out over the landscape I felt as if I had just been born again, for there was nothing like it in the world in which I had lived for sixteen years. Everything was below us, everything which we normally viewed from the side was viewed in miniature from above. The tiny green patches away out in the flats to the north I knew were North Elba, but now it was as if I had gone up in a balloon farther than I had intended and had drifted to some eminence on Mars from which I was looking back upon the earth. Eastward were pointed peaks with thousand-foot rock streaks racing down their flanks, the Gothic mountains Bill called them. To the south and west was such a confusion of jumbled hills and valleys that I got dizzy when Bill started to mention a few known localities in that uncharted domain. For tireless hours we sat and gazed at the spectacle, so lost from time in its magnificence that it seemed scarcely believable when Bill remarked that it was almost evening and high season for to be getting back to camp.

Bill Nye said he couldn't go along. No, there was no use talking, he couldn't go along. He had to go to Vermont, and anyway a man was crazy to go into the Bog River country at that time of year. He'd freeze to death, like as not. But if Mr. Colvin insisted on being a damn fool he'd better take somebody with no sense and young blood. Why not take Jim Allen's kid?

So Mr. Colvin came across the harvest fields to see me. He told me that the state had started a survey of the Adirondack wilderness for the joint purpose of mapping its territory and of relocating, before all the trace of them was gone, the old township and lot lines, many of which had not been surveyed for one hundred years. Such a catastrophe, he emphasized, would lead to endless litigation. He wanted three guides to go with him and his assistant into the unexplored Bog River country and would I be one?

I don't remember anymore if he mentioned anything about wages;

I had no idea what "endless litigation" meant, and "catastrophe" I had used only in connection with something like [the Civil War battles of] Fredericksburg or Cold Harbor. But to go into the Bog River country, synonymous with all that was most wild on the face of the earth, more remote from civilization than darkest Africa, the place where men went and never returned—I suggested that if Mr. Colvin would just sit down in the parlor I'd be ready in ten minutes and was much chagrined when he told me it would be ten days before he was ready to start.

It was one of those gloriously clear September afternoons, with the birch and aspen leaves falling so thickly they coated the surface of the lake all along the shoreline, that we shoved our boats into the waters of Lower Saranac. There were five of us: Verplanck Colvin, head of the expedition; Mills Blake, his assistant;[2] John Solomon and Albert Mackenzie,[3] a couple of bearded Saranac guides, and myself. The three boats were filled high with food, a tent, blankets and scientific instruments, between which the five of us barely found room for our legs. We traveled through several days of perfect autumnal weather along rivers and lakes whose names had always been to me the music of romance. Lower Saranac ("Lake of the Clustered Stars," Mr. Thornton had called it), the tortuous Saranac River, Round Lake, Upper Saranac, the Indian Carry, the Spectacle Ponds,[4] Racquette River, Tupper Lake and finally Bog River itself, with rapids it took us half a day to battle our way up, and a swift, clear current rolling fresh with the breath of the never explored.

Time inevitably rounds off the sharp corners of detail and leaves only a softly curving mass we call impression. After more than half a century the detail has largely departed from my memory of the six weeks we spent in the Bog and Beaver River wilderness. Dates I thought I could never forget, names of ponds we first discovered and mapped, mountains, distances, even adventures, have all blended into a hazy picture which is one of the most beautiful in the whole collection which hangs in the gallery of my mind.

I see as the background of my entire picture the deep mystery of primeval forests. Upon this setting many vague events are superimposed. I recall climbing over the shoulder of some rocky mountain and dropping in surprise onto a whole chain of little ponds, blue as the clear sky they reflected, encircled by a foliage of scarlet and yellow and darkest green. I recall unexpectedly coming out on the shore of another pond, which no human being even knew existed, and seeing three deer across its waters, grouped around the stump of some fallen giant of the forest. Another recollection is of an afternoon on a storm-swept summit, with snow being driven into our faces, while Mr. Colvin was sighting on mountains with his transit and reading his angles as carefully as he would have done in a steam-heated laboratory, and Mills Blake and I jotted down his readings and waited patiently for him to finish and shrugged our shoulders against the piercing blasts of wind. Attached to this is a vague recollection of a perilous night descent down slippery rock steps with a heavy transit strapped to my back and a wet night around a campfire without blankets or even adequate clothing.

I recall one morning when Mr. Colvin suddenly decided to head southward and cross over from the source waters of the Bog River into the even more remote Beaver River. I recall that John Solomon and Albert Mackenzie were sent back to Tupper Lake for more supplies. And I also remember one morning before they completed their one-hundred-mile journey that provisions gave out, and Mr. Colvin remarked grimly that we had food for thought but little else.

There were several days on very empty stomachs while geographic order was brought into the chaos of this unmapped wilderness, anxious days while we wondered whether some mishap could have befallen our guides. I recall the delight of meeting near the shore of a lost pond a couple of young trappers who had plenty of venison. Then the guides arrived with supplies, and the seven of us, for Mr. Colvin had hired the trappers, set out for the Beaver River.

The sharpest object in the whole picture is a dull November morning when we turned our backs to the frozen surface of Mud Lake, which I had always imagined as the wildest spot on the globe, and started through the new-fallen snow toward still remoter reaches. I remember Mr. Colvin likening it to midwinter in Labrador. We started out, one of the trappers picking the route, the rest of us following single file, some carrying supplies and instruments, one dragging the lightest of our boats like a sled, I myself bringing up the rear with the sixty-five-pound transit. I can still see that procession, battling through snow-laden brush, bridging hollows impassable for the boat, gritting teeth through long, exhaustive climbs up sloping hillsides and every moment, even through misery, aware of the elation of breaking into the unknown.

There followed more unsuspected lakes, more uncharted streams, which started no one knew where and flowed to swell the torrent of rivers we could only guess, more snow, more cold, and always the solemn depths of the lofty primeval forest. There was one half-frozen lake across which the guides tried to float the boat full of supplies and save the tedious backtracking by land. The rest of us walked easily around the shore until we were suddenly startled by a cry and saw the boat sinking, a great hole showed in her bow by the ice. For slow-beating, agonized minutes we watched, powerless to help, fearing both men would drown, fearing we would be stranded eighty trailless miles from the nearest supplies without a bite to eat and without a blanket, fearing as men only can when they must stand idly by. Finally, however, we saw them work the boat to shore and, dripping with icy water, step to the saving land.

After six days of severe traveling, with many delays to climb mountains and map lonely waters, we reached the Beaver River on a cold, moonlight evening late in November. Here we encountered the remotest outpost of civilization at a crude inn kept by a solitary old bachelor. It took several more days of journeying by trail before we reached the first settlement at Long Lake, from where it was still eighty miles of sleighing over the roughest sort of highway back to home.

NOTES

1   Bill Nye was a North Elba guide who lived from 1816 to 1893. Nye Mountain, one of the traditional forty-six High Peaks, is named after him.

2   For Marshall's tribute to the real-life Blake, see p. 229.

3   Marshall mentions these guides in his profile of Mills Blake. See p. 233.

4   This name for Stony Creek Ponds appears on an old map (Clarence Petty, personal conversation).

SUPPLEMENTARY
MATERIALS

RELATED ARTICLES

Contribution to the Life History of the Northwestern Lumberjack

This mock-academic article, a sociological study of loggers' table manners, exhibits Marshall's obsession with statistics and his refusal to take life too seriously. It isn't about the Adirondacks, though it might have been written about the Adirondack lumberjack. We include it to give the reader an impression of Marshall's quirky sense of humor. The article appeared in the December 1929 issue of Social Forces.

For it is the nature of man, to the extreme prejudice of knowledge, to delight in the spacious liberty of generalities, and not in the inclosures of particularity.

—FRANCIS BACON

If the social sciences are ever to justify such a dignified appellation they will have to submit to the same quantitative treatment which the more advanced physical sciences have long recognized as prerequisite. For entirely too long a time we have been in the habit of recounting individual conduct by a broad barrage of meaningless approximations of biometry. From the Malay Archipelago to the Court of St. James, we derive our knowledge of the deportment and colloquy of humanity not from the exact data of systematic investigation but from the ambiguous generalities of superficial impression. Historically it is impossible to draw representative pictures of past demeanor from such misleading evidence. Coevally the situation is only improved within the narrow orbit of personal acquaintance. Otherwise we still found our conception of the mores of the majority of mankind on the casual basis of shallow and often prejudiced assertion.

The more unusual or picturesque the mores are, the more essential it is that we forsake this almost universal subjective approach and adopt the modern scientific manner, because extraordinary customs are the ones most likely to be grossly exaggerated when reported in words, so that merely the oddest features are retained. Consequently the picture which is handed down to posterity is a crude caricature entirely devoid of honesty. The only way to overcome this deplorable result is to record the customs in a concise, objective fashion.

Perhaps no body of Americans has ever been described more picturesquely and less definitely than the lumberjacks. That is partly because of the great romance naturally inherent in the woodsman's dangerous and severe profession and partly because his habitat is so remote from that of the average citizen. Few qualities are less conducive to accuracy than romance and remoteness, and thus there have been woven about the lumberjack a great many fabulous fancies which have gone very well as poetry but have scarcely even approximated the truth. To remedy this defect in our comprehension of a unique participant in the American civilization I have undertaken a quantitative study destined to chronicle certain of the more outstanding peculiarities of the Northwestern lumberjack. The traits which I have chosen for mathematical analysis are: (1) the lumberjack's speed in eating; (2) his table manners; (3) the subjects of his conversation; (4) his use of profane and libidinous language.

These attributes will be discussed in the ensuing section in a strictly statistical manner, which will give them not only a precise present meaning but will render them capable of comparison with future narrations of similar characteristics.

II

When the consideration of a lumberjack's eating arises the obvious question is: how fast? To provide an answer I have timed three or four hundred men in nine north Idaho camps during 144 meals.

TABLE I

Mean number of minutes required for eating by:

Meal	Fastest man	Average man	Slowest man
Breakfast	6	10	15
Lunch	7	12	16
Supper	8	13	17
Daily total	21	35	48

Not only the first bolter and the last Fletcherizer [1] were clocked but also the average man, say the twentieth fellow to leave the table out of forty. As a result the mean figures in Table I were obtained.

Translated from arithmetic to prose this table implies that the average woodchopper spends just 35 minutes a day in food assimilation. Furthermore, there is in each camp a fastest man or group of men who waste but 21 minutes diurnally in the mad dash for sustenance. On the other hand there is generally some incorrigible laggard who requires as much as a quarter of an hour for the mastication of every meal.

It was only possible to gather data bearing on a few of those numerous specific habits of eating which an arbitrary society has established as table manners. Based on an actual analysis of 100 samples, it was found that 12 percent of the eaters were two-tool men—that is, employed both knife and fork to lift food into the oral cavity. As regards bread spearing, 33 percent of the diners commonly depended on their forks to harpoon the staff of life. That banal euphonism "please" preceded 93 percent of all the requests for the passage of sustenance. In the imbibition of soup the average auditory range to the nearest even unit was nine feet.

Since conversation is the principal absorber of the lumberjack's leisure, one naturally wonders to what fields he devotes his interlocutory abilities. As a silent listener, watch in hand, to 1,800 minutes of confabulation during the summers of 1927 and 1928, I have obtained the figures shown in Table II on subject matter.

TABLE II

Subject under discussion	Percent of time
Pornographic, stories, experiences and theories	23
Personal adventures in which narrator is hero	11
Outrages of capitalism	8
Prohibition, bootlegging and jags	6
Logging technique and lore	5
Acrimonious remarks about bosses and employers	5
Wildlife, excluding the human	5
Agricultural methods and failures	4
Tunney-Dempsey and Dempsey-Sharkey battles[2]	3
Scientific dissertations	3
Personal adventures in which narrator is not hero	2
Employment and unemployment prospects	2
Lindbergh and aeronautics	2
Forest fires	2
Religious discussions, more profane than spiritual	2
Automobiles, particularly Fords	2
Reform economic schemes to supersede capitalism	1
Sarcastic evaluations of the late war to end war	1
The meteorological outlook	1
Sears Roebuck vs. Montgomery Ward	1
The good old days of the golden past	1
Food and the culinary art	1
Sickness and quacks	1
President Coolidge, with mordant comments on pseudo-cowboys	1
Mr. Hoover and Mr. Smith[3]	1
The Forest Service	1
The Sacco-Vanzetti case[4]	1
A local murder	1
Miscellaneous	3
Total	**100**

But after all, it is not the subject matter which is most typical of the logger's conversation. It is the virility of his adjectives and interjections which differentiates his oral activities from those of ordinary mortals. To derive an exact measure of this vocal distinction, ten conversations were closely heeded for fifteen minutes each. All profane and lascivious utterances, assumed to be taboo in chaste circles, were tallied. From this record it transpired that an average of 136 words, unmentionable at church sociables, were enunciated every quarter-hour by the hardy hewers of wood. Divided by subject matter the profane words were overwhelmingly in the majority, for they constituted 96 of the 136 maledictions. Of the remaining 40 mephitic sounds enunciated every quarter-hour, 31 were of sexual import and 9 were excretory in nature. Unfortunately various heritages from Anthony Comstock's activities[5] make it impossible to mention individually these profanations and obscenities.

NOTES

1   The U.S. nutritionist Horace Fletcher (1849-1919) advocated chewing food a long time to reduce it to a liquefied mass. *The Random House Dictionary of the English Language* (unabridged, 2d edition) defines *Fletcherize* as "to chew (food) slowly and thoroughly."

2   Gene Tunney, Jack Dempsey and Jack Sharkey were champion prizefighters in the 1920s and 1930s.

3   Herbert Hoover defeated Al Smith in the 1928 presidential election.

4   Nicola Sacco and Bartolomeo Vanzetti were executed in 1927 after a controversial murder trial.

5   Anthony Comstock (1844-1915) was a U.S. author and reformer who advocated moral censorship of literature and art.

Approach to the Mountains

By George Marshall

When George and Robert Marshall began climbing the High Peaks, they would spend a full day just getting to the trailhead from their summer home on Lower Saranac Lake. Years later, George looked back fondly on that prelude to wilderness adventure. The article is from the March-April 1955 issue of Ad-i-ron-dac.

Fortunately our family did not have an automobile. Therefore, we took it as a matter of course that when we wished to climb the high peaks of the Adirondacks, we should approach them on foot. This had the double advantage of being a pleasure in itself and of helping prepare us physically and psychologically for the wilder country beyond the end of roads.

When Bob Marshall, Herb Clark and I first climbed Tahawus[1] in 1918, we hiked the eight miles of dirt road between Lake Placid station and South Meadows. In fact, on each trip to or from the high mountains during the following seven years or more, we walked and usually carried packs.

The day was generally started with a mile-and-a-half row across Lower Saranac Lake from Knollwood to Algonquin,[2] followed by a walk of about the same length to the Saranac Lake depot. The train ride to Lake Placid was our compromise with mechanical transportation, but even this had its active phase when the cars dashed wildly around sharp curves, throwing packages and pack baskets from the racks, amid much whistling at thirty miles an hour!

After the train docked at the Lake Placid station in Newman, we walked down the street to Sam Brennan's American House for lunch or stopped at Mullen's Corner Grocery to buy supplies and to chat with

Herb's brother, John, before we started in earnest for the mountains.

The joys of road walking in those days before pavements and heavy traffic were to us second only to those of tramping and climbing in the backwoods. The road lacked the freshness, superlative beauty, wildness and sense of great adventure and complete freedom of the wilderness; but it nonetheless possessed many of these elements and also awarded us with that satisfying sense of physical and mental exhilaration and well-being which can only be obtained through physical accomplishment. As we swung along, the dust rising from our feet, our energy seemed to be kinetic—the more we walked, the easier it seemed to be to walk. This process, especially when the sun was shining, also stimulated good conversation and the gaiety of open country. If at times fatigue stole upon us, it was banished readily by a short rest, a bite of food, a drink of water or a good night's sleep. After all, two of us in 1918 had the good fortune of being fourteen and seventeen.

The road from Lake Placid station to South Meadows wound over old glacial beaches and lake bottoms covered with second-growth trees and pastures. It afforded numerous inspiring views of the surrounding wooded mountains which were constantly changing from hour to hour and season to season with shifts in vegetation, light and color. We never tired of this route. The bright field flowers and humming insects welcomed us in June. The sticky hot, lazy days of July at some times tested our endurance and at others were strangely relaxing. The crystal-clear blue skies of August gave promise of perfect views from the high peaks. The intervening dark days of rain settled the dust and made the world fresher and greener. The chill, windblown, snow-blocked lanes of February brought the power of the wilderness nearer to civilization.

The pleasures of this road to the mountains were heightened further by its own peculiar history and lore which developed with the years. The Ausable River below the present Olympic ski jump was the Shenandoah, according to Herb. Here the *Monitor* and the *Merrimac* fought in deadly combat. Of course it was early spring at that time, so the water was somewhat higher. To verify his story, Herb told us that the little lame old lady with whom he was speaking, when we dropped behind to take some photographs, told him that she had had her shinbone smashed by a shell during the great battle and that that was why she limped and had been reduced to picking berries.[3] To overcome any possible lingering doubts, he pointed to some exposed gravel on the

The Plains of Abraham.

hillside where another shell had struck. As a matter of fact, if you look carefully, you may see this bare spot to this day.

The road climbs steeply from the river to North Elba. On the first trip on which we carried pack baskets, the straps began to pull a bit as the road mounted. Suddenly Herb burst into song:

> I saw three wayworn travelers,
> In tattered garments clad.
> They were struggling up the mountain
> And it seemed that they were sad.
> Their backs were heavy laden,
> Their strength was almost gone,
> And they shouted as they journeyed,
> 'Deliverance will come.'
> Then, crowns of victory, palms of glory,
> Crowns of victory they will wear.

As our laughter subsided, we gained our "palms of glory" by taking a shortcut across pastures and through the woods. This enabled us to escape the heat of the road and the remainder of the climb to North Elba Corners. Just before leaving the road, we looked with happy anticipation across the flower-studded Plains of Abraham to the high mountains, dominated by Tahawus and MacIntyre and cut dramatically by Avalanche and Indian passes. These, with their encircling wild country, were our objectives.

We thought of Emmons and Redfield and their first ascents of the highest peaks four generations before,[4] of Alfred Street and his purple-worded enthusiasm for Indian Pass, and of Verplanck Colvin who explored, surveyed and loved these mountains more than anyone before or since. These men were here when the wilderness spread far beyond its present bounds and before tragically large portions of the mountains were lumbered and burnt.

Before continuing, we also looked back across the Ausable River towards John Brown's farm and grave marked by the American flag flying above the trees. We thought of his courage and that of his family and neighbors in farming here in those difficult pioneer days and of his far greater bravery and foresight in his historic blows against slavery. We stood for a moment between these two great symbols of freedom—the wild mountains and the man of righteous passion.

We rested under a spreading maple at the far end of the pasture. Our serious mood vanished as Herb regaled us with a yarn about seventeen milk cows which had been chased down the grassy hill above us by a grizzly and had died of heart failure.

The trail through the woods passed a maple-sugar shed with a large brick stove and two huge iron kettles in which the sap was boiled in early spring. Nearby, we found an old wooden sign pointing to Adirondack Lodge. It must have been there since before the fire of 1903 which burnt the lodge to the ground along with much of the encircling forest. As the fires crept around the lodge, its proprietor, Henry van Hoevenberg, paced the piazza like a captain on the deck of a sinking ship.

We rejoined the road at the Wood farm, the last permanent settlement on the way to the mountains. We stopped here frequently over the years for a night's lodging, for a meal, for a drink of water or just to chat. The farm, which was one of the best in the region, was run by Mrs. W.K. Wood, who during the years we knew her was well into her seventies, and by her daughter Hattie, who had been a schoolteacher and had taught for a year or two at Fort Yukon, Alaska. They were assisted in the fields and in the barn by a farmhand or two.

The Woods' large table was always filled to overflowing with breads and cakes and other delicious foods in dishes which were crowded so closely together that one could scarcely see the tablecloth. They invariably were most hospitable and, once they knew us, always found a place for us to stop, if need be, even if it was in the hayloft over the munching horses.

Mrs. Wood had lived in this region for many years. When we knew her, she wore an old-fashioned full black skirt and blouse and high-laced shoes. She worked constantly, despite her advanced age, but now and then we persuaded her to sit in her rocker and tell us about the old days. Her husband, who died in 1906, was brought up by Rob Scott, who kept Scott's House at North Elba. She recalled when Alfred B. Street, state librarian and Adirondack writer, and Mrs. Street were thrown from a wagon nearby and were seriously injured. She was impressed by the strange fact that Street wore a copper plate in his shoe to protect one of his toes.

Rob Scott's father claimed to have discovered a silver mine on what since has been called Nye Mountain. Rob and his close friend, Bill Nye, a well-known North Elba guide, hunted for it. There were some who believed Bill found it because they observed him each year bending under a heavy pack basket on his way to Vermont.

Mrs. Wood spoke of Bill Nye as a "very nice, big, queer fellow with a shaggy beard, long hair and a little dog." She smiled as she told us of his famous "Hitch-Up, Matilda" exploit of 1868 at Avalanche Lake. In order to pass the foot of two precipitous granite cliffs on the side of Avalanche Mountain, the trail went through the water. When they came to the first crossing, the ladies of the party, which Bill was guiding, were dismayed. He persuaded them that the only solution was for him to carry them across on his shoulders. He started with an exceedingly stout woman. As he proceeded, she kept slipping farther and farther down his back, and when he came to the deepest part, she was practically sitting in the water. Her frantic husband in desperation shouted, "Hitch up, Matilda! Hitch up!" Matilda heeded and "hitched" and came across dry. To this day, these crossings on the Avalanche Lake trail, now spanned by floating logs, are called Hitch-Up Matildas.[5]

We stepped outside and looked at the two dark-green trailless summits to the southwest which commemorate Alfred Street and Bill Nye. We also thought of the high mountain pond beyond, close to Indian Pass, which is a memorial to the Scotts. Turning to the northeast, we noted the passes on either side of Pitchoff Mountain. John Brown almost froze to death when he followed the old road through the northerly pass on his way home in midwinter, 1850. He was so exhausted carrying a heavy satchel that he lay down in the deep snow by the side of the road and just rallied himself in time to drag himself to shelter at Rob Scott's. John Brown Jr. described going over a newly built road through the southerly pass by "Long Pond" (now called Cascade Lakes) in 1858 (the year before the historic Harper's Ferry raid) as "the most romantically beautiful that I ever saw in my life."

We also looked back towards the country surrounding North Elba, where Gerrit Smith settled a number of Negro ex-slaves and freemen in the 1840s and 50s. Among the former was Lyman Epps, friend of John Brown, singer of hymns, successful farmer and excellent guide. It was his trail that Street followed in 1865 on his famous trip through Indian Pass.

At last we continue on our way to South Meadows. A mile or so beyond the Woods' the road passes a shoulder of Van Hoevenberg Mountain. Herb claimed it was called "Calamity Mountain" after Joe McGinnis, who had the misfortune to contract the "fantod" right there. This dread disease made Joe shrink into a knot the size of a baseball.

Approximately halfway between Woods' and the South Meadows turnoff, we quenched our thirst with a long drink from "Alcohol Brook." The lumberjacks gave it this name because here they "cut" what remained in their pint bottles when they staggered back to the lumber woods after a high weekend in "civilization."

The pack baskets which Bob and I carried on our second trip to South Meadows were not too heavy, but they must have held us down pretty well. When we took them off, where the South Meadows Road turns to the east, something seemed to be missing. When we crossed the branch of the Ausable River and left the Heart Lake road to climb the then-trailless Mount Jo, we seemed to float to the top. We were like balloons freed of their ballast.

The descent was quite a different matter. While we picked our way with care through fire slash, Herb dashed ahead shouting as he ran that we had better hurry or we should be late for supper. When we caught up with him on the lower slopes, he was grazing contentedly on delicious June strawberries with all thought of hurrying gone.

A mile walk from where we had left our packs brought us to Abe Fuller's farm at South Meadows, where the sandy road ended. A two-story, four-room split-log cabin stood on the north side and a row of three log buildings, which comprised the barn, chicken run and one-room bunkhouse, stood on the south. One of these cabins was said to have been here since before the terrible fire of 1903.

The Fullers, who were about twenty-five years old, cultivated some fifteen acres. Their herd of a dozen or so cows grazed mostly on the meadows and in the woods beyond. The Fullers also raised some chickens, pigs, potatoes and a few vegetables for their own use and supplemented their diet with plenty of trout in the spring and venison in season. Water was brought in pails from a spring at the foot of the hill. Almost every day, someone drove the horse and buggy to Lake Placid with the excess milk and brought back any needed staple groceries. There was also communication with the outside world over a one-wire telephone line to the Woods'. It was so poorly grounded that during one storm the Fullers' adopted son was knocked down as he was passing the receiver just when the lightning struck.

In the evening, after a good country supper cooked by Mrs. Fuller, we helped with chores, or chased an escaped hog, or fished, or Bob and I strolled across the meadows while Herb and Abe played checkers. Sometimes frontier visitors stopped by like Charlie Wood, Hattie's brother, who was the local superintendent of the J.J. Rogers Company lumber operations and who had made first ascents of Wright in 1893 and of Phelps in 1904, or a young gum picker with a pack basket of spruce gum, or Ed Young, a half-Indian, who alternated between working at the lumber camps and roaming the woods, rifle in hand.

South Meadows were added to the Forest Preserve late in 1919, and the Fullers moved to the Notch House, west of Wilmington Notch. Abe returned about ten years later to carry heavy bags of cement to the top of Tahawus for the constructing of the stone refuge.[6]

We stopped at South Meadows a few times after the Fullers left but camped in our tent instead of a log cabin. Mr. Bowen, a friendly man in his fifties, with a big, black mustache, was dam tender at South Meadows Brook in 1920. Later he worked at the Woods'. He had an old-fashioned trumpet-type Victor Talking Machine on which he played a number of old favorites, including "The Preacher and the Bear." This was about "Allen's bear fight up in Keene" which was "the greatest bear fight ever seen." We were especially amused by the crisis,

When the preacher cried in great despair,
Lord, if you can't help me, don't you help that bear!

A more indigenous poetic version of the great fight dates it 1840 and calls Allen a census taker instead of a preacher. One folklore expert,

Edward P. Alexander, identifies our hero as Anson H. Allen and describes him as a "quip-making editor, who went his way enjoying life with his tongue in his cheek." Be this as it may, our enjoyment was heightened by the tradition which placed the fight just five miles to the east between Big Slide and Porter Mountain in "Tight-Nippin," the narrowest place in Biddlesome's old wagon road from Keene.

South Meadows was a jumping-off place for several of our trips into the roadless area which is the wilderness of the high peaks. From here, we made our first climb of Tahawus, circled the MacIntyre Range in a day, explored the wild Wallface-Scott Pond-Lost Pond plateau, packed to Panther Gorge to climb the Gothics Range, walked to the Saranacs by way of Indian Pass, Preston Ponds, Big Ampersand and Kettle Mountain Pass, and took numerous other trips into the backwoods.

When we entered these wilder regions, our eight-mile hike to the last frontier at the road's end had prepared us in ways that cannot be equaled today by driving an auto to the beginning of a trail. The road walk was a gradual transition, physically and psychologically, between the twentieth-century world and the primeval. Nowadays, this transition must be made beside a parked car in the few moments it takes to change into Bean boots and lock the door.

There is little choice today. One almost never sees a hiker along the roads—not that one saw too many in the old days. Thirty-three years ago we also lugged our pack baskets over fourteen miles of twisting dirt road from Lake Placid to Keene. This road has long since been paved and straightened and traffic has become much heavier. It has lost its meaning for me. Therefore, I now find myself driving over it as fast as I can go. Others seem to do the same, and most climbers speed to the trailheads.

Perhaps all this is merely one man's nostalgia. However, I believe it has this further meaning. Road walking having become a thing of the past, the transition to the mood of forest and mountain now must take place entirely within the wilderness itself. It really cannot occur by fiat at the car door or the trailhead with the speed and ease of switching off the ignition. Hours of walking and plenty of space are required for the transition alone. Much more of time and of big, roadless country are needed to give the opportunity for that complete and satisfying wilderness experience which thousands of people seek each year on their vacations into the backwoods. This re-emphasizes the continuing importance both to guard the boundaries of our Forest Preserve and to protect the wild-forest atmosphere within in order to preserve the wilderness and its unique, superlative values for generations to come.

NOTES

1   Apocryphal Native American name for Mount Marcy. Said to mean "Cloud-Splitter."

2   A hotel on the lake.

3   Bob Marshall also mentions this tall tale in his profile of Herb Clark. See p. 224.

4   The scientists Ebenezer Emmons and William C. Redfield were in the party that made the first ascents of Mount Marcy and Algonquin Peak, in 1837. Emmons also is credited with the first ascent of Nippletop. (Carson 1927, 261.)

5   The floating logs have been replaced by plank bridges bolted to the sides of cliffs.

6   Built in 1928, the stone shelter was removed in 1967 (Weber 2002, 166-171).

Lost Pond

By George Marshall

Like his brother, George Marshall loved a trek through the pathless woods. Here he writes about hiking to Lost Pond south of Street Mountain. The article was published in The Cloud Splitter *in June 1941.*

It was on the twentieth of June 1920 that we first visited Lost Pond. The afternoon before, Herb Clark, Bob and I had lugged our packs along the eight or ten blazing hot miles of road from Lake Placid to South Meadows. We had just pitched our tent and were preparing supper when a half-Indian hunter and lumberjack by the name of Ed Young came across the fields. We chatted for a while about the mountains, and Ed spoke eloquently of the shameful treatment of the Indians. This he thought symbolized by the fact that they were not even left a "monument" through the preservation of their ancient place names. As he was leaving he invited us to accompany him the next day to Scott Pond.

After an early breakfast and with a good supply of citronella, we walked over to Heart Lake and continued along the old tote road to the lumber camp which used to be at Scott's Clearing. The lumberjacks called the pond there "Mud Preston," where, as arranged the preceding evening, we met Ed Young. We followed him up the steep lumber road to Scott Pond, and as it was raining hard, we took shelter in the shanty which stood near the dam at the outlet.

While we were waiting, Ed told us of Lost Pond, and when the downpour diminished to a drizzle we set out along a blazed line which he had cut for his own pleasure a few days before. He was one of those old-timers who got the keenest enjoyment from the wilderness of the forest. As he expressed it, "No man likes a trip in the mountains any better than I do."

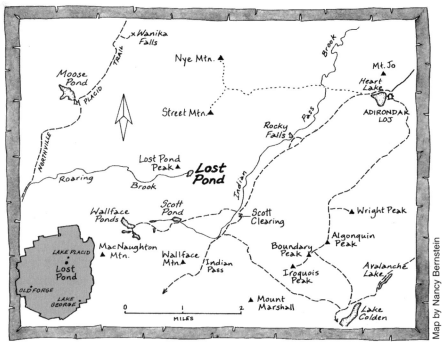

Map shows trails that exist today near Lost Pond.

The way to Lost Pond was superlatively beautiful as only the Adirondacks can be in June. It ascended through a deep coniferous forest which was brightened by the green tips of the spruce and balsam or by an occasional birch. At times it led between high rocks or across a little marsh. The ground was covered with a profusion of spring wildflowers and thick moss. I remember particularly the carpets of goldthread and discovering in a little marshy opening along the brook buckbean with its graceful pitcher-like blossoms.

Crossing a ridge we entered the high circular valley which surrounds the pond, and soon we saw water through the trees.

The pond itself, surrounded as it is by a splendid forest and with high hills rising from its steep banks, seemed one of the most beautiful and wildest spots we had ever seen.

We returned to Scott Pond by a slightly different route, and while we were on the plateau we also visited the Wallface Ponds. Alfred Street in his *Indian Pass* accurately described the ponds "on Wallface" which flow into three different rivers as among the great curiosities of the Adirondacks; but not having visited them himself, he failed to give an adequate idea of their rare beauty.[1]

The trip back to South Meadows was uneventful except for Herb's delightful good humor, which surpassed itself as the day ended with our diving into our tent just as a terrific thunderstorm was breaking.

One early morning, five Junes later, we started from the lean-to near Ouluska Brook and followed the old "Government Trail" to Lower Preston Pond, climbed MacNaughton Mountain and descended to the Wallface and Scott ponds. Before walking out to Lake Placid station, we thought we should revisit Lost Pond. Foolishly we tried to follow Ed Young's old "trail," and because in the meantime there had been a windfall and someone had blazed a trapper's line leading nowhere, we found ourselves over on the side of the mountain. As it was getting late, we concluded the pond was well named and descended directly to the dam at Scott's Clearing.

On August 1, 1929, Herb and I determined to find Lost Pond again. This time when we reached Scott Pond we wisely decided not to bother with old blazed lines and cut directly by compass to the pond. After circling it, we climbed to the top of Lost Pond Mountain and then cut by compass across a branch of Roaring Brook and a ridge of Street and down the long descent to the Moose Pond-Averyville trail, which we followed out to Averyville. A few years later Herb and Bob made another trip to Lost Pond and descended Roaring Brook to Cold River.

All of this is by the way of correcting the note in last November's issue of *The Cloud Splitter* which incorrectly stated that I had blazed a route to Lost Pond and that I said the pond was only "pretty nice." In conclusion let me add that I still think Lost Pond superb, that I hope the range from MacNaughton to Nye will forever remain trailless and wild,[2] and that I consider trailless cross-country travel in the Adirondacks, whether to the summit of a mountain or to a faraway pond, the most delightful form of recreation I know.

NOTES

1 Street refers to "the three lakes on top of Wallface, sending streams into the St. Lawrence by Cold River and the Racket, into Lake Champlain by the Ausable, and the Atlantic by the Hudson" (Street 1869, xxxiv). He probably has in mind, respectively, Lost Pond, Scott Pond and Wallface Ponds.

2 There are now well-worn paths to the summits of Street and Nye.

Paul Schaefer with his mentor, John Apperson, in 1947.

Bob Marshall, Mount Marcy, and–the Wilderness

By Paul Schaefer

On the day in 1932 when Bob Marshall climbed fourteen peaks (see p. 65), he happened to meet a kindred spirit, the conservationist Paul Schaefer, on Mount Marcy. Schaefer wrote about the encounter for the summer 1966 issue of The Living Wilderness, *the magazine of the Wilderness Society.*

Mount Marcy, also known by the Indian name Tahawus, which means "the cloud-splitter," is located in the midst of a jumble of high peaks in the northeastern Adirondack Mountains in the state of New York. More than a mile high, its upper slopes well above timberline, it is located seven miles from the nearest point of access and is wild and rugged. The trails to it thread through heavy coniferous and mixed hardwood forests and are steep and spectacular. A favorite trail goes through the precipitous Avalanche Pass, skirts Avalanche Lake and goes under huge blocks of rock broken off the towering cliffs above. The region abounds in streams and waterfalls.

Marcy is composed of rocks about as ancient as any on earth, and its storm-swept summit is scarred by glaciers of the ice age. The mountain provides magnificent views of hundreds of square miles of wild forest land, including most of the forty-six peaks exceeding four thousand feet in height[1] and probably a thousand lesser mountains which roll off to the horizon in all directions. Scores of glacial lakes fill the hollows of mountains and valleys which surround Marcy. Just below the summit, on its western shoulder, nestles tiny Lake Tear of the Clouds, ultimate source of the Hudson River. Panther Gorge, with its almost sunless rain forest, drops sharply nearly two thousand feet below its eastern shoulder. This is the land of the whitetail deer, the black bear, the beaver, the fisher, the otter and the lynx. Here also are the pileated woodpecker, the grouse, the owls, the hermit thrush and speckled brook trout. Ferns, mosses and a rich variety of wilderness flowers grow in profusion.

Into this wild setting one summer day in 1932 strode Bob Marshall, fresh from several years in the Arctic. The Adirondacks, where he and his brother George and Herb Clark first climbed all the forty-six high peaks, including many trailless ones before scarcely anyone else even thought of the idea, were Bob's first love. His father was Louis Marshall, renowned constitutional lawyer, noted for his pioneering defense of the Adirondack wilderness. The archives of the Association for the Protection of the Adirondacks, organized in 1901, are filled with letters and accounts of Louis Marshall's work with governors, legislators and members of constitutional conventions, of which he was a delegate, who sought his counsel. He was a prime factor in the defense of New York's constitutional guarantee of its Forest Preserve.

Before returning from the Arctic, Bob had decided to renew his acquaintance with the Adirondacks at his first opportunity. So, with the gusto that only he could muster, he decided to see how many high peaks he could climb in a single day and how many vertical feet he could achieve in the process. Beginning at 3:30 a.m. on July 15, 1932, he climbed fourteen peaks totaling 13,600 feet by 10 p.m. It was on that day, and under these unique circumstances, that I met Bob Marshall. It was a meeting measured in minutes, yet of unmeasurable significance to my life.

Robert Cromie and I had come to the summit of Mount Marcy from North River Mountain, where we had photographed the devastation of a forest fire. The fire, caused by lumbering operations, had destroyed much of the Opalescent River country. Our tripod was set on the highest rock, and we were photographing the high peak country with a camera loaned to us by Nobel Prize chemist Dr. Irving Langmuir, a devoted friend of the Forest Preserve.

To combat a constitutional amendment which would have permitted cabin colonies anywhere on state land, we were making a movie of beauty and devastation in the Adirondack Park. The state legislature had twice passed the "closed cabin" proposal, and it was to come before the people in referendum that November. Our strategy was directed by John S. Apperson, the foremost advocate of that era for the maintenance of the Preserve's constitutional protection. The Mohawk Valley Hiking Club, of which we were members, had been leading the crusade for about a year. We had traveled all over the state, distributed countless pamphlets and were preparing for a series of public forums before election day.

When we arrived at the summit we found Herb Clark, famed Adirondack guide. He carried a lunch for Marshall, who was due momentarily. It was about one o'clock when we looked down the steep, rocky eastern slope of Marcy and saw a tiny figure emerge from the conifers half a mile below. Bob was moving rapidly, and in a little while he bounded over the last rocks to the summit.

He greeted the guide and came over to us with a wide, welcoming smile. "I'm Bob Marshall," he said, shaking our hands with an iron grip. His eyes reflected a great joy for living, and his face was deeply tanned and ruddy with health. He was dressed in a light, well-worn plaid shirt, blue denims and sneakers.

We explained the cabin referendum to him and outlined the problems of public apathy. He grasped the situation at once. Perhaps our appearance underscored our earnestness; we were heavy with beard, unkempt and blackened with the char of the forest fire.

Munching his lunch, he seated himself on the rock summit. As we spoke he seemed to be chafing at the bit. A strong, cool wind whipped his hair. He exuded a restless, dynamic strength of purpose—a strength which had been nurtured in the remote Arctic wilderness.

"But this is only part of the Adirondack problems," I told him. Getting up, we walked to the western side of the peak where we could look down on Mount Adams, about six miles away. "They're stripping Adams of its virgin spruce, clear to the top. Three hundred lumberjacks," I informed him. "And over there—see the burned lands of the Opalescent? It was a crown fire. It leapt Lake Sanford and the river and burned deep, clear to the summit of North River Mountain."

Bob was shocked. "Before I left for the Arctic," he said, "they promised us there would be no more cutting above 2,500 feet elevation. Those are the most critical watershed forests in in Adirondacks. The Opalescent River valley was one of the loveliest we had and abundant with wildlife." He was plainly upset. He walked back and forth across the summit and circled it several times, in deep contemplation.

"We simply must band together—all of us who love the wilderness. We must fight together—wherever and whenever wilderness is attacked. We must mobilize all of our resources, all of our energies, all of our devotion to the wilderness. To fail to do this is to permit the American wilderness to be destroyed. That must not happen!"

"Good luck," he said. "I'll do all I can as soon as I get back to Washington.[2] We must keep in contact." He shook hands again and turned toward the valley. "Come on, Herb," he said to the guide.

With that he was off, loping swiftly and easily down the steep mountainside. We watched them. The guide picked his way carefully among the rocks and pockets of above-timberline flowers, scattered like a patchwork quilt on the open slopes. Bob quickly reached timberline. Just before he entered the forest he turned toward us and waved his hand sharply. Then he was gone.

Bob Cromie and I distinctly remember that moment. We were acutely conscious of having met a dynamic personality. He seemed to personify all that we saw before us: the limitless sweep of mountains rolling on and on to far horizons, the ancient rocks, the deep gorges, the unbroken forests, the scores of glacial lakes sparkling in the sunlight, and the rivers threading their way down through lovely valleys. There was about him the essence of a wild freedom and an utter determination to preserve wilderness for generations yet to come. Years later, he expressed in finest prose the sentiments he spoke to us that day:

> The universe of the wilderness, all over the United States, is vanishing with appalling rapidity. It is melting away like the last snowbank on some south-facing mountainside during a hot afternoon in June. It is disappearing while most of those who care more for it than anything else in this world are trying desperately to rally and save it.[3]

We gathered our equipment together and headed down the mountain. We camped that night near Bushnell Falls, and around our campfire we discussed our experiences of the day. We sensed at the time that this casual meeting foreshadowed more important events. Were we to be part of the "mobilization of all who love the wilderness"? Had we anticipated such mobilization?

Next morning we stopped at Johns Brook Lodge in the valley. Bob Marshall was there. We sat in the warm sun and reminisced. He told us about the Arctic for which he already had a certain nostalgia. We discussed the problems of the wilderness. I seem to recall his viewpoints clearly:

> Wilderness and roads are incompatible. The encroachment of roads into wilderness areas often goes by unnoticed until suddenly we find a mechanized vehicle already at a hitherto quiet and lovely wilderness lake. The gradual improvement of footpaths into wider trails invites mechanized use if there is no one on hand at the time to object. Hundreds of miles of improved trails of this kind penetrate into the very heart of many of our most remote regions. As I see it, control of the use of these trails is the heart of the wilderness problems in the Adirondacks.

Coming back to the immediate issue before us, we discussed it at length. He agreed to implement numerous phases of our work, and we left with mutual pledges of assistance.

That same day, probably at the lodge, he wrote a vivid account of his high peak adventure of the previous day. It was published in the October 1932 issue of *High Spots*, official magazine of the Adirondack Mountain Club. It included the following statement:

> I had wondered whether, after three summers and a winter of exploration in Arctic Alaska, I could still recapture any of the sense of wilderness I had always gotten from Mount Haystack. Gloriously enough, I did. It was still possible to forget the automobiles and machinery of the present in the vista from this rocky summit from which only in the extreme distance could any signs of man's meddlesome ways be observed.[4]

He followed that with an excellent article entitled "The Perilous Plight of the Adirondack Wilderness."[5] This was published in *High Spots* just before the referendum came to a vote.

A few weeks later the people of New York state sustained our position by a vote of 1,390,000 to 690,000. On January 17, 1933, I received a letter from Bob in which he expressed gratification at the results of the referendum and concluded by saying: "I hope we may meet again some day soon—perhaps on the top of Santanoni next time."

Four years later, on January 17, 1937, Bob called a meeting of New York members of the Wilderness Society, which had formally come into being in 1935. Among those present were Bob, George Marshall, James Marshall, Raymond Torrey, Arnold Knauth, John S. Apperson, Robert Sterling Yard and myself. Bob appointed several of us to a Truck Trail Committee.

As the years passed, the threat of mechanized invasion of the Forest Preserve became more menacing. Gradually, many of the most remote regions were being penetrated by jeeps and other forms of mechanized travel. After the war years this was accelerated.

Those of us who saw what was happening were not idle; but, for years, it looked as though we were waging a losing battle despite what seemed to be a clear mandate in the constitution to preserve the wilderness character of the region. Finally, we made an all-out presentation to the Joint Legislative Committee on Natural Resources for New York State, of which we were an advisory member.

Action began on a small scale when Conservation Commissioner Sharon J. Mauhs closed the Siamese Ponds trail to motorized vehicles. Gradually, the tempo was built up. The Association for the Protection of the Adirondacks led the supporting action on this issue. The Adirondack Mountain Club and the Izaak Walton League joined forces. Finally, the New York State Conservation Council threw its power behind the effort. Senator Robert Watson Pomeroy, chairman of the Natural Resources Committee, was of inestimable help.

On December 1, 1965, the conservation commissioner issued regulations protecting nearly one million acres of the Forest Preserve from motor vehicles and aircraft in the larger wilderness regions. Also, some five hundred lakes outside these areas were protected from planes and motorboats. The order was a long step in the right direction; it by no means accomplishes the whole job.

Bob Marshall clearly saw the whole picture more than thirty years ago. He had the kind of vision we need today.

The philosophy he advocated is the only one that can permanently preserve the wilderness. It is the mobilization of all those forces that care for wilderness; it is eternal vigilance and a determination that this is a resource which must be preserved as a heritage for future generations.

I cannot think of a more appropriate way to conclude these memories of Bob Marshall than to recall a few more of his words:

> To countless people the wilderness provides the ultimate delight because it combines the thrills of jeopardy and beauty. It is the last stand for that glorious adventure into the physically unknown that was commonplace in the lives of our ancestors, and has always constituted a major factor in the happiness of many exploratory souls. It is also the perfect esthetic experience because it appeals to all of the senses. ... It is vast panoramas, full of height and depth and glowing color, on a scale so overwhelming as to wipe out the ordinary meaning of dimensions. It is the song of the hermit thrush at twilight and the lapping of waves on the shoreline and the melody of the wind in the trees. It is the unique odor of balsams and of freshly turned humus and of mist rising from mountain meadows. It is the feel of spruce needles under foot and sunshine in your face and wind blowing through your hair. It is all of these at the same time, blended into a unity that can only be appreciated with leisure and which is ruined by artificiality.[6]

NOTES

1 Actually, only forty-two of the traditional forty-six High Peaks are over four thousand feet.

2 At the time, Marshall was living in Baltimore and working on his book *Arctic Village*. In September, he accepted an assignment with the U.S. Forest Service to write a report on recreation in the nation's woodlands.

3 From "The Universe of the Wilderness is Vanishing," which appeared in *Nature* in April 1937.

4 See p. 68.

5 See p. 183.

6 From "The Universe of the Wilderness is Vanishing." See note 2.

Mount Marshall from Iroquois Peak.

Mount Marshall: The Strange History of the Names of an Adirondack High Peak

By Philip G. Terrie

At 4,360 feet, the southernmost peak in the MacIntyre Range is far from the highest mountain in the Adirondacks. Yet when Bob Marshall bushwhacked up it in 1921, he exulted in its wildness. "On the whole mountain we could not see a single trace of the presence of any human being, not even an old blaze on a tree," he later wrote.[1] How appropriate that this peak later came to be called Mount Marshall. But therein lies a tale—and it was told by Philip G. Terrie in the July-August 1973 issue of Adirondac.

The 4,360-foot peak at the southwestern end of the MacIntyre Range has been known, at one time or another, by at least four different names: Clinton, Iroquois, Herbert and Marshall. For the last few years it has been known to various people as all of these except Iroquois and has been the source of a perplexing confusion. In December 1972, however, the United States Board on Geographic Names officially approved the name of Mount Marshall for federal use and thus finally settled a question that has plagued Adirondack climbers, cartographers and historians for decades.

The problem originated with Verplanck Colvin, who first called the mountain Clinton. But Colvin originally named the next peak north, the one we now know as Iroquois, Clinton and at times applied Clinton to the peak we know call Boundary as well.[2] From Colvin's published reports it is impossible to determine exactly what names Colvin intended for the three peaks south of Algonquin. "Indeed," wrote Russell M.L. Carson, author of *Peaks and People of the Adirondacks*, "the more one studies the Reports, the more complicated the question becomes." From unpublished maps and sketches found among Colvin's papers, however, Carson was able to decide that Colvin originally intended the name Clinton for the peak we now know as Iroquois and later moved it to the peak at the southwestern end of the range.[3]

When Robert and George Marshall and Herbert Clark climbed Iroquois in 1918, they thought that the peak on which they stood was unnamed and that the lower peak to the southwest was the one that Colvin had named Iroquois; considering the inconsistency and vagueness of Colvin's appellations, one can understand their confusion. Believing that they stood on an unnamed peak, the Marshalls decided to name it Herbert, for their friend and guide. In Robert Marshall's pamphlet, *The High Peaks of the Adirondacks*, the four main peaks are named, northeast to southwest, Wright, MacIntyre, Herbert and Iroquois.[4]

It was only after the Marshalls began to assist Russell Carson in the research for *Peaks and People of the Adirondacks* that they learned they had confused what Colvin had apparently intended for these mountains' names. To clear up the confusion, Carson suggested that people simply call Iroquois by its present name and the lower peak Herbert. For the time being, Clinton was lost in the shuffle, and to climbers the peaks were known by the names in Carson's book.

Another of Carson's suggestions had been that the conical peak southeast of Dix be named Marshall, since the Marshalls and Herbert Clark were the only men at the time to have ascended the forty-six peaks over four thousand feet above sea level. The Marshall brothers were opposed from the start to any mountain's being named after them and repeatedly asked Carson not to name any mountain after them. But he insisted that their accomplishment was worthy of some recognition, and after *Peaks and People of the Adirondacks* was published, climbers always referred to that peak in the Dixes, known today as Hough, as Mount Marshall.[5]

In this way the situation continued until 1935 when the Conservation Department decided that as part of its Fifty Years of

Conservation Celebration, a mountain in the Adirondacks should be named after some New Yorker prominent in the conservation movement. They chose Dr. Franklin B. Hough, a man instrumental in the preservation of the Adirondacks who later became an important figure in the acceptance and establishment of scientific forestry in the United States. Apparently the department was unaware that the mountain they decided upon, which had no official name, was unofficially known to hundreds of Adirondack climbers as Mount Marshall. The New York Board on Geographic Names approved the name Hough in 1937; little publicity was given the decision, however, and to most climbers and hikers in the Adirondacks the mountain continued to be known as Marshall.

In 1940 the Forty-Sixers of Troy decided to petition the state Board on Geographic Names for the official recognition of several names of mountains as used in *Peaks and People of the Adirondacks*; these were names that enjoyed wide currency among climbers but had never been officially approved or placed on the maps of the Geological Survey. The names on their first petition were Marshall, Blake and Couchsachraga. But the mountain to which they wanted Marshall officially applied was the mountain in the Dix Range for which the state board had already approved Hough. It had been three years since the approval of that name, but most of those climbers who knew the region most intimately had not heard of the new name. Once their petition was filed, however, they soon learned that they could not expect a new name to be given to a mountain for which a name had been officially adopted.

The Forty-Sixers found themselves in a quandary: they definitely wanted a mountain in the Adirondacks named after Robert Marshall, who after becoming a prominent figure in the field of conservation nationally had died at the age of thirty-eight, but they did not feel that East or South Dix was appropriate to his memory. Not wanting to take a mountain away from Herbert Clark but aware that since he was still alive he could not have a mountain officially named after him, the Forty-Sixers decided to request that Robert Marshall's name be given to the peak in the MacIntyres they had been calling Herbert. They amended their petition, and in June of 1942 Marshall was approved and the United States Board on Geographic Names notified of the New York board's decision.

But the issue was far from settled. Although the Forty-Sixers assumed that Marshall would appear in its rightful place on the maps of the Geological Survey, the Santanoni quadrangle that was surveyed and published in the mid-1950s placed the old name Clinton on the peak that most climbers had finally accustomed themselves to calling Marshall. A letter from L. Morgan Porter, then chairman of the Guidebook Committee for the Adirondack Mountain Club, to the Atlantic Region engineer for the Geological Survey, produced the alarming piece of information that the United States Board on Geographic Names had no record of ever having received notice of the New York board's decision to approve Marshall in 1942. The loss of this notification seemed strange in view of the fact that it had included the adoption of names of several other Adirondack peaks, all of which appeared correctly on the new quadrangles.

Nonetheless, the issue was dropped for the time being. The mountain in question, meanwhile, was known by three different names. Some people refused to let go of Herbert and continued to call the peak by the name originally suggested by Russell Carson. The Forty-Sixers, of course, had to go along with Marshall since they had first proposed it and had seen it at least through the state bureaucracy. The Conservation Department and hikers who relied on the quadrangles of the Geological Survey used the name Clinton. An unenlightened climber, walking from lean-to to lean-to at Lake Colden, could hear stories of three different mountains, which vaguely seemed to be in the same place: it all depended on whom one listened to.

Into this complicated situation I plunged last spring when I began to research mountain names for an introduction to a reissue of Carson's *Peaks and People of the Adirondacks*. As a climber I had been aware of the confusion, but I had never quite understood its source. Grace Hudowalski, historian for the Forty-Sixers,[6] loaned me her valuable file on the original Forty-Sixer petitions, and after examining it I began to get a clearer picture. It seemed that the first order of business was to write the New York Board on Geographic Names to see what they had in their files on their approval of the Forty-Sixer petition in 1942. To my dismay I learned that not only had the United States board lost all record of having received notice of the New York board's decision but the New York board had misplaced all its records on the matter as well. As far as any government body was concerned the names Herbert and Marshall had absolutely no official status. The Geological Survey maintained that its field workers in the 1950s had not found either Herbert or Marshall used by people in the area. Apparently they picked up Clinton from Colvin's reports and put it on the map, believing that it was the only name ever assigned to that mountain.

The United States Board on Geographic Names, however, was quite receptive to the suggestion that a name more appropriate than Clinton and already in use by Adirondack climbers be substituted. A petition was prepared and sent, with letters of support from a number of interested Adirondack groups and individuals, to the United States board. In its meeting of December 1972, the board approved for federal use the name Mount Marshall. The entry in the board's decision list will read: "Marshall, Mount: mountain, elevation 4360 ft., in the MacIntyre Mountains 3 mi. NE of Henderson Lake; named for Robert Marshall, conservationist who made the first recorded ascent of this mountain; Essex Co., N.Y.; 44° 07'40"N 74° 00'50"W. Variant: Mount Clinton."

One hopes that this is the end of a needless confusion, but it is hard to forget that the situation seemed to have been settled once before. It will probably be a couple of years before the Santanoni quadrangle is reissued. When it is, climbers will be checking eagerly to see if Robert Marshall's name has finally been given its rightful place.[7] Russell Carson originally suggested the name in a gesture of friendship and recognition of a relatively unimportant feat of mountain climbing. Now that name is a memorial to one of the giants of conservation in the twentieth century. It is only fitting that the Adirondacks, the area that first gave Robert Marshall a taste for the outdoors and love for wild country everywhere, should have a wilderness mountain[8] named for him. For while his interests and conservation activities eventually encompassed the continent, he never failed to come to the defense of Adirondack wilderness whenever it was threatened during his lifetime.

NOTES

1   See p. 17.

2   Boundary is a prominent knob between Algonquin and Iroquois. DeWitt Clinton was governor of New York from 1817 to 1823.

3   Carson 1927, 196-9. For Colvin's confusing references to the MacIntyres see his 1884 report, p. 159, and the two panoramic sketches of the high peaks bound in the 1886 report, in addition to the 1873 report, p. 134, cited in Carson. [Terrie's note.]

4   The mountains in this range seem to have had a peculiar proclivity for providing car-
tographical confusion; the main summit was originally named McIntyre after
Archibald McIntyre, who with others developed the iron deposit around Lake
Sanford. During the nineteenth century the name evolved to MacIntyre and eventually signified the entire range, while Algonquin was applied to the main summit
itself. [Terrie's note.]

5   At the time, some people objected to naming the mountain after the Marshalls,
since the brothers were still living. Marshall's father suspected that anti-Semitism lay
behind the objection. (Glover 1986, 88-92.)

6   Hudowalski died in 2004 at ninety-eight. The Forty-Sixers are campaigning to give
East Dix the name of Grace Peak.

7   The name Mount Marshall now appears on the Ampersand Lake quadrangle.

8   Mount Marshall lacks a maintained trail, but there is a well-defined herd path to the
summit.

A Short History
of Adirondack Peak-Bagging

By Phil Brown

In the 1870s, the Rev. F.F. Jones and G.T. M'Kenzie set out from St. Huberts one morning to climb Mount Marcy, New York state's highest summit, in a single day. The trip took them fourteen hours.[1] In the years to come, as more trails developed, marathon hikers found they could bag more than one High Peak in a day. When Bob and George Marshall climbed nine peaks on July 26, 1930, they inaugurated a fierce competition among several elite hikers that lasted several years.

The Marshalls had broken a record set thirty-six years earlier by Newell Martin, a bold climber who gained notoriety at Yale for scaling a church steeple and hanging from it the trousers of a Harvard man.[2] On August 5, 1894, when he was forty, Martin left St. Huberts at 6:50 a.m. and climbed in succession Gothics, Basin, Saddleback, Haystack, Skylight and Marcy—bushwhacking much of the way. He was accompanied by Wesley Lamb, a guide. Charlie Beede, another guide, waited for them with supplies at the Alderson Camp near Skylight.[3] They got back to St. Huberts at 11 p.m.

"I had been traveling for more than 16 hours (including rests)," Martin wrote. "None of us were very tired. None of us were stiff. But we all felt that we had done enough and went to bed without delay."[4]

Martin's six summits on the Great Range bettered the mark set just a few years earlier by two Princeton classmates, Walter Lowrie and Malcolm McLaren. One day in July 1892, they left Lowrie's summer home in Keene Valley at 5 a.m. and climbed, in order, Mount Marcy, Haystack, Basin, Saddleback and Gothics. They reached the Ausable Lake road, where a carriage was waiting, at 7 p.m.[5]

Lowrie, who later became a theologian and a translator of Kierkegaard, seemed miffed when Martin's hike was commemorated years later by Russell Carson in his book *Peaks and People of Adirondacks*.

291

Carson had wrongly attributed to Martin the first ascent of Saddleback. In a 1928 letter to Carson, Lowrie described his own feat and cast doubt on the worthiness of Martin's, suggesting that Martin had begun at Lake Tear of the Clouds and that he never recovered from his arduous outing. "I learned later ... that Martin was never able to work again and soon retired. My impression is that he died a few years later."[6] In fact, Martin stayed vigorous enough to continue climbing,[7] and he lived until 1941.

In another letter, Lowrie rightly emphasized the challenge faced by early hikers in climbing trailless peaks. "It is ... impossible to compare the difficulty of a climb without a trail with the climbs of today. The greatest effort was involved in traversing the zones near the summits where the dwarf balsams were so stiff that it was almost equally difficult to get under, over, or through them. I made a record that on Gothics it required 20 minutes of grueling labor to get from the peak nearest to Saddle Back up to the point where the trail stopped–whereas after the trail was made over the Range I could easily cover that distance in 3 minutes."[8]

The Marshalls did indeed enjoy the benefit of trails on their trek. The brothers departed Johns Brook Lodge at 5:30 a.m. and went over Marcy, Skylight, Haystack, Basin, Saddleback, Gothics, Armstrong, Upper Wolf Jaw and Lower Wolf Jaw, returning to the lodge at 7:45 p.m. The next day they sent Martin a telegram informing him of their accomplishment, asserting that it "does not approach in merit your six peaks record with five of them trail-less."[9] In extolling their feat, Martin wrote in *High Spots*: "The Marshall record should stand for another 36 years, till 1966. I can say only one word in depreciation of the Marshalls' achievement. Erosion has been at work, every day and night, for thirty-six years, on those bleak mountain tops. They are lower, therefore, than they were when I climbed some of them in 1894." [10]

As it happened, the Marshalls' record lasted barely a year. On August 21, 1931, Ernest S. Griffith, a dean at Syracuse University, ascended 10,720 feet while climbing nine High Peaks plus Mount Jo. Starting at Johns Brook Lodge at 5:30 a.m., he went up Upper Wolf Jaw, Armstrong, Gothics, Saddleback, Basin, Haystack, Marcy, Skylight, Algonquin and Jo. But this record lasted less than two months: On October 7, Herbert L. Malcolm racked up eleven High Peaks and ascended 12,000 feet. The next year, having returned from

Alaska, Marshall bested Malcolm's record with a solo hike up thirteen High Peaks and Mount Jo, ascending 13,600 feet.[11] Just six weeks later, Griffith ascended 16,930 feet in going over ten High Peaks and three lesser summits.[12] And that fall, Malcolm climbed twelve High Peaks and ascended 15,760 feet, afterward vowing to cover more peaks and more ascent on his next try.[13]

The following year saw a new competitor: James Foote of Port Henry. He calculated that, on June 21, 1933, he went over twenty-eight peaks, including twenty-four that surpass four thousand feet. Many of Foote's "peaks," however, were unnamed bumps or secondary summits not recognized as mountains in themselves. Still, Foote's accomplishment is impressive: He went over sixteen High Peaks—more than anyone else—and ascended 16,300 feet, just 630 feet short of Griffith's mark.[14] Moreover, he evidently spent much of the day bushwhacking.

The rules of this competition were not articulated, so it isn't clear whether the goal was to climb as many High Peaks as possible or as many vertical feet as possible or both. Malcolm, at least at the end, settled on vertical feet as the measure of a hiker's prowess. After Foote's hike, he went on two other expeditions in the Adirondacks, climbing only twelve High Peaks each time but setting new records for ascent. On the second of these hikes, a fifty-one-mile marathon in 1936, he piled up the vertical feet by going up and down Noonmark Mountain four times. Malcolm, then fifty-two, ascended 25,550 feet that day, which remains the twenty-four-hour record in the Adirondacks.[15]

In later years, hikers vied to climb all forty-six High Peaks in the shortest time. The Marshalls had completed their round over six summers. In 1948, Lillian and Daniel McKenzie took only twenty-three days.[16] By 1972, various hikers had whittled the time down to nine days. That year, Patrick Griffin and Chris Beattie set out to break the record but encountered strong winds and cold rain. Beattie gave up after climbing thirty-two peaks in four days. Griffin continued on his own. The next day he was found dead of a heart attack on Mount Marcy. In 1977, two local hikers, Ed Palen and Sharpe Swan, set a mark that would stand for twenty-five years: four days and eighteen hours. This was bettered in 2002 by Ted "Cave Dog" Keizer, a speed climber who had trained for more than a year. His time: three days, eighteen hours and fourteen minutes.[17] On his second day, Keizer reached the summits of seventeen High Peaks, but he fell well short of Malcolm's record for vertical ascent over twenty-four hours.

The single-day hikes discussed above are summarized below.

July 1892: Walter Lowrie and Malcolm McLaren climb Marcy, Haystack, Basin, Saddleback and Gothics.

Aug. 5, 1894: Newell Martin climbs Gothics, Saddleback, Basin, Haystack, Skylight and Marcy.

July 25, 1930: Bob and George Marshall climb Marcy, Skylight, Haystack, Basin, Saddleback, Gothics, Armstrong, Upper Wolf Jaw and Lower Wolf Jaw—in all, nine High Peaks. Estimated ascent: 10,000 feet.[18]

Aug. 21, 1931: Ernest S. Griffith climbs nine High Peaks (Upper Wolf Jaw, Armstrong, Gothics, Saddleback, Basin, Haystack, Marcy, Skylight and Algonquin) and finishes off with a lesser peak, Mount Jo. Estimated ascent: 10,720 feet.

Oct. 7, 1931: Herbert L. Malcolm climbs eleven High Peaks: Lower Wolf Jaw, Upper Wolf Jaw, Armstrong, Gothics, Saddleback, Basin, Haystack, Marcy, Skylight, Colden and Algonquin. Estimated ascent: 12,000 feet.

July 15, 1932: Bob Marshall climbs thirteen High Peaks (Big Slide, Lower Wolf Jaw, Upper Wolf Jaw, Armstrong, Gothics, Saddleback, Basin, Haystack, Marcy, Skylight, Iroquois, Algonquin and Wright) and finishes off with Mount Jo. Estimated ascent: 13,600 feet.

Aug. 25, 1932: Griffith climbs ten High Peaks (Giant, Lower Wolf Jaw, Upper Wolf Jaw, Armstrong, Gothics, Saddleback, Basin, Haystack, Marcy, Skylight) and three lesser peaks. Estimated ascent: 16,930 feet.

Oct. 10, 1932: Malcolm climbs twelve High Peaks (Colvin, Blake, Nippletop, Dial, Lower Wolf Jaw, Upper Wolf Jaw, Armstrong, Gothics, Saddleback, Basin, Haystack, Marcy). Estimated ascent: 15,760 feet.

June 21, 1933: James Foote climbs sixteen High Peaks: Lower Wolf Jaw, Upper Wolf Jaw, Armstrong, Gothics, Saddleback, Basin, Haystack, Marcy, Gray, Skylight, Redfield, Cliff, Colden, Iroquois, Algonquin and Wright. Estimated ascent: 16,300 feet.

Oct. 7, 1933: Malcolm climbs twelve High Peaks (Giant, Lower Wolf Jaw, Upper Wolf Jaw, Armstrong, Gothics, Saddleback, Basin, Haystack, Marcy, Skylight, Colden and Algonquin) and Mount Jo twice. Estimated ascent: 20,070 feet.

July 19, 1936: Malcolm climbs the same twelve High Peaks but in reverse order. He also ascends Mount Jo and Noonmark, the latter four times. Estimated ascent: 25,552 feet.

NOTES

1 The hike took place in 1874 or 1875 (*Cloud-Splitter*, Nov.-Dec. 1946, 4).

2 Martin 1993, 1.

3 From Alderson Camp, Martin went on to ascend Skylight and Marcy; it is not clear whether Lamb went with him up these last two peaks.

4 From Martin's trip notes, which were published in the July 1931 issue of *High Spots*, a year after the Marshalls broke his record.

5 Martin 1993, 430. Elsewhere, Lowrie says the year of his hike may have been as early as 1889.

6 The letter to Carson was reprinted in the September-October 1969 issue of *Adirondac*, p. 89-97. Note that if Martin had begun at Lake Tear, which lies below Marcy's summit, he would have climbed the Range from west to east, contradicting the account published in *High Spots*.

7 In 1896, for example, he and Milford Hathaway ascended the bare south face of Gothics, which today is regarded as a technical rock climb. Martin 1993, 433-7.

8 Martin 1993, 430.

9 Reprinted by Martin in the September 1930 issue of *High Spots*, 17-18. Martin's own notes suggest that only the route from Gothics to Alderson Camp–that is, over Basin, Saddleback and Haystack–lacked a trail. Nevertheless, he bushwhacked up Skylight as well, having been told the trail was overgrown.

10 Ibid., 18.

11 See p. 65 for Marshall's account of this hike.

12 *High Spots*, October 1932, 19.

13 *High Spots*, January 1933, 9-10.

14 *High Spots*, July 1933, 26.

15 Malcolm began at 6 a.m. on July 29, 1936, and finished at 5:55 a.m. the next day. *High Spots*, July 1936, 25-26.

16 *Adirondack Explorer*, September-October 2002, 17.

17 *Adirondack Explorer*, September-October 2002, 15

18 The estimates of vertical feet come from *High Spots* articles. Martin said the Marshalls "made upward climbing of 10,000 feet" (see note 8 for reference), but a later correspondent estimated the brothers climbed 8,790 feet (*High Spots*, October 1931, 21).

Forty-Six–But Who's Counting?

By Bill McKibben

The environmental writer Bill McKibben wrote this poem in 1997 to commemorate the seventy-fifth anniversary of the Adirondack Mountain Club. It appeared that year in a special issue of Adirondac, *the club's magazine.*

One day in midsummer
While climbing MacNaughton
I ransacked my brain
And found I'd forgotten
Just how many peaks
I still had to bag
Before I could send for
My Forty-Sixer tag
And so I composed
This mountainous ditty
To sing in my car
As I drive from the city

Oh I've been up on Haystack and Porter and Street
I've wandered on Saddleback, conquered Gray Peak
Up Rocky Peak Ridge to the summit of Giant
And then through the Wolf Jaws I've stumbled defiant
Up Blake and Emmons and Dial and Nye
They're all on my list in this summer up high

For I'm following Bob Marshall up all the High Peaks

My feet are so sore, and my polypro reeks
I'm flybit and rainsoaked and proud as can be
Before Labor Day comes a 46er I'll be

I climbed up Mount Marcy and crossed to Skylight
Lugging my stone to the summit that night
Donaldson, Seymour–they're part of my saga
As well as the peak that they call Couchsachraga
I've climbed down from Whiteface to pay Esther a call
Cascade, it caused me no trouble at all

For I'm following . . .

The trio of Dixes and Hough and McComb
Up Gothics and Sawteeth before I came home
Basin and Tabletop, and rocky Wright
I sat up on Big Slide awaiting first light
Santanoni and Allen and Nippletop too
From Colden to Colvin I've wandered right through

For I'm following . . .

Panther and Iroquois peaks I have crossed
On Seward and Marshall I found myself lost
From the top of Algonquin I had a great view
Saw Nippletop, Phelps and Redfield too
Why only last weekend I stumbled up Cliff
And now my notes show I've completed my list

For I'm following . . .

I thought I'd be happy but in fact I am sad
My blisters are healing but my heart's feeling bad
Why I've nothing to live for
I can think of no goal
Except for to climb them
All again in the snow

Bibliographical Information

Sources of Articles

The sources of articles published in this volume appear below. Unless otherwise noted, Bob Marshall is the author.

Introduction

George Marshall. "Adirondacks to Alaska: A Biographical Sketch of Robert Marshall." *Ad-i-ron-dac*, May-June 1951, 44-5, 59.

Peak-Bagger

The High Peaks of the Adirondacks (1922). Adirondack Mountain Club.

"Whiteface Mountain." Typescript in Bancroft Library, University of California at Berkeley.

"Mount Marcy." From typescript in Bancroft Library, University of California at Berkeley.

"Herbert Peak." From typescript in Bancroft Library, University of California at Berkeley.

"A Day on the Gothics." *High Spots*, January 1942, 10-12.

"A Winter Ascent of MacIntyre." February 1923. Manuscript in Bancroft Library, University of California at Berkeley.

"Climbing 42 High Adirondack Peaks." *New York Evening Post*, July 21, 1922, 12.

"Adirondack Peaks." *High Spots*, October 1932, 13-15.

"Night Trip on Ampersand." Typescript in possession of Roger Marshall.

"Wilmington Walk." Typescript in Bancroft Library, University of California at Berkeley.

POND-HOPPER

"Weekend Trips in the Cranberry Lake Region," 1923. Typescript in Franklin Moon Library, New York State College of Environmental Science and Forestry, Syracuse, N.Y.

"History of the Cranberry Lake Region." *Camp Log* 1922, 61-64.

"Dawn in the Woods." *Empire Forester,* 1923, 82.

"Why I Want to Become a Forester in the Future," 1918. Manuscript in Bancroft Library, University of California at Berkeley.

PRESERVATIONIST

"Recreational Limitations to Silviculture in the Adirondacks." *Journal of Forestry,* February 1925, 173-178.

"The Perilous Plight of the Adirondack Wilderness." *High Spots,* October 1932, 3.

"Comments on Commission's Truck Trail Policy." *American Forests,* January 1936, 6.

"Calkins Creek." *Ad-i-ron-dac,* Sept.-Oct. 1953, 101.

"Largest Roadless Areas in United States" (with Althea Dobbins). *The Living Wilderness,* November 1936, 11-13.

"Zoning the Forest Preserve."[1] *High Spots,* January 1934, 14.

"The Problem of the Wilderness," *The Scientific Monthly,* February 1930, 141-8.

PORTRAIT ARTIST

"Herbert Clark." *High Spots,* October 1933, 8-11.

"Mills Blake, Adirondack Explorer." *Ad-i-ron-dac,* May-June 1951, 40-48.

"Mills Blake." *High Spots.* March 1930, 13.

"An Evening with Professor Einstein: August 7th, 1936." Typescript in the Bancroft Library, University of California at Berkeley.

NOVELIST

Island in Oblivion. Typescript in Bancroft Library, University of California at Berkeley.

RELATED ARTICLES

Bob Marshall. "Contribution to the Life History of the Northwestern Lumberjack." *Social Forces*, December 1929, 271-3.

George Marshall. "Approach to the Mountains." *Adirondac*, March-April 1955, 24-7, 38.

George Marshall. "Lost Pond." *The Cloud Splitter*, June 1941, 2-3.

Philip G. Terrie. "Mount Marshall: The Strange History of the Names of an Adirondack High Peak." *Adirondac*, July-August 1973, 73-5.

Paul Schaefer. "Bob Marshall, Mount Marcy, and–the Wilderness." *The Living Wilderness*, Summer 1966.

Phil Brown. "A Short History of Adirondack Peak Bagging." Written especially for this book.

Bill McKibben. "Forty-Six–But Who's Counting?" *Adirondac*, Special Edition 1997.

NOTES

1 The article actually appeared with others under the title "Sabbath is for Man, Not Man for the Sabbath." The title used in this book was chosen by the editor.

Other Works Cited

1922 *Camp Log.* Syracuse: New York State College of Forestry.

Armstrong, George R., ed., 1961. *Forestry College: Essays on the Growth and Development of New York State's College of Forestry, 1911-1961.* Syracuse: New York State College of Forestry.

Beadle, G.W. 1953-54. "Up Doonerak: Climbing Bob Marshall's Mountain." *The Land*: 4.

Brumley, Charles. 1994. *Guides of the Adirondacks: A History.* Utica: North Country Books.

Brown, Eleanor. 1985. *The Forest Preserve of New York State: A Handbook for Conservationists.* Glens Falls: Adirondack Mountain Club.

Carson, Russell M.L. 1927. *Peaks and People of the Adirondacks.* Garden City: Doubleday, Page & Co.

Colvin, Verplanck. 1874. *Report on the Topographical Survey of the Adirondack Wilderness for the Year 1873.* Albany: Weed, Parsons and Co.

Donaldson, Alfred L. 1921. *A History of the Adirondacks*, 2 vols. Reprint 1977, with introduction by John J. Duquette. Harrison, N.Y.: Harbor Hill Books.

Forsyth, Alfred S., and Van Valkenburgh, Norman J. 1996. *The Forest and the Law II.* Schenectady: Association for the Protection of the Adirondacks.

Fowler, Albert Vann, ed. 1959. *Cranberry Lake 1845-1959: An Adirondack Miscellany.* Blue Mountain Lake: Adirondack Museum.

Glover, Jim. 1985. "Louis Marshall: A Visionary Who Helped Preserve the Adirondacks." *Adirondack Life.* June 1985.

Glover, James M. 1986. *A Wilderness Original: The Life of Bob Marshall.* Seattle: The Mountaineers.

Goodwin, Tony. 2004. *Adirondack Trails: High Peaks Region.* Lake George, N.Y.: Adirondack Mountain Club.

Gove, William. 2006. *Logging Railroads of the Adirondacks.* Syracuse: Syracuse University Press.

Graham, Frank, Jr. 1978. *The Adirondack Park: A Political History.* New York: Alfred A. Knopf.

Harlow, William H. 1923. *Weekend Trips in the Adirondacks.* Unpublished manuscript in Franklin F. Moon Library, New York State College of Environmental Science and Forestry, Syracuse.

Headley, Joel T. 1875. *The Adirondack or, Life in the Woods.* Reprint 1982, with introduction by Philip G. Terrie. Harrison, N.Y.: Harbor Hill Books.

Jamieson, Paul. 1994. *Adirondack Canoe Waters: Northern Flow.* Lake George: Adirondack Mountain Club.

Jenkins, Jerry, with Andy Keal. 2004. *The Adirondack Atlas: A Geographic Portrait of the Adirondack Park.* Syracuse: Syracuse University Press.

Keith, Herbert F. 1976. *Man of the Woods.* Introduction by Paul F. Jamieson. Syracuse: Syracuse University Press.

Ketchledge, E.H. 1996. *Forests and Trees of the Adirondack High Peaks Region.* Lake George: Adirondack Mountain Club.

Kogut, Kenneth. 1990. "A Look at Fish and Wildlife Resources of the Adirondack Park in the Twenty-First Century." *The Adirondacks in the Twenty-First Century Technical Reports,* vol. 1. Published by the New York State Commission on the Adirondacks in the Twenty-First Century.

Laskey, Paul. 2003. *The Fire Observation Towers of New York State.* Ballston Spa, N.Y.: MKL Publishing.

Marshall, George. 1951. Unpublished letter to Grace Hudowalski, dated March 1, 1951. In Adirondack Room of Saranac Lake Free Library.

Marshall, Robert. 1922. "Summer Camp." Unpublished manuscript in the Bancroft Library, University of California at Berkeley.

Martin, Newell. 1930. "Expunging Old Records." *High Spots.* September 1930, pp. 16-18.

Martin, Newell. 1993. *Spinach and Zweiback: The Writings of Newell Martin.* Edited by Cynthia Parsons. Millbrook: Grinnell and Lawton Publishing.

McMartin, Barbara. 1994. *The Great Forest of the Adirondacks.* Utica, N.Y.: North Country Books.

McMartin, Barbara. 2001. *Discover the Northwestern Adirondacks.* Caroga, N.Y.: Lake View Press.

McMartin, Barbara. 2004. *The Privately Owned Adirondacks*. Caroga, N.Y.: Lake View Press.

Podskoch, Marty. *Adirondack Fire Towers: The Northern Districts,* Vol. 2.

Schaefer, Paul. 1989. *Defending the Wilderness: The Adirondack Writings of Paul Schaefer*. Syracuse: Syracuse University Press.

Smeby, Susan Thomas. 2002. *Cranberry Lake and Wanakena*. Charleston, S.C.: Arcadia Publishing.

Street, Alfred Billings. 1869. *The Indian Pass: Source of the Hudson*. Reprint, 1975. Harbor Hills Books: Harrison, N.Y.

Terrie, Philip G. 1993. *Wildlife and Wilderness: A History of Adirondack Mammals*. Fleischmanns, N.Y.: Purple Mountain Press.

Wallace, E.R. 1894. *Descriptive Guide to the Adirondacks*. Syracuse: Watson Gill.

Waterman, Laura and Guy. 1989. *Forest and Crag: A History of Hiking, Trail Blazing, and Adventure in the Northeast Mountains*. Boston: Appalachian Mountain Club.

Weber, Sandra. 2002. *Mount Marcy: The High Peak of New York*. Fleischmanns, N.Y.: Purple Mountain Press.

The 409,000-acre Bob Marshall Great Wilderness would provide a safe haven for nearly all the creatures of the Adirondacks, including moose.

Bob Marshall Great Wilderness
A big idea for the western Adirondacks

In 1940, less than a year after his death, the federal government recognized Bob Marshall's contribution to conservation by designating a vast roadless area in Montana the Bob Marshall Wilderness, which today encompasses more than a million acres.

The Adirondack Council believes New York state should take a similar step by establishing a 409,000-acre Bob Marshall Great Wilderness south of Cranberry Lake, the region Marshall explored as a forestry student in the summer of 1922.

Nicknamed the Bob, it would be the biggest Wilderness Area in the Adirondack Park—big enough to represent most the Park's ecosystems and, the council says, big enough to harbor two extirpated predators, the wolf and the cougar. The Bob's territory contains 441 lakes and ponds and more than seventy miles of rivers. As with other Wilderness Areas in the Park, no motorized use would be permitted.

Marshall himself recognized the importance of this wild country: In an article published in 1936,[1] he included it in a list of the nation's largest roadless areas. The list was intended to be the first step toward protecting these wild lands from motorized incursions.

The council, a private environmental group, first proposed the Bob in 1990. At the time, the state owned 230,000 acres within the boundaries. Since then, the state has aquired thousands of additional acres in the region and protected other land by conservation easements that forbid development. All told, about eighty-five percent of the Bob is in the state Forest Preserve or protected by easements.

The state has not endorsed the proposal, but it does want to preserve the wild character of the region, albeit through a mixture of public and private ownership. The council is not asking the state to seize the land by eminent domain. Rather, it hopes that over time—perhaps many generations—the private owners will sell their land to the state voluntarily, enabling the state to piece together the Bob.

But Brian Houseal, the council's executive director, sees no reason to wait to create a smaller version of the Bob. "The state could lump together the existing Forest Preserve units in the region and call it the Bob Marshall Great Wilderness today," he says.

To learn more about the Bob Marshall Great Wilderness, call the Adirondack Council at 877-873-2240 or visit the group's Web site, **www.adirondackcouncil.org.**

NOTES

1 Reprinted in this volume, p. 199.

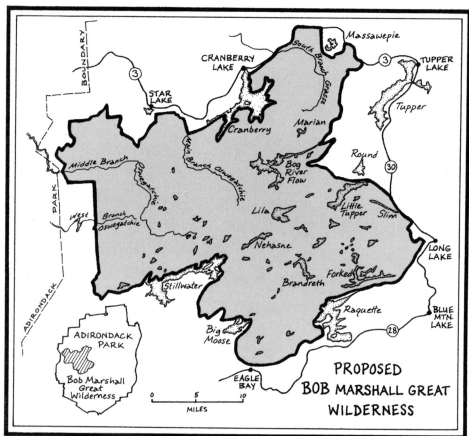

PROPOSED
BOB MARSHALL GREAT
WILDERNESS

Map by Nancy Bernstein